Praise for *A Stra*

'This long–awaited publication wil[   ]>f an author whose reputation has never [   ], and who is now being rediscovered in Britain, the USA, France, and Italy. All these countries have recently published his last, posthumously published novel [*Alone in Berlin*], thus demonstrating his rare ability to attract the common and the literary reader alike.'
Modern Language Review

'Recording his experiences of Nazi Germany while confined in an asylum in 1944, Hans Fallada wrote in real life what Günter Grass later wrote in fiction. An intriguing literary testament, expertly edited by two leading Fallada scholars, and skilfully translated by Allan Blunden.'
Geoff Wilkes, The University of Queensland

'This wonderful volume, painstakingly transcribed from his microscopic handwriting by his gifted biographer, Jenny Williams, and her fellow Fallada scholar and archivist, the poet Sabine Lange, is a conversational memoir: blunt, whimsical, outrageous, anecdotal and often hilarious. Allan Blunden's translation conveys the exasperwated humour.'
Irish Times

'This is certainly a revelatory book. As its author intended, it reveals much about the pernicious nature of Nazi rule during the Third Reich; the compromises demanded, the tribulations endured, the lives ruined.'
The Financial Times

'A gripping and revelatory prison diary. Thanks to Polity Press and Allan Blunden's skilful translation, we now have it in English for the first time . . . Colourful and anecdotal reflections of life under Hitler. Fallada's diary turns out to be not a record of quotidian events inside but reminiscences of scrapes, challenges and day–to–day reality outside, from the advent of Nazi misrule to the final stages of the war.'
The Sunday Herald

'*A Stranger in My Own Country* is the story of one individual who rejected the Nazis and their central philosophy for a variety of reasons, many more personal than political . . . A rare account of living close to an edge that you can't quite locate in the darkness.'
Tribune

'Fallada's strengths as a novelist permeate his narrative. He is a master of the brief character sketch, bringing friend and foe to life on the page with economy and wit.'
The Australian

'Fallada, one of Germany's most well–regarded writers of the 20th century, tells the tale of a writer and his friends, and how the swell of Nazism means there's always a listening ear outside the door – except this time he's telling his own story.'
South China Morning Post

A Stranger in My Own Country

The 1944 Prison Diary

HANS FALLADA

Edited by Jenny Williams and Sabine Lange

Translated by Allan Blunden

polity

First English edition © Polity Press, 2014
This paperback English edition © Polity Press, 2016
Reprinted 2017, 2021

The translation of this work was supported by a grant from the Goethe-Institut London
which is funded by the German Ministry of Foreign Affairs

Polity Press
65 Bridge Street
Cambridge CB2 1UR, UK

Polity Press
350 Main Street
Malden, MA 02148, USA

ISBN-13: 978-0-7456-6989-2

A catalogue record for this book is available from the British Library.

Library of Congress Cataloging-in-Publication Data

Fallada, Hans, 1893-1947.
  A stranger in my own country : The 1944 Prison Diary, 1944 / Hans Fallada.
    pages cm
  Includes bibliographical references and index.
  ISBN 978-0-7456-6988-5 (jacketed hardback : alk. paper) 1. Fallada, Hans,
1893–1947--Diaries. 2. Authors, German--20th century--Diaries. 3. Authors,
German--20th century--Biography. 4. Prisons--Germany--Neustrelitz--History--20th
century. I.nTitle.
  PT2607.I6Z46 2014
  833'.912--dc23
  [B]
                          2014019994

Typeset in 11/15 Adobe Garamond by
Servis Filmsetting Ltd, Stockport, Cheshire
Printed and bound by CPI Group (UK) Ltd, Croydon, CR0 4YY

For further information on Polity, visit our website: politybooks.com

Contents

Introduction

On 4 September 1944 Hans Fallada was committed to the Neustrelitz-Strelitz state facility, a prison for 'mentally ill criminals' in Mecklenburg, some seventy miles north of Berlin, where he was to be kept under observation for an indefinite period of time. His fate was entirely uncertain.

This was not the first time that this son of an Imperial Supreme Court judge found himself behind bars. In 1923 and 1926 he had already been jailed for six months and two and a half years respectively on charges of embezzlement. In both cases his drug addiction had been a key factor. In 1933 he had been accused of involvement in a conspiracy against the person of the Führer, and had been taken into protective custody for eleven days. In the autumn of 1944 the charge was a different one: Fallada was accused of having threatened to kill his ex-wife on 28 August 1944.

The divorce had been finalized on 5 July 1944. Yet the couple continued to live together, with others, on the farm in Carwitz: Anna (Suse) Ditzen in the house with their three children, her mother-in-law and a constantly changing number of bombed-out friends and relatives, Hans Fallada in the gardener's flat in the barn. On that Monday afternoon at the end of August the heavily intoxicated Fallada fired a shot from his pistol during an argument. Anna Ditzen took the gun away from him, threw it in the lake and alerted Dr Hotop, the doctor from the neighbouring town of Feldberg. Both Fallada and Anna Ditzen later testified that the gunshot was not intended to kill. Dr Hotop sent the local police constable to escort his patient to Feldberg to sober up. The matter might have ended there, but the story came to the ears of an over-zealous young prosecutor. He insisted on having Hans Fallada transferred to the district court in Neustrelitz for questioning. On 31 August the accused was ordered to be 'temporarily committed to a psychiatric institution'. On 4 September the gates of the Neustrelitz-Strelitz state facility closed behind Hans Fallada. He was placed for an indefinite period in Ward III, where insane or partially insane criminals were housed. It looked like the end of the road for him: an alcoholic, a physical and mental wreck, an author who was no longer capable of writing.

Yet Fallada used his time in prison to recover from his addictions – and to write. As early as 1924, when he was in prison in Greifswald, he had kept a diary as a form of self-therapy. So now he requested pen and paper once more. His request was granted. He was given ninety-two sheets (184 sides) of lined paper, approximating to modern A4 size. As well as a series of short stories, Fallada wrote *The Drinker*. On 23 September, noting that his novel about alcoholism remained undiscovered, he was emboldened to start writing down his reminiscences of the Nazi period. He was one of 'those who stayed behind at home' (as distinct from those writers and artists who went into voluntary exile when Hitler came to power): he spent the years of the Third Reich in Germany, for the most part in rural Mecklenburg, where he 'lived the same life as everyone else'. Now he wanted to bear witness. Here in the 'house of the dead' he felt the time had come to settle personal scores with the National Socialist regime, and also to justify the painful compromises and concessions he had made as a writer living under the Third Reich.

In the autumn of 1944 the catastrophic war was entering its final phase, and the collapse of Hitler's Germany was clearly imminent. The Allies were approaching from all sides, American troops were at the western frontier of the German Reich, while the Red Army was advancing towards East Prussia. At the same time the Nazi regime was stepping up its reign of terror and tightening its stranglehold on the

German people. In committing his thoughts and memories to paper, Fallada was now putting his own life at risk.

Surrounded by 'murderers, thieves and sex offenders', always under the watchful eye of the prison warders, he wrote quickly and frenetically, freeing himself, line by line, from his hatred of the Nazis and the humiliations of the past years. He proceeded with caution, and in order to conceal his intentions and save paper he used abbreviations – 'n.' for 'nationalsozialistisch' (National Socialist), for example, and 'N.' for 'Nazis' or 'National Socialism' – while the minuscule handwriting was enough in itself to deter the prison warders. But Fallada went further in his efforts to 'scramble' the text, turning completed manuscript pages upside down and writing in the spaces between the lines. The highly compromising notes, part micrography and part calligraphic conundrum, became a kind of secret code or cryptograph, which can only be deciphered with great difficulty and with the aid of a magnifying glass.

On 8 October 1944, a Sunday, Hans Fallada was allowed out on home leave for the day. He smuggled the secret notes out under his shirt.

The 1944 Prison Diary

(23.IX.44.) One day in January 1933[1] I was sitting with my esteemed publisher Rowohlt[2] in Schlichters Wine Bar[3] in Berlin, enjoying a convivial dinner. Our lady wives[4] and a few bottles of good Franconian wine kept us company. We were, as it says in the Scriptures, filled with good wine, and on this occasion it had had a good effect on us too. In my case you couldn't always be sure of that. The effect wine had on me was entirely unpredictable; generally it made me belligerent, self-opinionated and boastful. But this evening it hadn't, it had put me in a cheerful and rather jocular, bantering mood, which made me the ideal companion for Rowohlt, who is increasingly transformed by alcohol into a huge, two-hundred-pound baby. He sat at the table with alcohol evaporating, in a manner of speaking, from every pore of his body, like some fiery-faced Moloch, albeit a contented, well-fed Moloch, while I regaled everyone with my jokes and anecdotes, at which even my dear wife laughed heartily, even though she had heard these gags at least a hundred times before. Rowohlt had by now reached the state in which his conscience sometimes directs him to make a contribution of his own to the general entertainment: he would sometimes ask the waiter to bring him a champagne glass, which he would then crunch up between his teeth, piece by piece, and eat the lot, leaving only the stem behind – to the horror of the ladies, who couldn't get over the fact that he didn't cut himself at all. I was present on one occasion, though, when Rowohlt met his match in this quasi-cannibalistic practice of glass-eating. He asked the waiter for a champagne glass, a quiet, placid

man in the company did the same. Rowohlt ate his glass, the placid
man did likewise. Rowohlt said contentedly: 'There! That did me good!'
He folded his hands across his stomach, and looked around the table
with an air of triumph. The placid man turned to him. He pointed to
the bare stem of the glass that stood on the table in front of Rowohlt,
and taunted him: 'Aren't you going to eat the stem, Mr Rowohlt? But
that's the best part!' And with that he ate the stem himself, to gales of
laughter from the assembled company. Rowohlt, however, cheated of
his triumph, was furious, and he never forgave the placid man for this
humiliation!

But appearances could be deceptive with Rowohlt: even though
he sat there like a big, contented baby, with eyes half-closed as if he
could barely see a thing, he was actually wide awake and right on the
ball – scarily so, when it came to figures. Not realizing this, one time
when I was strapped for cash I thought to pull a fast one on him in this
baby state and negotiate a particularly favourable contract with him. I
can still see us both sitting there, scribbling endless columns of figures
on the menus. The contract was finally agreed in something of a boozy
haze, and I was laughing up my sleeve at having finally put one over on
this sharp businessman. The end result, of course, was that I was the
one who'd been suckered – and how! Afterwards Rowohlt himself was
so horrified by this contract that he voluntarily gave back most of what
he had taken from me.

But on this particular evening there was no eating of glasses or
transacting of business. The mood on this particular evening was one
of satisfied contentment. We had done full justice to Schlichter's
wonderful chilled salads, his bouillabaisse, his beef stroganoff and his
peerless mature Dutch cheese, and with the wine we had taken the odd
sip of raspberry brandy to warm our stomachs. Now we were gazing
at the little flames of the alcohol burners under our four individual
coffee machines, heating up our Turkish coffee while we sat back and
savoured another mouthful of wine from time to time. We had every
reason to be pleased with ourselves and with what we had achieved.
True, *Little Man – What Now?* had already peaked as an 'international

best-seller';[5] like every international best-seller, it had been succeeded by something else that did even better, and I can't remember now if it was Pearl Buck's *The Good Earth*[6] or Mitchell's *Gone With the Wind*.[7] In the meantime I had written *Once We Had a Child*, which the public didn't like, although the author liked it very much, and now I was working on *Jailbird*.[8] Maybe *Jailbird* wouldn't be a new international best-seller either. But give it time – all in good time. It was the easiest thing in the world to create an international best-seller; you just had to really want it. For the present I was busy with other things that interested me very much: if it interested me one day to have an international best-seller, then I could easily manage that too.

Listening to these remarks, which were more drunken ramblings than seriously intended, Rowohlt nodded like a Buddha and seconded my words with an occasional 'Quite so!' or 'You're absolutely right, my friend.' Our good lady wives were by now rather tired of hanging on the lips of the famous author and his famous publisher and imbibing words of pure wisdom, and were now talking in whispers at the other end of the table about housekeeping matters and bringing up children. The coffee, giving off its rich, intense aroma, was slowly starting to drip into the little cups positioned beneath the spouts . . . Into this supremely relaxed and contented scene there now burst an agitated waiter, to remind us that beyond our perfectly ordered private world there was a much larger outside world, where things were currently in a state of real turmoil. With the cry 'The Reichstag is burning! The Reichstag is burning! The Communists have set fire to it!' he dashed from room to room spreading the word. That certainly got the pair of us going. We leapt from our seats and exchanged a knowing glance. We shouted for a waiter. 'Ganymede', we cried to this disciple of Lucullus. 'Fetch us a cab right now! We're going to the Reichstag! We want to help Göring play with fire!' Our dear wives blanched with horror. Göring had probably only been in the government for a few days,[9] and the concentration camps had not yet entered the picture, but the reputation that preceded the gentlemen who had now seized control in Germany was not such that one could mistake them for gentle lambs meek and mild. I can still see it all in my mind's eye – a confused, anxious, and yet ridiculous scene: the two of us seized with a veritable *furor teutonicus*, looking straight into each other's eyes and shouting that we absolutely must go and play with fire ourselves; our wives, pale with terror, frantically trying to calm us down and get us out of this place, which was reputed to be Nazi-friendly; and a waiter standing at the door, hurriedly writing something on his pad – an extract from our manly declamations, or so we assumed from the amused applause. Eventually our wives succeeded in steering us out of the door, onto the street and into a cab, under the pretext, I assume, of going with us to see the burning Reichstag building. But we didn't go there all together; first we took Rowohlt and his wife home, then our car headed east out of town, to the little village on the banks of the Spree[10] where my wife and I were living at the time with our first son. Meanwhile my wife's soothing words had calmed me down to the point where, when we drove past the Reichstag, I could look into the leaping flames of the burning dome – that sinister beacon at the start of the road that led to the Third Reich – without feeling any incendiary cravings of my own. It's a good thing we had our wives with us that evening, otherwise our activities, and very possibly our lives too, would have come to an end on that January day in 1933, and this book would never have been written. We also heard nothing more about the head waiter and his furious scribblings, although his spectre haunted us for several anxious days: he was probably just making a quick note of the bills for his tables, since all the customers were then getting up to leave.

(24.IX.44.) This little episode says a great deal about the attitude with which many decent Germans contemplated the advent of Nazi rule. In our various journals – nationalist, democratic, social-democratic or even Communist – we had read quite a bit about the brutality with which these gentlemen liked to pursue their aims, and yet we thought: 'It won't be that bad! Now that they're in power, they'll soon see there is a big difference between drafting a Party manifesto and putting it

into practice! They'll tone it down a bit – as they all do. In fact, they'll tone it down quite a lot!' We still had absolutely no idea about the intractability of these people, their inhuman cruelty, which literally took corpses, and whole heaps of corpses, in its stride. Sometimes we had a wake-up call, as when we heard, for example, that a son of the Ullstein publishing family, when they came to arrest him,[11] had asked if he could brush his teeth first; perhaps his tone had been a touch supercilious, because they promptly beat him half to death with rubber truncheons and dragged him away. People were being arrested left, right and centre, and a surprising number of these detainees were 'shot while trying to escape'. But we kept on telling ourselves: 'It doesn't affect us. We are peace-loving citizens, we have never been politically active.' We really were very stupid; precisely because we had not been politically active, i.e. had not joined the one true Party and did not do so now, we made ourselves highly suspect. It would have been so easy for us; it was in those months from January to March '33 that the great rush to join the Party began, which earned the new Party members the scornful nickname 'March Martyrs'. From March onwards the Party put a block on new membership, making it conditional upon careful vetting and scrutiny. For a long time the 'March Martyrs' were treated as second-class Party members; but the distinction became blurred with the passing years, and the March Martyrs for their part did all they could to demonstrate their loyalty and reliability. In fact, most of the Nazis who were later described as '150 per cent committed' came from their ranks; in their zeal they sought to outdo the older Party members in the ruthlessness with which they enforced the Party line – as long as such measures didn't affect them, of course. I shall shortly have occasion to speak about some of these fragrant flowers, whose acquaintance I was soon to make.

Strictly speaking, Rowohlt and I had every reason to be very careful indeed: we were both compromised, he more than I, but compromised nonetheless, and that was quite enough for the gentlemen in power, who didn't bother with the finer nuances. They have always ruled by brute force, mainly by the brutal threat of naked physical violence, intimidating and enslaving first their own people, and then other nations. Even the relative subtlety of the iron fist in the velvet glove is too sophisticated for them – way beyond their powers of comprehension. All they ever do is threaten. Do this, or we'll cut your head off! Don't do that, or we'll hang you by the neck! These utterly primitive ideas constituted the sum total of their political wisdom, from the first day until what will hopefully soon be the last.

So, Rowohlt and I were both compromised. He was known to be a 'friend of the Jews', and his publishing house had once been described by a Nazi newspaper as a 'branch synagogue'. He had published the works of Emil Ludwig,[12] whom the 'militant journals' persistently referred to as 'Emil Ludwig Cohn', even though he had never been called Cohn in his life. Rowohlt was also Tucholsky's publisher, and in his magazine *Die Weltbühne* Tucholsky had conducted a dogged campaign to uncover the secret extra-curricular activities of the Reichswehr.[13] Furthermore, Rowohlt had published *Das Tagebuch*,[14] a weekly journal for economics and politics, which supported the League of Nations and the world economy, exposed the secret machinations of the 'chimney barons', and was generally opposed to all separatist or nationalist tendencies. He had also – the list of his crimes is truly shocking – published Knickerbocker,[15] the American journalist who gripped his readers with his account of the 'Red Trade Menace' and the rise of Fascism in Europe, and who, on the personal orders of Mr Göring himself, had been denied a press pass to attend the opening session of the Reichstag under the aegis of the Nazis. Finally, Rowohlt had also published a book entitled *Adolf Hitler Wilhelm III*,[16] which pointed out the remarkable similarities in character and temperament between these two men; he had published a little book called *Kommt das Dritte Reich?* [*Is the Third Reich Coming?*],[17] which was less than enthusiastic about the prospect; and worst of all he had printed and published *Geschichte des Nationalsozialismus* [*A History of National Socialism*],[18] in which all the contradictions, infamies and stupidities of this emerging political party were mercilessly laid bare. This book was subsequently sold under the counter for vast sums – officially, of course, it was immediately consigned to one of those book bonfires[19] that burned all over Germany when the Nazis came to power, and on which pretty much everything with a Jewish-sounding name was burned indiscriminately. (The standard of literary education among the Nazi thugs was pretty dire, as was the standard of their education in general.) Add to that the fact that Rowohlt also had any number of Jewish literary authors on his list, and that his publishing house employed quite a few Jewish staff members. Enough already? More than enough, and then some! (One of these Jewish employees would later – officially at least – turn out to be his nemesis, but I shall come to that later.) Rowohlt had no interest in politics, and in mellow mood he liked to describe himself as a 'lover of all forms of chaos'. He really was, and probably still is, someone who feels most energized in turbulent and chaotic times. The heyday of his publishing house was during the bad years at the end of the revolution and the beginning of the introduction of the *Rentenmark*.

I hardly need to relate my own catalogue of sins at such length, and in the pages that follow it will become clear how much I was loved, how fervently my work was encouraged and supported, and what joyous years I and my family experienced from 1933 onwards. I probably only need to mention that leading and 'respected' Nazi newspapers and journals described me as 'the poster-boy goy for all the Jews on the Kurfürstendamm', that they called me 'the notorious pornographer', and right up until the end disputed my right to live and write in Germany.

From the other side of the fence it has been much held against me that I didn't draw the natural conclusions from these hostile attitudes towards me and leave Germany like the other émigrés. It's not that I was short of generous offers. Back in the days when Czechoslovakia was being occupied, I was invited to escape the impending war and travel with my family to a nearby country, where a comfortable home, excellent working conditions and a carefree life awaited me, and where I would have been naturalized overnight. And once again, even after everything I'd been through since '33, I said 'No', once again, obstructed in my work, constantly under attack, treated as a second-class citizen, menaced by the approaching shadow of a necessary war, I said 'No', and chose rather to expose myself, my wife and my children to all the dangers than to leave the country of my birth; for I am a German, I say it today with pride and sorrow still, I love Germany, I would not want to live and work anywhere else in the world except Germany. I probably couldn't do it anywhere else. What kind of a German would I be if I had slunk away to a life of ease in my country's hour of affliction and ignominy? For I love this nation, which has given, and will continue to give, imperishable sounds to the world. Here songs are sung as in no other country upon earth; here in Germany were heard strains that will never be heard again if this nation perishes! So true, so forbearing, so steadfast, this nation – and so easily led astray! Because it is so trusting – it believes every charlatan who happens along.

And I'll say it here and not mince my words: it wasn't the Germans who did the most to pave the way for National Socialism, it was the French and the British.[20] Since 1918 there have been many governments who were more than willing to cooperate – but they were never given a chance. It was repeatedly forgotten that they were not only the executors of measures forcibly imposed by foreign countries, but also the representatives of an impoverished and starving people, whom they loved! It is those others who have thrust us into the abyss, into the hell in which we are now living!

So yes, I have stayed, and many others with me. We have given each other courage, and we have made something of ourselves in Germany; let it be said without arrogance, in all modesty indeed, that we have remained the salt of the earth, and not everything has lost its savour. It was inevitable, of course, that people in my neighbourhood would realize that I was a black sheep, nobody in my house has ever said 'Heil Hitler!', and in such matters the ears of people in Germany have become remarkably acute over the years. Many people have spoken to me very openly about their true feelings, and that has given me and them the strength to carry on and endure. We didn't do anything so preposterous as to hatch conspiracies or plot coups, which is what people in other countries always expected of us, utterly failing to recognize the seriousness of our situation. We were not intent on committing suicide when our death would be of no use to anybody. But we were the salt of the earth – and if the salt has lost its savour, with what shall it be salted?

Although it doesn't actually belong here, I will tell a little story at this point that happened to me in the first years after the Nazis came to power, and which will perhaps give some idea of how the atmosphere in my house immediately encouraged those of like mind to emerge from the silence they so anxiously maintained the rest of the time. One day a repair man from Berlin called on us to fix some appliance or other. He was a real Berliner, quick on the uptake, and he had immediately grasped what kind of house this was. At the table – we always eat together – he loosened up more and more, finally regaling us with the following delightful and instructive story, from which one can see that in Germany, even in the worst of times, there were still (and there always will be) plenty of upright and unwavering men in every walk of life. Anyway, this repair man told us the following story in his strong Berlin accent: 'So the doorbell rang, and when I opened up there was one of the Chancellor's tin-rattlers standing there with a list in his paw. "I'm from the WRO",[21] says the man, "and we can't help noticing that you have never contributed to the great relief effort for the German nation. The Winter Relief Organization, that is . . ." And he reels off his spiel, and I let him rabbit on, and when he's finished I say to him: "Look mate," I say, "you can save your breath because you're not getting anything out of me!"

"Well," says he, "if you're still not going to give anything even after I've paid you a personal visit, then I'll have to put a circle after your name on my list of addresses, and that could have very unpleasant consequences for you."

"Look mate," I say again, "I don't give a monkey's what kind of geometric shapes you draw after my name, I'm still not going to give you anything!"

Now he tries a bit harder. "Look here," he says, "don't be like that, don't get yourself into trouble when there's no need! Just give me a fifty and I won't put a circle on the list – job done!"

"You think?" says I. "But a fifty, that's a whole loaf of bread, and a loaf of bread is a big thing for me: I've got five kids."

"What!" says this fellow, all excited. "You've got five children? Then you're a man after our Führer's own heart!"

"Whatever," says I, "but just so you know: we had all the children before your lot came to power!"

"You know what?" says he, "you'll never make a good National Socialist as long as you live!"

"You've got it, mate!" I reply. "I won't even make a bad National Socialist!"'

I must admit this little story made a lasting impression on me, and the line about not even making a bad Nazi proved very helpful to me in many of the situations I would find myself in during the times ahead.

If I ask myself today whether I did the right thing or the wrong thing by remaining in Germany, then I'd still have to say today: 'I did the right thing.' I truthfully did not stay, as some have claimed, because I didn't want to lose my home and possessions or because I was a coward. If I'd gone abroad I could have earned more money, more easily, and would have lived a safer life. Here I have suffered all manner of trials and tribulations, I've spent many hours in the air-raid shelter in Berlin,[22] watching the windows turn red, and often enough, to put it plainly, I've been scared witless. My property has been constantly at risk, for a year now they have refused to allocate paper for my books – and I am writing these lines in the shadow of the hangman's noose in the asylum at Strelitz, where the chief prosecutor has kindly placed me as a 'dangerous lunatic', in September 1944. Every ten minutes or so a constable enters my cell, looks curiously at my scribblings, and asks me what I am writing. I say: 'A children's story'[23] and carry on writing. I prefer not to think about what will happen to me if anyone reads these lines. But I have to write them. I sense that the war is coming to an end soon, and I want to write down my experiences *before* that happens: hundreds of others will be doing the same after the war. Better to do it now – even at the risk of my life. I'm living here with eighty-four men, most of them quite deranged, and nearly all of them convicted murderers, thieves or sex offenders. But even under these conditions I still say: 'I was right to stay in Germany. I am a German, and I would rather perish with this unfortunate but blessed nation than enjoy a false happiness in some other country!'

Reverting now to Rowohlt and me and that time of innocence in January '33: yes, we were badly compromised, and sometimes we admitted as much to ourselves. But then we kept on reassuring ourselves with the fatuous observation: 'It won't be that bad – at least, not for us.' We fluctuated wildly between utter recklessness and wary caution. Rowohlt had just told his wife the latest joke about G., only to turn on her angrily because she had told the same joke to my wife. Did she want to ruin them all? Did she want to land them all in a concentration camp? Was she completely mad, had she taken leave of her senses?! And then the very same Rowohlt went and pulled the following stunt. His wife was actually by far the more cautious of the two, and since she knew very well that they were not exactly renowned in the neighbourhood as a model Nazi household, she took great care to greet everyone she met with the proper Hitler salute and the words 'Heil Hitler!' Trotting along beside her was her little daughter, who was probably four at the time[24] and just called 'Baby', who raised her arm in greeting just like her mother.

But her dear father, Rowohlt, who was always full of bright ideas and loved to play tricks on his wife, took Baby aside and trained her and drilled her, so that the next time her mother was out on the street with her, dutifully greeting everyone with 'Heil Hitler!', Baby raised her left fist and yelled in her clear little voice: 'Red Front! Blondi's a runt!' What tears and fits of despair the poor mother went through to get the child to unlearn this greeting, which really wasn't exactly in step with the times! But Rowohlt, the overanxious and cautious one, just laughed; his enjoyment of this excellent joke far outweighed any fear of the very real danger. Giving the 'Red Front' salute meant being sent to a concentration camp at the very least – and probably much worse than that.

At other times Rowohlt would phone me in my little village, where the young postmistress, with too much time on her hands, was always very curious about the telephone calls of the 'famous' local author, and he would greet me with a full-throated: 'Hello, my friend! Heil Hitler!'

'What's this, Rowohlt?' I would ask. 'Have you joined the Party now, or what?'

'What are you on about!' cried the incorrigible joker. 'We're all brown at the arse end!'

That was Rowohlt for you, and basically he never changed. And I was the same, perhaps not quite so active or inventive, and certainly not as witty; but in those days I developed a dangerous penchant for little anecdotes and jokes poking fun at the Nazis, I stored them up in my mind, so to speak, and shared them readily with others – though I was often rather careless in my choice of listeners, especially if the anecdotes were particularly good and I was bursting to tell. This was bound to end badly, and end badly it very soon did. But before I tell the story of my first serious clash with the Nazi regime, I need to say a little more about the circumstances in which we were living at the time. As already stated, the success of *Little Man* came and went very quickly, I had spent the money none too wisely, and when my wife called a halt to my extravagance we had a little money left, but not very much. To ensure that what little we had left would not drain away too quickly, we decided to move out to the country, far removed from the temptations of bars, dance halls and cabarets. After looking around for a while we found a villa on the banks of the Spree in the little village of Berkenbrück; we rented the upstairs rooms and decided to use this as a temporary base, living here while we looked for a place of our own to buy further out from the city. Everything about the place seemed to suit us down to the ground. The villa lay at the far end of the village, overlooking the forest, one of a small number of townhouses that had been built on the outskirts of what was basically a rural farming village. The garden facing the road, which had hardly any passing traffic, was on the level, while round the back it sloped steeply down to the river, which here flowed past in a straight line between engineered banks.

There was an abundance of fruit trees, lots of outbuildings, and it all looked a touch neglected, on the brink of dilapidation. The reason for this was that our landlords were entirely without means. The husband, Mr Sponar, in his seventies, with a smooth, chiselled actor's face and snow-white hair, always wore velvet jackets and little loose, flapping cravats, and fancied himself a bit of an artist. He certainly had an artist's lack of business acumen. He had owned a small factory in Berlin, where they manufactured alabaster shells to his own designs in a range of attractive soft colours, intended for use as lampshades. At one time the factory had been doing very well, when these alabaster lampshades were all the rage, but then people's taste turned to other kinds of lamps. Sponar had doggedly defied this shift in taste, continuing to produce his beloved alabaster shells to his own designs. He had sunk all his savings into this pointless protest, mortgaging his house on the Spree down to the last roof tile. And then the economic collapse had come, before alabaster lampshades were back in fashion again. When you heard the seventy-year-old talk about this, his dark eyes flamed beneath his white hair; he still believed in the enduring appeal of alabaster lampshades, as others believe in the second coming of the Messiah. 'I shall live to see the day when everyone will be buying alabaster shades again!' went up the cry. 'This present fashion for parchment lampshades, paper lampshades even – what on earth is that? It shows a complete lack of taste. Firstly, an alabaster shade gives out a soft light that can be tinted to any colour you like, and secondly . . .' And he would launch into a lengthy excursus on the advantages of the lamps made by him. Mrs Sponar, his espoused wife, had something of the dethroned queen about her, an air of Mary Queen of Scots in the hour before her execution. Her hair too was snowy-white, crowning a face that was white and almost wrinkle-free, there was something Junoesque about her figure, and she had what one might call an ample bosom – which she knew how to carry off. It was not hard to tell who wore the trousers in that marriage. The retired artist obeyed the dethroned queen in all matters without question. I rather doubt if it had always been this way. This undoubtedly clever, or at least wily, woman would surely not have allowed her husband to ruin himself so foolishly while she stood idly by. I imagine he did it all behind her back, and only when she discovered the full extent of his business failure did she seize the reins of government. But it was too late. They had become impoverished – worse than that: they were on welfare. The rent that I paid them – and it was no small amount – all went to the mortgage lenders, who were happy to get a little interest at last on the money they had lent. In the meantime the Sponars were living off the meagre pension that the social services paid them during those lean years, which probably amounted to something like thirty marks a month – that's for husband and wife together, of course! As the saying goes: not enough to live on, too much to die for. Things were made easier for them, of course, in that they were still living in 'their' own house and could feed themselves from 'their' own garden. In other times, needless to say, the mortgage lenders would have long since lost patience and forced them to put the house up for auction; but in order to prevent total chaos in the property market one of the previous governments had introduced something called 'foreclosure protection', which meant that a foreclosure could only be initiated if the borrower gave his consent, which of course happened only in very rare instances.

Such were our landlords, and such were the circumstances of their lives at the time, which they made no secret of. In general we got on very well with them; as tenants we were not the petty-minded type, and if something needed repairing I had it done at my expense, even though it was technically the landlord's responsibility. The fact is that the Sponars were destitute. I even paid the old man a small monthly allowance, in return for which he pottered about a bit in my part of the garden, strength and health permitting. But we were more cautious in our dealings with the dethroned princess: she acted all condescending and friendly, but we never quite trusted her. Her big eyes often lit up with something like pain, and I sometimes thought that she hated us because we had what she had lost: property, a carefree life, happiness. The days passed and turned into weeks and months, and we felt more and more at home in our villa on the Spree. Our little boy cheered every tug boat that went past almost under our windows, belching thick black smoke and towing long lines of barges in the direction of Berlin. We went for long walks in the woods, and sometimes we forgot for hours on end that Berlin even existed, even as the Nazis there continued to strengthen their hold on power, banning other political parties and confiscating their property. I remember saying to my wife in outrage, when the Liebknecht House was taken over and changed into the Horst Wessel House with a lot of pomp and ceremony (as if they had won a huge victory or something): 'It's so brazen, the way they carry on! It's just theft, pure and simple! But they get away with it precisely because they are so shameless about it, as if it's the most natural thing in the world!'

But if we happened to be in Berlin and came across formations of brownshirts or stormtroopers marching through the streets with their standards, singing their brutish songs – one line of which I still remember clearly: '. . . the blade must run with Jewish blood!' – then my wife and I would start to run and we would turn off at the next corner. An edict had been issued, stating that everyone on the street had to raise their arm and salute the standards when these parades went past. We were by no means the only ones who ran away rather than give a salute under duress. Little did we know at the time that our then four-year-old son[25] would one day be wearing a brown shirt too, and in my own house to boot, and that one day I too would have to buy a Nazi flag and fly it on 'festive days'. If we had had any notion of the sufferings that lay ahead, perhaps we would have changed our minds after all and packed our bags. And when we returned home to Berkenbrück we congratulated ourselves on our peaceful village existence. We looked at each other and said: 'Thank God! The farmers out here in the country are not bothered about the Nazis! They till the soil and are happy just to be left in peace!' What naive fools we were! Our eyes would soon be opened to the realities of Nazism in rural life!

Meanwhile we had grown to like our villa so much that we decided to stop looking for somewhere else and to stay where we were – but to become owners rather than tenants. That would not be possible without the consent of the Sponars. So we went to see them and made the following proposal: I would buy up the mortgages from the individual mortgage lenders, and he would agree to let the house be put up for compulsory auction. At the sale I would then acquire the house for the value of the mortgages, the property being so heavily mortgaged that there was no danger of anyone outbidding me. In return for his consent to the auction I would grant him and his wife a lifelong right of residence in the ground-floor apartment – admittedly half the size of what they had now – and in addition I would pay them both a monthly annuity that was twice as much as the pension they were getting from social services. In return, he would help out in the garden as far as his strength permitted.

I was offering the Sponars an incredibly good deal here. The protection against foreclosure would not last indefinitely; the house would come under the hammer one day, and he would lose the right of residence there, lose the garden, and not get a penny in compensation. So I was astonished when the couple seemed unsure about accepting my proposal. I pressed them, and eventually he came out with it. He felt that by agreeing to let the house be put up for auction he was placing himself entirely in my hands. Once the house had been sold at auction, he said, the Sponars would have no rights at all, and I could do with them whatever I wanted. It was easy to make promises – no offence intended – but keeping them in these uncertain times was even less certain . . . I said with a laugh that his concerns could very easily be laid to rest: all we needed to do was go and see a notary together and put our mutual obligations in writing. He promised to think it over for a day or two. I couldn't understand it – I thought he should have been grateful to me, simple as that. What I was offering was a pure gift. But people are strange, and old people especially. But he came to me next morning – it always pays to sleep on things – and gave his consent. I suggested that we go straight to the notary and get it all down in writing, exactly as he wanted. But all of a sudden he wasn't in such a hurry any more. He had a touch of bronchitis, he claimed. Besides, there was no great hurry, he said: he knew I was a man of my word, the end of this week or the beginning of the next would be soon enough.

Which was fine by me. I was exhilarated by the prospect of owning a house of my own, when just a short time ago I had had nothing to my name. Thinking that everything was settled, I travelled to Berlin and went to one of the big banks to arrange the transfer of the prime mortgage. They were happy enough to give it to me, and were just pleased to be rid of this instrument that had hardly ever yielded any interest. Then I set about buying up five or six smaller mortgages with a value of a few thousand marks each, which Sponar had presumably taken out when he was really up against it, in order to keep his head above water from one month to the next and carry on making alabaster lampshades that nobody wanted to buy. Having sorted all this out, I sat at home feeling very pleased, and waited for my landlord to get over his mild attack of bronchitis so that he could come with me to the notary.

Now comes a strange interlude, not without deeper significance, on the eve of Easter, when we planned to organize an Easter egg treasure hunt for our little boy. On Maundy Thursday[26] we had a visit from a Mr von Salomon,[27] who worked at my publisher's. Mr von Salomon was not Jewish, as one might assume from his name (and as some people did assume), but came from Rhineland aristocracy. Salomon was a Germanized form of the French 'Salmon'. He had three brothers, and anything more different than these three brothers it would be hard to imagine. They perfectly exemplified the condition of the German nation: disunited and riven by conflict. One of the brothers was a respectable bank clerk,[28] an upright citizen, who was only interested in his own advancement. The second was a committed Communist,[29] and if one is to believe his brother, the one I knew (although one certainly shouldn't believe everything he said!), this brother had been honoured by Stalin in person with a distinguished award. At all events, this Mr von Salomon was soon one of Germany's 'most wanted' men, defying the Nazi terror regime as he travelled constantly back and forth between Paris and Moscow as a courier, wearing a hundred disguises, braving dangers of every kind, and stopping off regularly in Berlin too, where the brothers met up from time to time. The third Salomon brother was a big cheese on the staff of the later notorious Mr Röhm, with whom, however, he did not perish: on the contrary, he rose ever higher through the ranks. He had the – for me – unforgettable first name 'Pfeffer'. Pfeffer von Salomon – now that's what I call aristocracy! And my Salomon too, still young as he was, had already had a fairly chequered past. As a young lad he had fought with the Iron Division in the Baltic,[30] then he had joined the Consul Organization,[31] had taken part in the Ruhr resistance campaign, and finally had been involved somehow in the murder of Rathenau.[32] For that he spent some time in prison, where the fiercely nationalist sympathies of the prison staff at the time meant that he was feted as something of a celebrity. He even made a habit of going into town with the prison governor for an evening in the pub, where he found an admiring audience among the bar-room regulars for the tales of his exploits, although it was not unknown for him to get so carried away in the heat of the moment that he mixed up other people's exploits with his own – for example, telling anecdotes from the Battle of the Marne as if he had been there in person, whereas he couldn't have been more than twelve or thirteen at the time. When he came out of prison he wrote a couple of books about his experiences; he wrote well and fluently, as long as he stuck to his own adventures. In one of these books, *Die Geächteten* [*The Outcasts*],[33] he sought to glorify the murder of Rathenau, turning things round somewhat to present the murdered Rathenau as a better kind of man, but with a dark and sinister side to him, while the poor murderers were forced to go on the run in Germany, innocents hunted like wild game. Another book, called *Die Stadt* [*The City*],[34] is something of a curiosity, a hefty volume, written and printed as a continuous stream of words without any chapter breaks, or even paragraphs, to enliven the tedious uniformity of the text, or give the reader's eye a chance to rest and pause. Booksellers were quick to dub the book 'the book with no returns' – and they were right on both counts: no paragraph breaks, and the book failed to sell, much to the chagrin of my good friend Rowohlt. Mr von Salomon soon discovered, however, that the business of writing books requires a lot of hard work, and often brings in very little money. Like many people who have bright ideas and don't care for hard work, but do like to live well, he went into films instead. That suited him very well, and when I last saw him on the Kurfürstendamm he had put on a lot of weight, and the acquaintance of a minor writer was clearly a thing of very little importance for a man who was constantly hobnobbing with the film stars of the day. But back then, when he visited me that Maundy Thursday, all this still lay in the future. At that time Mr von Salomon was as lean as a whippet, to which he bore a striking resemblance with his aristocratic, sharp-featured face. I don't remember any more why he came to see me, he probably just wanted to tell me the latest jokes about Hitler and the Party: back then it was a sort of parlour game – people couldn't spread the word fast enough! Von Salomon was a funny and talkative man, who knew everybody in the world of literature and art, and the hours passed quickly enough in his company. It would have been a bit wiser, perhaps, to have had this conversation not out in the hall, but in a room where we could have closed the door behind us: but which of us is wise all the time? At that time, certainly, we were anything but. And which of us can always keep in mind that someone downstairs only needs to leave a door ajar in order to hear every word that's spoken upstairs? The acoustics of a house are unpredictable: sometimes you can hear everything, sometimes nothing at all, and on this Maundy Thursday afternoon someone damned well heard just a little too much!

Now comes interlude Number 2, again not without deeper significance, particularly for the study of the human character. By now it was Good Friday, my wife and I were walking in the garden, while our son tottered gamely along between us on his three-year-old legs. It was still mid-morning, the bell up in the village had just started to ring for the morning service, so it must have been shortly before ten o'clock. We were just admiring the crocuses and tulips and hyacinths that had pushed their way up through the withered leaves, their blooms a blaze of colour in the bright sunshine. We did our best to stop our son picking the flowers – with varying degrees of success.

And then the Sponars emerged from the house, prayer books in hand, ready to set off for church; she looked, more than ever, every inch the dethroned queen, while he, having exchanged the velvet jacket for a black frock coat, was the eternal artist, playing the part of a graveside mourner. They marched straight up to us and halted in front of us. 'It is our custom', said Mrs Sponar in that deep and slightly doleful voice of hers, 'to take Holy Communion on Holy Friday.' (This excess of holiness was already making me feel uncomfortable.) 'It is also our custom', Mrs Sponar went on, 'before we take Holy Communion, to ask forgiveness of our friends and acquaintances and relatives for any evil that we might have done them in thought or deed, either knowingly or unknowingly. And so, Mr Fallada, Mrs Fallada, we ask your forgiveness – please forgive us!' Tears of emotion actually welled up in their eyes, while we, my wife and I, felt so angry and embarrassed that we wanted the ground to swallow us up. 'They can keep their private religious claptrap to themselves!' I thought, thoroughly infuriated. 'It's all sanctimonious humbug! The queen never regrets anything, is without fault, and cannot ask for forgiveness, and he's just an old fool! It's sickening – why can't they just leave us alone!'

But what can you do? We're brought up to hide our true feelings and just put on a good face in these situations. I'm afraid my face wasn't up to much as I assured them we had nothing to forgive them for, and as far as we were concerned they could take communion with a clear conscience. They thanked us again very emotionally, while the tears coursed down the old hypocrites' faces. Had I known then what I suspected twenty-four hours or so later, and what I knew with absolute certainty some twelve days after that – that these two bastards had already shopped us to the Nazis even as they begged us for forgiveness, and that in return for money they had stored up trouble, illness and mortal danger for us – I think I would have strangled them there and then with my bare hands! But as it was, I just watched them walk out of the garden in their solemn black garb, prayer books in hand, and turned to my wife: 'What do you make of that?'

'It makes me sick!' she burst out. 'We could have done without their play-acting. Or did you believe a single word they said?'

'Not a word', I replied, and then we walked down through the garden to the Spree, where our little boy's delight in the rippling waves and river barges soon made us forget all about the two old hypocrites.

(25.IX.44.) The next morning came, it was the Saturday before Easter, and mother was busy with cooking and baking. So father and son went out by themselves, down to the banks of the Spree again, walking side by side with Teddy in the middle. Teddy was a wonderful and indestructible creature; I'd bought him when we were still living in 'straitened circumstances' for the sum of 33 marks, much to the horror of my wife. Teddy stuck out his jolly red tongue, and he seemed to take as lively a pleasure in the sunny spring sky and the bustling river traffic as my boy did. For a while we were content just to stand there and watch, and then we started to play more actively, poking about in a little patch of reeds and disturbing some birds, which flew up, chirping indignantly. We'd parked Teddy on a molehill while we played. We were still rummaging about when suddenly there were two figures standing in front of us, wearing those brown shirts that I didn't care to see even then, and the sight of which still unsettles me to this day. Each of the figures had a pistol in his hand, which was unmistakably pointed at me. 'Uh-oh!' I thought to myself. 'Are you Fallada?' one of them asked. Except that the speaker didn't say 'Fállada' with the stress on the first syllable, which I prefer, because it sounds a bit like a triumphant blast on the trumpet; instead he pronounced it 'Falláda', which always sounds like someone who's about to trip over and fall flat on his face. In a way he was right, because I *was* about to take a tumble – out of all my dreams of a joyous Easter, at any rate: but I was not going to be floored and laid low on that account! 'Yes, that's me' I said, and tightened my grip on my little boy's hand, finding this whole show of force wildly histrionic, given my peace-loving nature. 'You're to come with us!' the man barked. 'And don't even think of running, because we'll shoot the moment you try it.'

'Do you mind if I fetch our Teddy first?' I asked amiably, and in sullen silence they allowed us to collect Teddy from his molehill. And so we marched back up through the garden, towards the villa at the top: my son and I, with Teddy in the middle, and the two brownshirts with pistols drawn. Personally I thought I completely ruined the dramatic effect for them, but they didn't see the funny side; no-one has ever been more lacking in a sense of humour than Mr Hitler and all his hangers-on, right down to the last lackey. To them everything was deadly earnest, and in the end that's exactly what it all turned out to be – in the most literal sense of the word.

For the rest, I wasn't unduly concerned about this morning visitation. It was probably just another of those searches for weapons or Communist literature that they were so fond of – and they were welcome to search my place, because I was sure they wouldn't find anything. (Sweet innocent that I was, I had no idea back then that people can bring with them what they want to find – a sure-fire method of getting rid of undesirables, come what may. But on that day I gave no thought to such things. Politics seemed a long way off, and money matters were uppermost in my mind; but I would learn my lesson soon enough!)

I found our quiet house at the end of the village in a state of uproar. The place was crawling with SA stormtroopers, at least twenty or twenty-five of these gentlemen had graced me with their presence, including a big man wearing some sort of gold insignia. Was he a 'Standartenführer'? A 'Rottenführer'? A 'Scharführer'? I've no idea, and to this day I have not wasted mental energy on learning to tell the difference between all these silly uniforms that the new Germany has gone to town on since 1933. I'd like to die without insignia or decorations of any kind; if I reach a ripe old age, they can put me on display by the Brandenburg Gate in Berlin with a sign saying: 'This is the only German who never received a medal or decoration, never earned a rank or title, never won a prize and never belonged to a club.' In this regard I'm doubtless very un-German.

So anyway, some kind of senior SA officer was involved, but what cheered me was the presence of a good old country policeman, wearing the familiar green uniform complete with shako-style helmet. An edict had only recently been issued by Mr Göring to the effect that house searches and arrests were no longer to be carried out by Party echelons acting alone, but that a regular police officer must always be present. The abuses and brutalities that Party members had permitted themselves in their dealings with opponents had caused quite a stink, and in those early days there were even a few Party noses that were still sensitive to excessively rank odours. But that sensitivity was short-lived. The powers that be soon saw that they could take all the liberties they wanted with the German people, who were too acquiescent by half.

So the sight of a policeman, putting me in mind of that edict, gave me a certain feeling of security: at least things would be conducted with a semblance of 'legality'. (In the next two hours I would find out just how much this 'legality' was worth.) The policeman was very polite and proper: 'We have to conduct a search of your house, Mr Fallada, a complaint has been lodged against you. Give me your keys!'

'Be my guest!' I replied, and handed them over. I was reassured by the courteous tone, but knew better than to inquire as to the nature of the complaint. 'Ask too many questions and you'll get too many answers' – or none at all, and that's certainly true when dealing with court officials and anything to do with them.

We processed solemnly into the house, my little boy, who had been following everything that happened with big blue eyes and without a sound, and Teddy still holding on to my hand.

For a moment Mrs Sponar peeped round an open door in the hall. There was a burning look in this evil woman's eyes, and the way she looked at me made me feel distinctly ill at ease. Although I didn't know it at the time, I was right to feel that way: she thought she was seeing me for the last time in her life. We climbed the stairs, and in the kitchen I saw my wife busying herself with the dishes. She was a little pale, but there was no clattering of plates as she worked. I sent the boy in to her, and the policeman said: 'For the moment you are not allowed to have any contact with your wife or anyone else.' I nodded. 'And now you can start by showing us where you keep your correspondence!' Which I did.

I have always been proud of the good order in which I keep my private affairs, and my double-entry bookkeeping would not put a professional accountant to shame. My correspondence is clearly filed in alphabetical order by addressee. I unlocked the cupboard where it was kept. The first folder they took out was not the letter A, but the letter S. 'Aha!' I thought to myself. 'This early-morning visit is all about Mr von Salomon! Who knows what that adventurer with his hard-line Communist brother has been up to this time – and now I'm in trouble too because of it!'

But they didn't find a single letter to or from Mr von Salomon, who was someone I'd only ever spoken to.

But that didn't discourage them, even if it was initially a disappointment. They went through the correspondence folder by folder, and when they had finished that they started on my books. They took every book and shook it out vigorously, which didn't do the bindings much good. I didn't have very many books at the time, but there were still a good few – so it took them quite a time. Every now and then they would trot across to their gold-braided leader and show him a book that had caught their attention, such as the book of memoirs by Max Hölz[35] – *Vom weissen Kreuz zur roten Fahne [From White Cross to Red Flag]* – or Marx's *Das Kapital* or an issue of the journal *Radikaler Geist*.[36] But the leader shook his head. He was not interested in such trifles: he was after bigger game. I rightly took that to be a bad sign. This wretched Mr von Salomon had doubtless been planning another little putsch of some kind, they'd been keeping him under surveillance, and that's how they knew about his visit to me. Well, whatever: they wouldn't find anything in my house! Incidentally, the policeman took no part in this house search. He just stood by and watched, looking pretty bored, and let the brownshirts rummage about by themselves. After searching for a whole hour, all they had to show for it was a piece of paper they had found in my work folder for *Jailbird*. Written on the paper next to a small drawing was the one word 'Maschinengewehr' – 'Machine gun'.

'Why are you interested in machine guns?' I was asked. 'And what's the meaning of this drawing?' They had all clustered around me, listening intently. Written across their faces was a mixture of schadenfreude and curiosity – they thought they had got me. 'Gentlemen', I said with a smile, 'as you can tell from the manuscript folder there, I am working on a novel about the fate of people who are sent to prison. To that end I have collected a good deal of material about prison life. And this 'machine gun' is part of that. But this is not a real machine gun: as you can see from the drawing, it's eight prisoners who have got hold of a ninth prisoner, who's made himself unpopular by stealing, say, and they've wrapped him in a blanket and are now about to beat him up in a particular way. They have a special word for this in the nick, they call it "machine gun" . . .' I beamed at them. But in their faces all I saw was naked disbelief, and their leader screamed at me in fury: 'Don't try and pull the wool over our eyes! Do you think we're going to fall for a pack of lies like that? Tell us right now where you've buried the machine gun, or I'll start getting rough with you. I'll come down on you like a ton of bricks, my friend!' He glared at me threateningly. My heart sank as I realized I had no other proof if these men chose not to believe me. I was entirely at their mercy, and they had no interest in my innocence, since they were determined to find me guilty. But now, in my hour of need, help came from an entirely unexpected quarter: from a coarse, thuggish-looking man in a brown shirt. 'No', he cried, 'that's right! We once worked a guy over in the dormitory like that, and "machine gun" is what we called it . . .' He broke off, cowed by a look from his leader, who probably thought it not quite the thing to be discussing the past history of an upstanding SA fighter in the presence of an outsider like me. 'Fine', growled the leader, and pushed the piece of paper into the cuff of his uniform sleeve – for possible use at a later date. 'I'll look into the matter later. But for now we need to search the other rooms.' They did so thoroughly, but not overly skilfully. I was gratified to note that a house guest we had at the time, a Jewish lady, managed without much difficulty to evade these gentlemen by slipping from one room to the next. They never even saw her, despite the fact that the few rooms I had were fairly swarming with SA men. At one point I saw the lady sitting in a corner on the balcony. I signalled to her by blinking my eyes slowly, and she nodded back with a smile. I was glad they didn't find her – for her sake and also, a little bit, for mine. Having a Jewish woman in the house would have been one more item on the charge sheet against me.

The search of the remaining rooms also failed to yield anything remotely incriminating. In sullen silence they then climbed up into the attic and proceeded to search through our empty suitcases and boxes. I stood by one of the attic windows, while the SA leader and policeman stood by the next one, deep in conversation. Suddenly I heard the policeman say firmly: 'There's not a shred of evidence against him. I can't arrest the man.'

The SA leader replied heatedly: 'But look here – we've received very definite information. You've got to take him in.'

The policeman put on his helmet and tugged at his belt. 'I can't – and I won't', he stated as firmly as before. 'Then I'll just have to arrest him myself!' retorted the SA leader waspishly. 'Do what you like. But I'm having nothing to do with it!' replied the policeman, and left the attic. When he left the house, all 'legality' went out the door with him: so much for compliance with Göring's edicts[37] . . . Up until this moment I had looked upon the whole thing as a rather tiresome but amusing game: these fellows had nothing on me – I was innocent! But now I realized that this was beside the point, if they really had it in for me. I realized that I was in real danger, and that it would be better for me not to take the whole thing so lightly. It might be that I would need all my strength and courage to get out of this business in one piece!

I was taken back to my study and kept there, guarded by two SA men, while the others left, along with their leader. But when I looked out of the window I saw that an SA sentry had been posted by the garden gate that led to the street. Doubtless there was another one behind the house, on the side overlooking the Spree. I really did seem to be very valuable to them. I listened for any sound in the house: dead quiet everywhere. The waiting was torture. What had they got planned for me? Why were they leaving me here? I looked into the faces of my two guards – and thought it better not to ask. They had the coarse faces of thugs, veterans of a hundred brawls at political meetings, where they drove home the words of their Führer with knuckledusters and chair legs; the vicious faces of ruthless men who were ready to smash heads in here – anyone's head – if someone gave the word. I've always thought that this archetypal SA visage, which became a familiar sight after the Nazis had seized power, was perfectly epitomized in the face of Gauleiter Streicher,[38] that intimate friend of the Führer and editor of the anti-Semitic paper *Der Stürmer* – a filthy rag, and far filthier than any muck-raking scandal sheet. Whenever I saw that man in a photograph, I felt the hatred rising up within me, a hatred that had absolutely nothing to do with politics. Those little piggy eyes, the low brow, the overdeveloped chin, and above all that thick neck with its six or seven rolls of fat: for me he was the embodiment of evil, the devil incarnate – so much so that I had taken to calling him 'the Hangman'. My two guards had faces just like him, the kind of people who wouldn't hesitate to grab a child by the legs and smash its head against the radiator of their car until it was dead. (This is what eye-witnesses later told me about the Führer's praetorian guard, the SS, the elite formation that employed such methods to solve the Jewish question . . .)

I was waiting two or three hours like this. I had no idea what was going on. Later I learned that the SA had problems finding a suitable car to take me away. It eventually arrived, though – the oldest vehicle I have ever set foot in, a decrepit, rattling conveyance from the year dot, which didn't even have a starter motor, but had to be hand-cranked from the front. I was squeezed in between two SA men in the back of this ancient vehicle, whose upholstery was all torn and ripped, while the group leader sat up front and drove, with another SA man beside him. We set off in the direction of Berlin. I looked back at the house. It was a lovely spring day. The sun was reflected off the window panes, and if there was a face at the window looking out at me, I didn't see it. I didn't dare wave. But I noticed that the sentry on the garden gate had not been stood down after my departure, but continued to wander up and down the street. So were they now keeping my wife under guard too? My heart sank.

We rattled through the village, across open country between fields, and entered the forest, a monotonous expanse of scrawny young pines: a characteristic feature of this sandy region, amounting to nothing more than a bunch of thin poles topped with a bit of greenery.

The leader was now oddly courteous to me, constantly turning around (the car had a top speed of twenty kilometres an hour, no more) and inviting me to smoke if I wanted to, and even asking if we were not too cramped back there. The change in his manner made me uneasy. His friendliness seemed so forced, there was something about it that felt like fear; whatever it was, the man was very agitated. I was very much on my guard, and had the feeling: he's up to something. Perhaps the moment of truth is at hand.

Suddenly the car stopped in the middle of the barren forest, the road was completely empty. The two SA men got out, as did the two men in the front. I stayed in my seat. I watched the four of them step to the edge of the road and relieve themselves. And then they stood there, while they lit up cigarettes and talked quietly among themselves. One of them tugged at his belt and pushed his holster more towards the front. I was getting more uneasy by the second . . . The leader crossed the road towards me. His voice sounded strangely low and agitated as he spoke: 'Perhaps you'd like to get out? Please.' His face was very pale. He went on: 'We'll be on the road for quite some time yet, and this old jalopy isn't up to much!' He tried to laugh.

I replied coolly: 'Many thanks, but I don't need to get out. But thanks all the same.'

He was insistent: 'No, no, it really would be better if you did it now. Otherwise I'll have to stop later when it just isn't convenient. And this old jalopy is hard to get going again. So please!' Now it sounded more like an order.

But as he was speaking, I kept seeing a headline that I'd recently read in a newspaper: 'Shot while trying to escape.' It all fitted: the quiet, empty road, the secluded forest setting – they would carry me into the house and tell my wife 'Shot while trying to escape. We're sorry that he was so foolish . . .' No, they would just send her my things, with a note:

'Shot while trying to escape.' No apology necessary.

I said coolly: 'Thank you, but I'm fine. I don't need to get out. I'll be all right for hours yet.' His face flushed red with anger. He looked across at his men, who had stopped talking and were looking at us, still smoking their cigarettes. 'Look, don't make a fuss!' he said brusquely. 'You will get out now, I am ordering you. I don't want any trouble from you!'

I looked straight at him. 'And I am not getting out of this car!' I cried, and dug my hands into the seat cushion. I shouted in his face: 'You'll not shoot me "while trying to escape"! If you want to shoot me, you'll have to do it in the car! And even if the seats *are* all torn and ripped, people will see it!'

For a moment we gazed at each other in silence. His face was white as a sheet, and I dare say mine was too. Suddenly he spun round and shouted across to his men. 'You lot, come over here!' I gripped the seat cushion even more tightly, and my whole body was shaking. 'I'm not letting them drag me out of here', I thought to myself. 'They'll have to shoot me in the car.' All I could think about now was making sure they shot me *in the car*. The fact that I would end up getting shot hardly interested me at all in that moment.

The men slowly crossed the road towards the car, cigarettes dangling from their mouths, their eyes fixed on me. The moment of decision had come. But the decision turned out differently from what we had all been expecting. While we were engrossed in our altercation, a big car had arrived on the scene from Berlin. Now it came to a stop, and our own good doctor called out to me from the window: 'Mr Fallada, what are you doing out here in the middle of nowhere?'

'Oh', I said, 'I'm just going to the courthouse in Fürstenwalde with these gentlemen. Please say hello to my wife, and tell her that I am well.'

'I'm glad to hear it', said the doctor. 'I'll pass that on. I'll wish you bon voyage, then!' But he did not tell his chauffeur to drive on. The car remained stationary. My escorting party exchanged glances with each other. Now they came to a decision and got back in the car. The last man turned the hand crank and started the car. We set off, leaving behind the barren spot where I was supposed to die. I had a definite feeling that I was safe for the moment – if the sour and morose look on my companions' faces was anything to go by. And then, when I cautiously turned my head to look back, I saw the doctor's big car still there, as he watched us crawl away at a snail's pace. The dear man had not driven on: back then, in Germany, people knew well enough what it meant when they saw a car with SA men inside and a civilian sitting between them!

We drove into the little town of Fürstenwalde. It's only a one-horse town, a miserable, provincial little place with wretched cobbled streets, but I greeted it like the City of Zion on high, the City of the Redeemer: the humblest citizen, the children playing in the street, everything increased my confidence that now I was safe. The worst of the danger was past; back then even the Nazis were not quite ready to kill their opponents out on the street in broad daylight.

We stopped in front of the police station, and my leader disappeared inside with a couple of his minions. We had a long wait, and once again it seemed that not everything was going to plan with me. And it really wasn't going to plan: even if Göring's own stormtroopers were not following his edicts, other people were. After a while my leader reappeared with a blue-uniformed police officer, pointed at me and said: 'That's him. Take him into protective custody!'[39]

'No, I'm not doing that', said the policeman obstinately. 'Without papers I'm not doing it.'

'But I've told you already, I'll get you the papers! I can't leave the man running around on the loose in the meantime! He's not going to wait for me! So just do it!'

'Papers first!' came the reply. 'Without papers we can't take in anyone here.' The man was adamant. 'Bloody hell!' swore the leader angrily. Then he had a thought – he'd found a way round it. 'Well, come back inside, then. I'll make out the papers myself.'

They disappeared inside, and this time the negotiations were successful. When they reappeared, the blue-uniformed officer muttered: 'All right, come with me.' Before I followed him inside, I cast a last glance at the brownshirts. The several hours I had spent in their company had not deepened my fondness for them. I felt a pressing desire not to have anything to do with them or their like anytime soon – and preferably never again.

The cell they took me to was the scurviest and most disgusting hole I had ever been in in my entire life. I'm not even talking about the obscenities that covered the once-whitewashed cell walls from floor to ceiling, either scribbled in pencil or scratched into the chalky surface with a nail. I'm talking about the appalling standards of hygiene. The straw mattress, which was falling apart, the mouldy, flattened straw spilling out of it, the filthy floor covered with bits of dirt – it all pointed clearly to the fact that all was not well with the administration of the good town of Fürstenwalde – even under the Third Reich. When I gingerly lifted the straw mattress between two fingers, I uncovered swarms of bedbugs; alerted to their presence, I now saw their trails everywhere, on the walls, around the bed – wide, reddish-brown splats of blood or squashed bedbug corpses with their trails of blood tapering to a point behind them. But the worst thing about this disgusting place was the bucket in the corner. It was badly battered and hadn't been emptied for a long time, so that a big puddle of faeces and stale urine had formed all around it. Although most of the window panes in the high-level window of the cell were broken, the air in the cell was thick with this hellish stench, which made it a torment just to draw breath. The act of breathing made you want to throw up at the thought of letting this filthy stench into your body even for a single breath. You couldn't sit and you couldn't lie down, and you couldn't really pace up and down; there was just one small spot that was clean enough to stand on at least.

And it's a strange thing: I'd just managed to escape almost certain death, and in a manner of speaking I was now safe, yet the outrage I felt about the pigsty they'd put me in outweighed everything else. I had not been anything like so furious with my brown-shirted friends – who did, after all, try to kill me – as I was with the policeman who had put me in this hole. I had only been taken into protective custody, and yet they had the nerve to put me in this squalid hole, fit only for some verminous lowlife! Had these people forgotten the meaning of the words 'law' and 'justice' in Germany, or what? Then it was high time that I reminded them! And I began to hammer on the iron-plated door, alternately using my fists and my heels. I could hear a muffled echo in the corridor, but it had absolutely no other effect. I hammered on the door again from time to time, and in between I shouted, but nobody came. It didn't surprise me: I knew what nerves of steel police officers can have, able to sleep through the night on standby on a hard bed while some drunk who's just been brought in is raving deliriously in the cell next door, or some woman high on alcohol is bawling out obscenities. So I could well imagine that my blue-uniformed friend out there in his front office was taking a quiet afternoon nap while I was making all this racket, especially as this was the first really fine and warm afternoon of the spring. But I carried on hammering and shouting all the same; it was a way of passing the time.

I was right in the middle of one of these hammering and hollering sessions when suddenly the cell door opened without warning, and a man in a blue uniform was standing there in front of me. But it was not the same man I had seen earlier. 'What's all this noise about, then?' he inquired mildly, and without any real interest. 'First of all, I demand a decent cell and not a shit-hole like this!' I shouted in fury. 'And secondly I demand some lunch! I am here in protective custody, and I have a right to insist on that!'

'Well then, just be happy that you've got such a right!' he replied, slamming the door shut and sliding the bolt home. Through the sound of my renewed angry bellowing I could hear him quietly giggling in the corridor.

The hours crept past, spent partly in studying the pornographic scribblings on the wall, partly in kicking up more din. I had to do something with my time, after all. I'd have liked to take a look out of the window, and get a little fresh air after this noisome stench. But in order to pull myself up to the window I'd have had to come into contact with the wall, and the thought of that was just too revolting.

Then again, I was quite sure that they planned to do something else with me before nightfall, and at the time I just couldn't believe that they would dare to leave me sitting (or rather standing) in this hole for the entire night. After all, we were living in a country under the rule of law, and a dirty trick like that would cost them dear. Child that I was, I still didn't get it: since January 1933 Germany had ceased to be a country under the rule of law, and was now a police state pure and simple, where those in charge decided what was lawful and what was not. But on this occasion my instinct was right, and as it was starting to get dark my cell door opened again. 'Come with me!' he said, and led me to the front office of the police station, where he handed me over to a man in a grey uniform with the words 'This is the man.' Then he turned on his heel and promptly dismissed me from his mind for good. 'Come with me', said the man in the grey uniform, and I thought: 'I wonder where your fate is taking you now', and followed him. But we didn't go far, just across the street to a red building that bore the legend 'Courthouse'. 'Aha!' I thought to myself, 'the courthouse jail – at least it can't be any worse!' We entered the building and went into an office, where an elderly, decrepit-looking man with moth-eaten hair was sitting chewing on his pen. 'This is the man', said my escort; the lexicon of social intercourse around here seemed somewhat impoverished. The clerk gave me a sidelong look, searched at length through a great stack of files, but in the end decided to plump for a single sheet of paper lying on the desk in front of him. 'There!' he said.

I unfolded the letter. It was from the district council leader for the Lebus district, and informed me in a single sentence that he had ordered my arrest on the grounds that I was involved in a 'conspiracy against the person of the Führer'.

'I deny the charge!' I protested. 'That's complete and utter nonsense! I have never been involved in any conspiracy, and certainly not against the person of the Führer. I'm not even interested in politics . . .'

'That's nothing to do with us', said the clerk evenly, and scratched his ear. 'We're only here to process the arrest order. Is there anything else?'

'Then I'd like to contact my lawyer immediately!' I said. 'You can write to him', replied the clerk, and handed me a sheet of notepaper and an envelope. 'Anything else?'

'I can't think of anything right now . . .' I said hesitantly.

'As someone taken into protective custody', said the man, suddenly looking me full in the face, 'you can cater for yourself, that is to say, you can have your lunch and evening meal brought in from a local hostelry.' He looked at me again. Then he added quickly: 'As long as you've got the money to pay for it.'

'That I have!' I cried, and produced my wallet. 'Constable, see that this man has his meals fetched regularly from the *Poor Knight* on the market square.' And to me: 'Anything else?'

At that moment I really couldn't think of anything else, or at least nothing that the clerk could have done for me. 'Constable, take this man to his cell!' Thank God, it was a clean cell, as I could just make out in the fading evening light, and it was also bug-free, as I discovered after the first night I spent there. I woke early, made my bed, and wrote my two letters. My lawyer I simply asked to visit me; the letter to my wife contained the same request but also a few other things, whatever I felt able to say under the circumstances. I could see her there before me; she was having a hard time of it right now, expecting a child, in fact she was expecting twins, as we knew, and she was in a lot of discomfort. And then I pictured myself driving away from the house, in this clapped-out car commandeered by the SA, while a sentry stayed behind outside her door. How would she cope with all this – in her condition? I was somewhat comforted by the thought that at least she need not fear for my life, since the good doctor would have passed on my message. And then my heart sank as I realized that there was no guarantee of this. Would the sentry let visitors through to see her? Wasn't the whole point of the sentry to keep her isolated? And I could see her there before me, alone in the house with the boy, the telephone now cut off, with only our landlords downstairs, an elderly couple, to call on for help and advice. The Sponars! I suddenly remembered the hate-filled look that Mrs Sponar gave me as I went upstairs escorted by the SA men. A horrible feeling crept over me: did the Sponars have a hand in this dirty business? Then I remembered the Thursday afternoon, the little jokes that Mr von Salomon had made – but how could that possibly be? What interest could the Sponars have in doing me harm? On the contrary, they had every interest in helping me, because I had offered them more than anyone else had: a carefree old age! No, the Sponars would surely help my wife, in so far as strangers like them could really do anything to help. That encounter before morning communion on Good Friday had really been so distasteful – Suse would never be able to trust such people completely. But then again, now that I thought about it there was something reassuring in this encounter too: surely these old people couldn't be so two-faced and so vicious as to come and ask our pardon with treachery in their hearts? Impossible! And they didn't need to. No, it had to be that incorrigible schemer and hothead von Salomon who had landed me in this mess! 'Conspiracy against the person of the Führer' – that was just his kind of thing! But how did they get the idea that I was some sort of co-conspirator? They couldn't just arrest every person that Mr von Salomon had visited lately, without further investigation, and take them all into protective custody as suspected co-conspirators! Whichever way I looked at it, there was something about it I couldn't explain; and however much I tried to avoid it, I kept on seeing that look of hatred in Mrs Sponar's eyes.

These thoughts kept on going round and round in my head, and so I was really pleased when the police constable finally unlocked the door and handed me my breakfast – a dry crust and a cup of watery chicory coffee. He took the letters I handed him, looked at me, then looked around the cell. His gaze came to rest on the bed, which had been made in regulation fashion and folded up against the wall. 'This isn't the first time you've been inside', he observed. 'Only an old lag makes his bed like that.'

Unfortunately he was correct in his observation. In the course of my eventful life I had indeed inhabited a prison cell from time to time. But it still annoyed me a little that he had noticed. In the meantime I had become a famous writer, and the days of my youthful follies lay

far in the past. I made no reply. He looked me in the face again and
said: 'Well then . . . I'll look in again before lunch and see what you
want.' 'Some sort of meat dish with soup and stewed fruit', I said, 'and
a large glass of beer. And twenty cigarettes.' (I had ordered the glass
of beer – I actually don't like beer at all – because beer always makes
me feel nice and sleepy. I was hoping for a good long afternoon nap.
It would make the time pass more quickly.) 'Okay, done', he replied,
and left. The long day stretched out before me, and I knew from bitter
experience what a long and endless torment a day in a prison cell can be
if you have no work to do, and are just left alone with your thoughts. I
don't have the ability to 'doze', and my talent for sleep is limited at the
best of times. So I had decided on a program of work for myself. My
cell was clean enough, but by my Hamburg-born wife's[40] standards of
spring cleaning it was a pigsty. I had calculated that my lawyer probably wouldn't come to see me for another two or three days, so I had
allocated these three days for window cleaning, washing the walls and
polishing. I knew that one could spend a whole day polishing up the
zinc lid of a pail until it shone like a mirror, with not a dull patch the
size of a pin-head. So let's get to it! First, the windows – and the hours
just flew past so quickly that I was really surprised when the constable
unlocked my cell door and brought in my lunch from the hotel in a
tiffin box.

(26.IX.44.) The lunch was tasty enough, and I even got my glass of
beer, which was more than I had dared hope for. Ignoring the rules, I
let my bed down from the wall and flung myself on it, weary enough
and ready for sleep. But then of course my thoughts, as if they had just
been waiting for this moment, immediately began to revolve around
my wife, left alone without protection, and around this mysterious
'conspiracy against the person of the Führer'. No stranger to such
troublesome intrusions, I countered them by silently reciting poetry to
myself from memory, starting with some lines from Hofmannsthal[41]
('Noch spür ich ihren Atem auf den Wangen') and moving on to

Münchhausen's ballads[42] ('Es ritt nach Krieg und Reisen . . .'). No sooner had I managed to escape the torment of my obsessive thoughts and fallen fast asleep when I heard the key rattling in the lock of my cell door, and I leapt up guiltily from my bed. The police constable didn't say anything about my using the bed when I wasn't supposed to, but looked at me instead in silence for a while. Then he asked me a rather surprising question, considering where I was: 'Do you play cards by any chance?'

I replied: 'I do indeed, constable!'

He looked at me again, and seemed to be turning something over in his mind. Then he came to a decision. 'The thing is', he said, and gestured with his thumb down the corridor of the cell block behind him, 'back there in the cell there are two old Yids and they're looking for a third man to play cards with them. Have you got anything against Yids?'

'Not really, no', I confessed.

'Well then', he said, 'you come along with me and I'll put you in with them.' He led the way down the corridor, then stopped again. 'But you mustn't say a word about this to anyone', he whispered. 'I won't, constable. There's nobody here I could tell.' He went on: 'And especially not my colleague, who's on duty tomorrow afternoon. He's a Nazi, you see, and I'm Stahlhelm,[43] do you understand?'

I understood well enough. The hostility between the Stahlhelm and the Nazis, and more specifically the SA, with which the Stahlhelm had been forced to merge, was well known. The worthy leader of the Stahlhelm, a Mr Düsterberg,[44] had been ousted as a result, but the second-in-command, Mr Seldte,[45] had landed the job of Reich Minister for Labour in return for selling out his organization. But the struggle between the die-hard Stahlhelm men and the SA continued behind the scenes, and that fire is still burning to this day.

So I indicated by a nod that I understood completely, and assured him that his colleague would learn absolutely nothing from me. To tell you how this little story ends, I now need to fast-forward one day. At lunchtime the next day the key rattled in the lock again, and again I was caught sleeping when I wasn't supposed to by a police constable, only this time it was the other one, the bad-cop Nazi. Again I didn't get shouted at for sleeping during the day, but was taken – again – to the other cell and locked in to 'play cards with the two old Yids' – but given strict instructions not to say a word to his 'colleague': 'The thing is, he's Stahlhelm and I'm Nazi, and if he can drop me in it, he will!'

It really wasn't a bad little jail at all, that courthouse jail in Fürstenwalde an der Spree. Nobody made my life a misery, nobody bawled me out, nobody got worked up because I had been arrested for conspiring against the blessed person of the Führer. It was still 1933, and the Nazis had only been in power for a few months; they had not yet managed to stamp out all sense of decency and humanity. I very much doubt if such a thing would be possible in any German jail today, in 1944. People like these two police officers simply don't exist any more, because whatever sense of justice they still had has been systematically destroyed. Today it is seen as a disgrace to display leniency, or even common decency, towards one's enemies. It's become a crime, in fact. The Nazis have been going about their dirty business out in the open for so long now, and shouting about it as if it's something to be proud of, that they've got everyone used to it now. Everyone's just so apathetic. It's quite something if someone so much as sighs these days – only to say in the next breath: 'But what can you do? That's just the way it is!'

The truth is I had chosen a good time to be arrested, a time of transition, and the remnants of decency that had not yet been destroyed allowed me to live a pretty tolerable life. The pair I played cards with, 'the old Yids', were cultivated and amusing companions. The card games were just a pretext for us to socialize, and we spent most of the time just sitting and talking. They had been teachers at a school not far from Fürstenwalde, which combined classroom teaching with a large farm estate; the idea was for young Jews to learn a trade that was unusual for Jews, namely agriculture. Both these gentlemen, the headmaster and one of his teachers, were idealists and Zionists; their dream was to bring world Jewry back to Palestine, the land promised to the Jews by God Himself, and to persuade all Jews to turn away from money and become a nation of farmers. They were so innocent and naive that they actually welcomed the arrival of the Nazis, believing that Hitler's reign of terror would help their plans. For now their school had been shut down and expropriated by the Party, and the pupils and teachers had been carted off and scattered to the four winds – but all this just made them smile. They sat there in their cell, pretty shabbily dressed, with the hands of men used to working in the fields, and looking very Jewish. They said: 'The Jews have suffered so many persecutions and have successfully survived them all. In fact, the persecutions only served to focus their minds on their strengths as a nation, and persecutions made the Jews stronger, not weaker. During the Russian pogroms a huge wave of nationalism swept through world Jewry. Jews in every country, who were normally at daggers drawn, now helped each other.'

All three of us were dismissive of the 'thousand-year Reich' that the Nazis wanted to establish, which Hitler, and in particular the delusional Mr Rosenberg,[46] were always rabbiting on about. I was more sceptical than the others, giving the Nazis four years, five at the most. (I turned out to be a false prophet.) One of the Jews, the headmaster, smiled and said with that inimitably subtle, ironic Jewish smile: 'A thousand years! I tell you, Mr Fallada, you'll wake up one day and rub your eyes in astonishment and cry: "What, have the thousand years ended already? It felt more like one day!"'

I must just tell a little story at this point about my dear old publisher, 'friend Rowohlt', who sometimes liked to boast that he was always ahead of his time. By way of example he cited the time he stopped making his payments. What happened? Four weeks later the Dresdner Bank copied his example, and then hundreds and hundreds of firms followed suit. 'And then take my family life, my friend. As you know, I've been married twice before and am now on my third marriage. What is that if it's not the third Reich? Else was the first Reich, Hilda was the second Reich, and now Elli is my third Reich.[47] And now I'll let you into a little secret, friend Fallada', dropping his voice to a hollow whisper, 'whenever I quarrel with Elli I'm convinced that the fourth Reich will be along soon! Mark my words, friend Fallada, we'll both live to see the fourth Reich yet!' A few pages further on it will become clear that there are indeed some prospects of a fourth Reich – not least in Rowohlt's private life.

Anyway, outwardly I had very little to put up with in the courthouse jail at Fürstenwalde. They did take away my big glass of beer a week later, after some official, having got wind of this alcohol abuse, which was completely inadmissible in the prison system, had forbidden it. It was no great sacrifice. What was harder to bear was the brief message from my lawyer that they finally gave me after five or six days of fruitless waiting: he'd been forbidden to contact me or represent my interests.

So I didn't need any legal counsel. They took care of it. They gave the prisoner in protective custody five-star treatment: he could feed himself at his own expense, wear his own clothes, smoke, and he didn't need to work. But those basic legal rights that even the most depraved murderer is granted, the right to retain legal counsel and the right to defend himself, were denied me and all others in my situation. Normally anyone placed under arrest in Germany had to appear before an examining magistrate within twenty-four hours, to be told the reason for his arrest and be given an opportunity to explain himself. Depending on the outcome of that explanation, the examining magistrate then issues a definitive arrest order or releases him from custody.

But it's a different story altogether for someone taken into 'protective custody'! The gold-braided brownshirt went to the district council leader and accused me of conspiring against the person of the Führer. So they put me behind bars – where I remained: I was not expected to defend myself, nobody wanted me to defend myself, and I was not even given the opportunity. So and so was safely tucked away, so and so could not do any more damage – and that was all they cared about. This striking characteristic of the Nazis, treating people like cattle for the slaughter and never giving a thought to their distress or suffering, was starting to become apparent even back then. Questions of guilt and innocence never interested those gentlemen. The only thing that mattered to them was expediency. Whatever suited their plans was right, whatever didn't suit their plans simply didn't exist in their eyes. When later on during the war – and I've just remembered this example – some little postmistress was sentenced to several years' imprisonment because she had taken a single bar of soap that fell out of a damaged parcel, the powers that be did not care a fig about the grotesque mismatch between the 'crime' and the punishment. Nor do they care that they ruined a human life, and perhaps more than one, for the sake of a trifle. They didn't care about people, and despite all their big talk they have never cared about people. All that mattered to them was expediency. And it was expedient to keep the German population down and in a constant state of fear and terror. They terrorized people until the prisons, jails and mental institutions were full to bursting, they terrorized them with the gallows and the guillotine until nobody cared if they lived or died. Life was cheap; a careless jest could send you to your death. So what does any of it matter? 'You're done for one way or the other', as they say in Berlin – and as usual they are right. We're all of us well and truly done for.

When I received the message from my lawyer that he had been denied permission to talk to me, I knew straightaway that my wife wouldn't be allowed to visit me either, and my letter to her probably hadn't even been forwarded. It was only now, as the days and weeks passed, that I realized how hopeless my situation was. They could leave me here to rot until the end of the thousand-year Reich . . . Nobody cared what happened to me, nobody was able to contact me. The judicial authorities were not responsible for me: I was a 'political' prisoner, only held in custody here behind bars. The district council leader who had issued the custody order, and who had taken a decision with such grave consequences on the unproven say-so of an SA leader – this zealous district council leader viewed my case as closed the moment I was put away. And what about the SA who had arrested me, whom I had caused so much trouble by refusing to oblige and let them shoot me while trying to escape? Well, the fact was that the SA men had achieved their purpose; I was living the life of a dead man in here, dead to the world, unable to get a message out or receive any message from outside. And whenever my thoughts had taken me this far, the moment always came when I said to myself: something's not right here. The SA really had gone to an awful lot of trouble over me, as if they took a very personal interest in my case; first of all the argument with the country policeman, then their attempt to make it look as if I was shot while trying to escape. You don't go to all that trouble over some faceless prisoner whose arrest order has come down from Berlin! Because the investigation will have to be conducted in Berlin. That's where Mr von Salomon lives, and if he was really preparing a putsch they'll have to take me there for interrogation and not leave me mouldering here. It was no good: try as I might, the pieces of this jigsaw puzzle just would not fit together. And then my thoughts kept coming back to the dethroned queen, and that hate-filled look of hers. There were many times when I felt certain that the Sponars were behind all this, but then I asked myself the question the ancient Romans used to ask, which should be asked whenever a crime has been committed: cui bono? Who benefits from this? And in the case of the Sponars I could not see any way in which they would benefit. Rather the reverse, if anything.

But as the weeks passed I became more and more concerned about my wife and child, and sometimes I would stand beneath the high window of my cell late into the night, quite convinced that Suse was now standing at her window, looking down at the SA sentry still patrolling outside, and thinking of me. I shook with helpless rage and despair. But in the end I would always go back to bed and sleep a little. What could I possibly do? Poor blighter that I was, they had me where they wanted me, and I could do absolutely nothing about it.

And then suddenly everything changed. One morning the policeman was suddenly standing there in my cell – it was the Stahlhelm man – and saying: 'Come with me, Fallada, you've got a visitor.'

'What?' I cried, and couldn't believe my ears. 'A visitor – ?! Who on earth would be visiting me here?!'

'Well, who do you think?' he said, viewing my agitation with astonishment. 'Who else but your wife?'

'My wife – ?' I exclaimed, and for a moment I was so shaken that I wanted to burst out crying with happiness. 'Ah, my wife! Well, that's all right, then!' And I composed myself, adjusted my clothing, which was looking pretty shabby by now, and followed my leader. And it really was my wife, standing there in a wide corridor, holding my son's hand and looking towards me. Her pale face lit up with her smile, such a patient, kind and gentle smile!

So I had a visitor, but let me say straightaway that this visit was a 'clerical error' on the part of the court office, because this visit should never have been allowed. But as I have already said, in these early days after the Nazi seizure of power it was still possible to find basic human decency and also personal courage (completely eradicated in the meantime) in many parts of the system. By now I had been in the jail for weeks on end, and although I had only had any real contact with 'my' two police constables – Mr Nazi and Mr Stahlhelm – the message had filtered through that I was a quiet and well-behaved man with tidy habits. Nobody in prison is more highly regarded than the man who doesn't make trouble. I had never made any applications or complaints, I hadn't even written any letters, and smuggling out secret messages was the last thing on my mind. I had been like a man who doesn't exist, the complete opposite of a conspirator in my innermost being – and as for what the people downstairs really thought about a conspiracy against the beloved person of the Führer, that is anyone's guess. And so on this particular morning a woman had turned up with her little boy holding on to her hand, clearly in an advanced stage of pregnancy, and had implored them to let her speak to her husband. The husband was only here temporarily, having been taken into protective custody on 'political' grounds: all the more reason why visits would not be allowed. But someone must have said to the constable: 'Oh go on, take the lady up to the corridor – no, not into the visiting room. This isn't a proper visit, we'll just pretend it didn't happen. It's just so that husband and wife can see each other again, do you see – just for a minute or so, that's all . . .'

I wasn't there in the office, but that's more or less how the conversation will have gone. And that's how we saw each other again, the two of us, standing there and looking at each other. The Stahlhelm constable sounded almost threatening: 'You know you can't discuss your case, not a single word. And I can give you five minutes, maximum!' He gave us a very severe look, then did an about-turn and walked to the far end of the corridor, where he turned his broad back on us and found something very interesting to look at in the street.

We hugged and embraced and smothered each other with kisses, weeping a little with emotion and joy, and our little boy was there in between us and asking: 'Daddy, why aren't you at home with us any more? Why are you here in this horrible house? Do we have to live here for ever in this horrible house, Daddy?'

But then came the moment in the midst of all this rejoicing and excitement when my wife surreptitiously glanced over her shoulder at the policeman, who had his back turned towards us the whole time, and urgently whispered a single word, and that word was the name of our landlords, traitors and Judases: 'Sponars!' And then we talked at length, or rather Suse talked, since my life had been so uneventful that there was little to tell. This visit that never happened definitely lasted longer than five minutes, it may have been fifteen, or then again fifty minutes – the time just flew past, until the policeman finally turned round and said: 'Right, now it really is time for you to stop!' And when we looked at him imploringly: 'Oh, all right then, another two minutes. But I really do mean two minutes this time!' And so finally we parted; my wife went back to a life of freedom, while I returned to my cell, my heart seething with emotion. In my mind I went back over everything she had just told me, nearly choking with fury and hatred at the despicable vileness of it all. So my dark foreboding had been right, and I had seen aright: that look in the eyes of the dethroned queen had been a look of hatred, the villainous hatred that a murderer feels for his victim. And that woman was not much better than a murderer, one who lacked the courage to do the deed herself, a coward who got others to do it for her.

When I was taken away and Suse had been left alone in the house with our boy, the first thing she had tried to do was telephone my publisher. But when she dialled there was no answer from the exchange, and that's how it had been the whole time since: they'd blocked the connection. The postman too had only called on the couple downstairs, and had not even delivered the newspaper to her. She had approached the sentry posted on the street and tried to go past him, but he had told her curtly that she was not allowed to leave the house, and that she would be shot if she attempted to escape. And when she asked how she was supposed to buy food for herself and her son, he had just told her that was up to her. Perhaps, he suggested, Mrs Sponar would be kind enough to buy for her when she did her own shopping, although it was a bit much to expect her to help out when traitorous scum like that had been planning an attempt on the Führer's life. This was the first gentle hint that Mrs Sponar was perhaps on the other side – it was almost imperceptible, but still, it was enough to make my wife suspicious.

It would have been good if the Jewish lady friend had still been in the house, because she could have taken a message to Berlin for us. But she had slipped away during the final phase of the house search, and didn't even know that I had been arrested. My wife sat at home, deeply worried. 'Where have they taken my husband?' she wondered. 'When will he be home again?'

Thank God, she hadn't remembered that headline in bold print: 'Shot while trying to escape!' She was not afraid for my safety, only worried because we were apart. But she had always been patient and longsuffering, accepting without complaining whatever fate threw at her; she had her work and the child, and so she kept her dark thoughts at bay by working and playing. She was a little surprised that in the wake of such an event and such an upheaval in their house the Sponars hadn't even looked in to see if she was all right, so as it was getting dark she went downstairs to ask them if they could get some fresh milk and vegetables for the child. She found the old couple sitting in their darkened room in dead silence, the queen working away blindly on a delicate piece of lace, as she liked to do, and the old man with his actor's face nodding off in his chair, as he liked to do.

They gave her a warm welcome, and showered her with effusive expressions of regret and sympathy – the sort of thing she hated, but now had to listen to patiently – and quizzed her about what had been going on, and what it was I had done.

My wife's assurance that I hadn't done anything, and that the whole thing must be some kind of misunderstanding that would soon be cleared up, was met with a coolly sceptical silence, and when she added, in some agitation, that it might all have something to do with the visit from Mr von Salomon, whose name might have led them to think he was Jewish, whereas in fact he came from French (and later Rhenish) aristocracy, this too was met with cool scepticism. That evening Mrs Sponar went so far as to say that she was sufficiently well acquainted with the SA and its leaders to know that mistakes simply never happened. It was probably just the old, familiar story – a husband up to his tricks without the wife knowing, and she having to pick up the pieces afterwards. It was too dark to tell whom Mrs Sponar was looking at when she spoke these words, whether my wife or her own husband, but Mr Sponar did heave a deep sigh at this point. The dethroned queen added that she was well acquainted with, not to say good friends with, the local Party branch leader, a building contractor by the name of Mr Gröschke; she would contact him tomorrow and ask what the charge against Mr Fallada was. She would be happy to report back to my wife, as long as that was allowed.

My wife didn't care either for the tone or for the substance of our landlady's remarks, and she quickly asked if they could do the food shopping for her and then made as if to leave. But she wasn't going to get off so lightly, because now the Sponars launched into a litany of complaint about my irresponsible behaviour, which, they noted, jeopardized their future as well. They pointed out that there'd been talk of a firm agreement about paying them an annuity and giving them the right to live in this house for the rest of their lives – so where did they stand with that now? Had the mortgages at least been bought up? My wife took the greatest possible exception to their complaints, which made it sound as if I was out of the picture for good. She stood up and said curtly that we would stand by our commitments, regardless of whether it was the husband or the wife who fulfilled them, was somewhat taken aback to hear them heave a huge sigh of relief, and left the room.

I won't dwell on the details of how my wife's eyes were gradually opened to the guile of the Sponars, how she came to see more clearly with each passing day how the fearful prospect of an impoverished old age had turned our landlords into heartless criminals. Most of her news came via a little old lady who delivered newspapers and bread, who had taken pity on the lonely and heavily pregnant woman. Isolated though our house was, it was the object of close scrutiny in the village. People there knew a lot – and suspected more than they knew.

On the evening when I had put what I thought was a very generous proposal to the Sponars, namely to provide for them in old age in return for their consent to the auction sale, they hadn't taken time to 'think things over', as they had said to me, but had gone straight to their friend, the building contractor and local Party branch leader Gröschke, to seek his advice. I can't say much about this man from my own observation, I only saw him the one time, much later, a slimly built man with a curiously small head and a hard face. Like many small skilled tradesmen during the worst years of unemployment he had declared himself bankrupt, probably not because of his own incompetence, but either because of the general hardship of the times or because of his Party commitments – or else for a combination of all three reasons. Anyway, he'd been declared bankrupt, and it's not hard to imagine what a wretched life such a little man would have led as a bankrupt in a village of hard-nosed farming folk who placed a high value on money and property. But now the Führer had come to power, and with him tens of thousands of these bankrupted little men had seized their own opportunity, determined to get their share of power and property. Overnight they had acquired the power of life and death over their fellow men, or if not that, then at least the power of making them or breaking them: and if they themselves had been harshly treated in the past, they were determined to treat their fellow citizens much more harshly now.

So what kind of advice was such a man going to give his good friend Sponar, when the latter explained his and my situation to him? He knew this friend was living on a pitiful pension from social services, in a house that could be taken away from him at any time. The conversation will doubtless have gone something like this: 'The man is a writer and he's not a Party member, and we know from the jokes he was told by his Jewish visitor that he is no friend to the Party. We could have him put away for that alone. But that isn't going to help us much, in six months or a year he'll be out again, and we'll be right back where we started. No: what we need to do is charge him with something serious and conduct a house search – we'll probably find something. But even if we don't, it doesn't really matter; we'll lock him up anyway on the serious charge, and since he won't be questioned he won't be able to talk his way out of it either. Best of all, of course, is if he tries to make a run for it. Then we'll be rid of him for good, one way or the other.

But of course we won't do anything until he has bought up the mortgages and has effectively become the owner of the house. You'll agree to his proposals, but not give your consent to the foreclosure. I know these city types, they can't wait, things can't go fast enough for them, and he'll buy on the strength of your word alone. So then he'll be the owner, and safely out of the way, and we'll have no trouble with the wife. She can't put the house up for auction without your consent, and we'll make her life there a misery – leave that to me. But we won't let her move out until she has paid rent for the longest possible time, and definitely not before she has paid out the allowance that has been promised you and your wife for the rest of your lives. And I can guarantee, Sponar, that you and your wife are going to live to a ripe old age!' That's more or less what the hard-boiled old bruiser, leathery veteran of many a brawl at political meetings, will have said: not all at once, of course, but one little plan will have led on to another, until the whole villainous scheme had been cooked up to perfection. All three of them will have appeased their consciences by arguing that I was an enemy of the Party, and over the next ten years this neat little excuse was used to justify so much brutality in Germany that the trick they planned to pull on me was just a minor thing by comparison, quite benign and harmless.

My wife only learned of all this in dribs and drabs, noticing something when she was with the Sponars, or picking up on something said by her delivery lady. It's a good thing the whole business didn't just drop on her all at once, like a cold downpour; it might well have proved too much for her. The body can habituate itself to the most potent poisons, it's just a matter of increasing the dosage gradually. Meanwhile the days passed, one after another, the sentry was still posted out in the street, another stood guard at the back down by the river, and nothing happened. If she had only known where I was she would have tried earlier to escape from this prison, but she knew nothing. (The good doctor had not been able to get a message to her, of course – that's why the sentry was there.) In the end it was the old lady who told her they were saying in the village that I was in the nick in nearby Fürstenwalde. No sooner had my wife received this tip-off than she made up her mind. She waited until the late evening, after supper, when it was getting dark. Then, in order to throw the evil Sponars off the scent, she turned the taps full on to fill the bath noisily and turned up the volume on the radio, got our sleeping boy out of bed and dressed him. Holding him in her arms and leaving everything else behind, she slipped out into the garden in her stockinged feet, put on her shoes and crept along to the garden gate. She had already observed, especially at night, that the sentries, while still in place, were so tired after their long hours on duty that they relaxed their guard somewhat, often wandering a long way up and down the street. So she waited for such a moment, when the SA man was eighty or a hundred paces away, crossed the street and disappeared into the dark forest of thin pine trees, where she walked on through the night, with no path to follow. The hardest thing to cope with was the child in her arms, who had picked up on her agitation, wouldn't go to sleep, and kept on asking questions. In the end she managed to calm him down (and herself too, therefore) by telling him little stories in a low voice. She pressed on through the dark, trackless forest, bumping into unseen

branches, stumbling over roots, sometimes falling over: but always she
was driven on by her single-minded resolve. She wasn't far from the
railway station, but she was frightened to go there. She had reached
the point where she thought our enemies capable of anything. Perhaps
they had sent her description through to the station, a description that
was easy enough to recognize: a tall, heavily pregnant woman. So she
carried on feeling her way through the forest, further and further, until
she had left the village behind her. Then she struck out for the road,
found it, and carried on along it, finding the going a little easier now. It
was the same road that I had travelled a few weeks earlier in the 'jalopy'.
She also passed the spot that I'll never forget as long as I live, where I
was supposed to get out and where I had to fight for my life. I had seen
it in the sunshine, and will always see it bathed in sunshine, with the
thin poles of the scrawny pine trees. She walked past the place at night,
it meant nothing to her, and her heart did not beat any faster on that
account. It's a strange planet we live on, and those who are closest to
each other still live a long way apart.

It's not that far from our village to the town of Fürstenwalde, not
much more than ten kilometres, but for a heavily pregnant woman
with a three-year-old child in her arms it is a very long way indeed.
For weeks on end she had just been sitting in the house and getting no
exercise: now she had to step out and keep on going. Sometimes the
boy would run along beside her for a bit, and then she would sit down
on a milestone and rest for a while. She was also thinking about the
two babies she carried inside her, of course, and told herself that all this
agitation, worry and over-exertion couldn't possibly be good for them.
But it didn't help at all. And it didn't help at all that every kilometre
felt like a mile, and that her feet hurt terribly from all the extra weight
she was carrying. Nor did it help that she was fretting and worrying
about me and about what the future would bring for us. But she was
driven on by sheer willpower, and she travelled the road that she had to
travel; rough or smooth, she had no choice. The night was all around
her, perchance the stars were up above her head, and a wind helped
her on her way. But as she was walking she also thought about the

people whose actions had brought her to this, having to creep around in secret at night like some tramp. She thought about the men who had seized control in Germany, destroying at a stroke the freedom of the individual in every area of personal life, inviting every kind of arbitrary abuse and putting people at each other's throats. But it helped her to think like that. It taught this kind, forgiving heart how to hate, it made these eyes, which otherwise only ever looked for the good in life, clear-sighted, and not once in the ten years that followed, not for one second, did she ever falter in her hatred. She knew these men are evil, and want only what is evil. It may be that here and there along the way they do something good, but since they want what is evil, it doesn't count, and their downfall is certain. What is acquired by evil means cannot stand. And now hopefully the hour is nigh when the whole evil edifice will collapse in ruins!

She reached Fürstenwalde, by then it was already morning, and she went to the railway station. She used the washroom to freshen up herself and the child, and had a bit of breakfast. Then they went to visit me, she saw me again, healthy and in good spirits, and both of us felt our hearts a little lighter. As for what to do next, the only word of advice I could give her was: 'Go and see Rowohlt, good old Rowohlt – he'll know of a way out!'

And so she went to see him, the man who stood by his authors when they were in any kind of trouble, and he knew what to do. 'You must always go straight to the top', said Rowohlt, and telephoned a high-profile lawyer,[48] a man who had defended the Reichstag arsonist on the authority of the Party, who in the end was executed himself. They arranged a meeting: the famous lawyer, the famous publisher Rowohlt, and the writer's wife. The wife was rather indignant when she realized that the lawyer, a man of the utmost coarseness and an old Party member, found nothing remotely surprising about her story; to him it was just another run-of-the-mill case. Instead the lawyer cheerily assured her: 'You've come to the right man, dear lady! The district council leader of Lebus is an old school friend of mine. We'll take a car and scoot straight over there, and I'll bet you anything: in half an hour

I'll get your husband released!' This completely unexpected prospect of my early release banished all my wife's indignation at his blasé acceptance of such a blatant injustice. She gladly climbed into a car with the lawyer, waved goodbye to the publisher, and off they went. What the lawyer and the district council leader talked about in private, regarding conspiracies against the person of the Führer, good and bad political jokes, and Mr von Salomon, we shall never know. We are and always have been entirely unpolitical people, and this kind of thing is a closed book to us. At any rate, the lawyer came hurrying into the anteroom where my wife had been waiting with pounding heart, pressed a sheet of paper into her hand and said: 'Take the car and drive like the wind to Fürstenwalde! This is an order for your husband's immediate release, but it's Saturday today, and after twelve noon no German courthouse jail will release a prisoner until the Monday! So if you get a move on you might just make it!' And make it she did: at five to twelve she got the decrepit-looking clerk of the court to stop chewing his pen and stir his stumps, and by five past twelve we were standing out on the street together again – and oh so happy!

The first thing we did, of course, was to drive to Berlin to my publisher and thank him for his splendid intervention. Then we went for a celebratory dinner (we viewed my release as a definitive victory over our enemies!), collected our son and went home – for my part, I must admit, with a heart full of feelings of triumph and revenge.

It was still light when we got back to our village. From the railway station we walked along the narrow path through the forest to our house. The sentry in the street had gone, but Mr Sponar happened to be standing in the garden, and he just stared at the three of us, stared and stared . . . We walked past without a word and went upstairs to our apartment. Oh, if only I had been a little more worldly-wise and diplomatic, I would have done nothing now and just left Sponar and his friend Gröschke to fret and stew, safe in the knowledge that I had the district council leader's release order in my pocket. In time everything would have settled down again, I would have acted as though I knew nothing about the treachery of the Sponars, somehow or other I would have got rid of these dangerous enemies and so would have quietly and gradually come into possession of the villa.

But I just couldn't wait, I couldn't hold my tongue, I had to charge at it like a bull at a gate! I sat down at my typewriter and hammered out a letter to Mr Sponar: 'Dear Mr Sponar, 1. I hereby give you notice that I am terminating your tenancy. 2. I hereby withdraw my offer of such and such a date giving you rights of residence and a lifetime annuity. 3. . . . 4. . . .' The list went on, as I exacted my revenge by numbers. I sealed the letter, put it downstairs on the hall table, and climbed into the bathtub, where I bathed my body in hot water and my soul in hot feelings of revenge.

And what did it all get me? A second visit from the SA! Next morning, when we had barely finished our breakfast, they turned up again. This time there were only three of them, accompanied by a leader I hadn't seen before, who was not wearing quite so much gold braid; but still, there they were, and just as determined as their predecessors to do whatever it took. I pointed to my release order, and to my civic right to terminate agreements: but to no avail. He told me I had tried to exploit the plight of a fellow German national in order to gain a personal advantage. That contravened a basic Nazi principle, and for that alone he could place me under arrest again forthwith. I had no right, he said, to deprive old Mr Sponar of his villa just because I had loads of money. Either I must agree immediately to withdraw the letter and fulfil all the obligations I had entered into earlier – or else! And he made a dramatic gesture to underline his meaning. And, he added, this time they would make sure I ended up in a place where even the most wily lawyer would not be able to get me out!

It was the first time in my life that I had been confronted by attempted Nazi blackmail of this kind, and I must confess that the brazenness with which it was presented to me really knocked me back. 'But surely I am at least allowed to terminate my rental agreement', I cried angrily. 'I have no desire to carry on living here!'

'You are not allowed to terminate your rental agreement', he replied, 'because by doing so you will aggravate the plight of a fellow German national. Of course, you are free to live wherever you like, but you must carry on paying the rent here! And of course, if you so wish, Mr Sponar will try to find an alternative tenant, at your own expense. If that works out, then of course you are off the hook. As you see, we are bending over backwards to accommodate you here. So: what is your decision? Are you coming with us, or are you going to meet your obligations?'

What choice did I have? I complied, inwardly raging. Perhaps the leader read something of my feelings in my face, because he said: 'And I would advise you to be extremely polite in your dealings with the Sponars. Any cause for complaint, and we'll come down on you very hard!' And with that they left.

(27.IX.44.) As for us, we just sat there wondering where it had all gone wrong. I especially didn't dare look at my wife, having now realized just how much damage I had done to us both by my ill-advised outburst of anger. Neither of us wanted to speak. But in the end I got to my feet and said: 'Yes, I've made a mess of things again, I can see that, you don't need to look at me like that, Suse! But I'm not going to carry on living here on that account. I can't stand the sight of those two sanctimonious creeps, and if I had to clap eyes on them every day I'd end up doing something really silly. I'm going to the village to see if I can't get a car to Berlin, and while I'm gone you can start to pack. Just pack what we'd need for a long trip, and use the big wardrobe trunk too, Suse. I have a feeling that we won't be living here again!' And I cast a long and rather wistful look around my large, bright study, the first room for which we had had furniture made to our own design by a master carpenter who still loved his work. Suse followed my gaze, and she doubtless felt a little wistful herself; but she said stoutly: 'Of course it's best if we move away from these two-faced people, I can't stand the sight of them either, and especially not her. He's just a weedy little man, and he reminds me of a rabbit with that velvet jacket of his. But I do wonder if Berlin is the right place for us? We're just coming into the hot season, and it would surely be better for the boy to have trees and

grass and water, like we had here. It would be good for me too. And it would definitely be better for you.' (Now she's thinking about the bars in Berlin, I thought to myself.) 'Not at all!' I cried, suddenly excited at the thought of a change of scene and different company. I was already realizing that it would be quite impossible for me to sit around quietly in the countryside after the last few eventful weeks. 'Not at all, we'll just move into the Stössinger guesthouse[49] for now, I'll phone them right away and see if we can have a nice big room. And what happens after that, we'll just have to wait and see. At times like this it's best not to make any plans at all. As you see, nothing turns out the way you expect it to!'

Having thus entrusted our collective future to pure chance, I got started on the work of moving house – which proved quite entertaining for me and our boy. The one unpleasant moment for me came when I knocked on the Sponars' door downstairs and went in with a receipt and a wad of notes in my hand to pay the rent and the annuity in advance for the next quarter. He could not conceal his agitation, and was almost shaking as he darted about looking for pen and ink. He normally signed his name with a flourish, but now he could barely manage a scrawl. The queen, meanwhile, sat by the window, bolt upright and stiff as a ramrod, and she was back at her lace-making again, the wooden bobbins clacking away balefully. Her dark eyes darted restlessly back and forth between her husband and me, and suddenly she laid aside the bobbins, reached out her hand and said imperiously to her husband: 'Sponar, let me see that!'

He responded with alacrity, she counted the notes, read and reread what was written on the receipt, handed it to me between the tips of two fingers, and said spitefully: 'But the furniture and all the other things stay here, as a security for our claims! From now on nothing more is to be removed!' I could have taken issue with her on that, but for one thing we already had all our essential belongings loaded into the car, which was parked outside the garden gate – I had put off this unpleasant parting visit until the last moment, when Suse and the boy were already sitting in the car. And for another thing, I had only just been hauled over the coals for my precipitate actions, and the effects of such a drubbing lasted for a few hours, even with me. So I moved not a muscle in my face – the mark of supreme self-control in moments of dire peril, as all the adventure stories tell us – and walked to the door without a word. The queen called after me in a deep, malevolent voice: 'And tell your wife I hope all goes well with the birth!' Coming from her, it sounded so malicious and hateful that for two pins I would have turned round and strangled the evil woman with my bare hands.

But I controlled myself again, and focused on getting out of there as quickly as I could so as not to have to listen to any more. Breathing a sigh of relief, I climbed into the car with my loved ones and called to the driver: 'Go! Go!' I was afraid they might come running out after me. My wife asked anxiously: 'Was there a problem? You look so pale!'

'No', I replied, 'it all went fine. But let's not think about any of this any more.' And as we took our leave I gazed out at the village as we drove through, and when we passed the house with the sign 'Karl Gröschke – Building Contractor' I pointed it out to Suse and showed her what an ugly house it was: the misbegotten brainchild of a country builder with pretentions, and a blot on the sandy landscape. And I began to rhapsodize about the beautiful buildings one sees in southern Germany, where even the humblest dwelling has something of beauty in it, be it only in the way its form is structured and articulated; and where even the simplest woodcutter has something of the artist in him, be it only in the way he carves a wooden spoon with his penknife. Warming to my theme, I soon forgot the little village of Berkenbrück and its inhabitants, and then we were in Berlin and arriving at the Stössinger guesthouse, at which point our lives entered a new and interesting phase, and all our troubles – for now – faded somewhat into the background. We had stayed at the guesthouse once before, in a quiet, tree-lined street in the old west end of the city, but only for a short time on that occasion. But we had enjoyed our stay. It was a very elegant guesthouse, but quite small – it won't have had more than fifteen or twenty rooms at most. The proprietor[50] was an elderly and very shrewd Jewish lady, whom my wife and I came to regard highly.

She was very precise in money matters, and her bills were not cheap. But she knew how to keep the business side and the personal side quite separate, and while she was the guesthouse proprietor, she was always the perfect lady. Actually, the term 'lady' is somewhat misleading: she was a cultivated and very motherly woman, who was always on hand to offer help and advice. With her motley international clientele she encountered every kind of peculiar and bizarre behaviour, but had learned to smile and turn a blind eye. No doubt she had her fair share of shady customers staying under her roof, international con men at large, but she wasn't bothered, just as long as they didn't play the fool in her house and paid their bills on time. But she would not tolerate any kind of smuttiness, such as bringing women of dubious character into the house, or flirting with the very pretty housemaids. If that happened, the eyes of this little old rotund Jewish woman would flash, and even the most well-heeled guest would get his marching orders there and then. If the odd guest came home drunk once in a while and kicked up a racket in the small hours, she would dismiss it with a smile. But when it came to cleanliness she was remorseless, both towards her guests and her maids, who were constantly cleaning the huge rooms from top to bottom.

It was of course absolutely typical of the writer Hans Fallada that five minutes after the Nazis had seized power he should have sought out a Jewish international guesthouse – of all things – as his place of residence and gaily started sending out his letters from there. I really was naive to the point of stupidity! For one thing, my application for membership of the Reich Chamber of Literature[51] was pending at the time, and our future livelihood depended on the outcome. The fact was that any writer whose application had been rejected was immediately banned from publishing anything at all in Germany, either in book form or in a newspaper or magazine. So I had every reason to be cautious, since I was already quite compromised, as I have said. But caution was the last thing on my mind. To those who warned me that it would be suicide to go and live in a Jewish guesthouse, which couldn't be kept secret, given the growing number of spies and informers – another fruit of the

Nazi regime! – I replied loftily: 'But I like it there! If they ban Aryans from living in Jewish guesthouses, then I'll move out. But until then, I'm staying put!'

Incidentally, the story of my application for membership of the Reich Chamber of Literature has a curious ending: despite several written submissions from me and my lawyer, I never heard back from them. I never did become a member of the RCL, I was just allowed to carry on working 'provisionally', since my application had not been rejected as such, i.e. it had not yet been processed. And that is still the case today, eleven years after the Nazi seizure of power. For the gentlemen at the RCL this arrangement has the advantage that they won't need to expel the author if he makes a serious nuisance of himself, since he was never a member in the first place! Moreover, an author in that situation, living in a constant state of uncertainty, is going to behave himself better than one who is already a member, and against whom formal proceedings have first to be initiated before he can be expelled. (Not that it did make me behave myself any better: I continued to cause those gentlemen a good deal of trouble.) In the early years I used to ask my lawyer from time to time how things were going with my membership application, to which he replied with a wave of the hand: 'Let sleeping dogs lie! Whatever you do, don't remind them! As long as they haven't turned you down, you can carry on working. So there!'

Although we have hardly got our foot in the door at the Stössinger guesthouse, so to speak, I must just mention the biggest *faux pas* that I committed round about that time. I received a letter from the Reich Minister for Public Enlightenment and Propaganda, signed by Mr Goebbels himself, which read as follows: 'Dear Mr Fallada, I am obliged to point out that your works in Swedish translation are published by the Bonnier publishing house, which is in the forefront of anti-German agitation. I must ask you to be mindful of this in future. p.p. Dr Goebbels'

I showed this letter to my trusty Rowohlt. We thought the letter uncommonly well composed – for a minister. We particularly liked the closing sentence, which followed on so lyrically from the one before.

But much as we enjoyed it, we still had the problem of having to write a reply, and in particular of having to 'be mindful in future', which we were not at all disposed to do. In the end we drafted something along the following lines: 'Dear Minister, At the time when I signed my long-term contracts with the Bonnier publishing house, I was not aware that it engaged in anti-German agitation. What I was aware of, however, was that the memoirs of Reich President von Hindenburg[52] were published under this imprint, and remain in print there to this day. Heil Hitler! Hans Fallada.' And I actually sent this wonderful missive to the Minister! So neither of us should really be surprised that this seed, so foolishly and rashly sown, would one day bear evil fruit. I myself haven't been all that badly affected, but poor Rowohlt had to pay dearly for this and other matters that I may get round to talking about later.

Anyway, we enjoyed our time at the Stössinger guesthouse very much. Not just on account of the food, which really was uncommonly good – my wife learned a great deal there. Not only were there beautifully prepared Austrian pastries, from apple strudel to *Kaiserschmarren* [sugared pancakes with raisins], but we were also introduced to colonial dishes such as chicken with curried rice, stuffed peppers, and all kinds of good things. But the most interesting part of the experience was the constant succession of other guests. Most of them were just passing through on their extended 'trip', spending four or five days in Berlin, while Paris always rated four or five weeks, which offended my sense of local patriotism hugely at the time, before I discovered that magnificent city for myself. Some of them were real oddballs, and Mrs Stössinger would often bring them to my table. We'd then sit for a quarter of an hour over an excellent cup of strong coffee, smoking foreign cigarettes and chatting. There was one lady I recall from the USA,[53] a real lady, but divorced from her husband, who earned her living – and a very good living too, judging by the fact that she was staying in an expensive guesthouse – entirely from doing parachute jumps. At the time, in 1933, parachute jumping was not yet the commonplace activity that it has now become as a result of this war. And especially not for a woman! She was an attractive woman, aged around thirty, with a wonderfully toned body. When she walked, she didn't so much walk as waft. She had fascinating stories to tell about her life of adventure, moving around from one city to the next in the vast expanses of the States, with six or eight old Army aeroplanes and a couple of veteran pilots from the World War, who performed their aerobatic stunts for paying crowds of onlookers. They lived a kind of itinerant circus existence, often short of money, then suddenly, if the crowd for some unknown reason took a special liking to them, very comfortably provided for. The star attraction was always her parachute jump. She described very vividly what it felt like to step out into the void. Back then parachutes were not the perfectly reliable affairs they are today. They often failed to open. So far she had been lucky, but one day. . . . And then she would hug our little boy tightly to her, which he didn't like at all. She had a boy like him back home in the States, and she was always thinking about him. So for her our lad was a kind of surrogate. We really had to keep an eye on him all the time in the guesthouse, and even then we were always looking for him. There were so many women staying in the guesthouse who had left their own children at home, and who now took every opportunity to spirit our lad away for a few hours in order to play with him or spoil him. There was nothing we could do about all the sweets he was given – he must have had a cast-iron stomach to cope with that lot without serious harm! And then there was the big toy shop directly across the street from the guesthouse. Every two or three days our son would be dragged in there by one of our fellow guests, and allowed to choose whatever he wanted – price no object! Personally, though, I think his admirers of both sexes liked buying him the toys that they enjoyed playing with themselves, and many is the time that I have gone to fetch our boy from one or other of the large, grand bedrooms and found him with his new lady friends, worthy matrons in amazing pyjamas, lying on the floor and 'squealing with delight' as he made some clockwork duck waddle back and forth between them, or busily changing the points on the track of a brightly-lit electric train set! It was always a struggle to get him back to our own, much quieter room, and my protests against all this crazy splurging on presents were always quite futile. I have to say that our stay in this elegant guesthouse was definitely not very good for our little boy.

One of the strangest characters I encountered in the guesthouse was a dark-skinned, slender man from India,[54] who had spent time in Soviet Russia as a buyer of precious stones. He bought up choice precious stones there for some prince or other. I assumed that he bought the stones illegally, then smuggled them out of the country without paying any duty. The way he stored them certainly seemed to indicate as much. He used to carry them around on his person, wrapped up in dirty pieces of paper and secreted inside various pockets and pouches. It never ceased to amaze me, the way he would suddenly reach inside his waistcoat pocket while we were talking and pull out a grubby little ball of paper, which he would then unwrap with his dusky fingers and produce a glittering cut diamond. By then I had already discovered that the precious stone that suited my wife best was an aquamarine, a stone that can appear sea-green or sea-blue, depending on the light, and which is sometimes suffused with a grey sheen, especially in daylight, like early-morning mist over the sea. I once asked the Indian if he had any aquamarines. Without a word he reached into his trouser pocket and pulled out a grey cone of paper, like the bags grocers use when you buy half a pound of sugar or semolina, and shook the contents out onto the table. We caught our breath for a moment: aquamarines of every size and shade lay there before us, thirty or forty of them, all polished and unmounted, and not a bad one among them. But there was one that immediately caught our eye, not just because of its size, but also because of its bright, limpid deep-blue glow. Our friend had immediately noted our interest. He picked up the stone and placed it on his open palm. 'From an icon', he said, and mentioned the name of a Russian town that I've long since forgotten. 'From an icon there!' he said. We were completely bowled over. We had never seen such a stone before, and I have never seen one like it since. It was as big as the palm of a baby's hand, and only ground at the edges. The man held the stone against my wife's neck, gazed at me with his gentle eyes, and whispered: 'Only three thousand marks – and I give you!'

I fought a hard struggle with myself. We had already decided to give
up the villa in Berkenbrück for good and to buy something else. Our
way of life had swallowed a lot of money, on top of that we had the
lawyers' bills, the financial settlement with Sponars – there was no way
I could afford it! And yet it was not the price as such that stopped me
buying it. I might have been able to stretch to that with an advance
from my publisher. What held me back was the sheer size and beauty
of the stone. All my life I have never been able to stand vulgar ostentation, and I just thought that we were not the kind of people to wear a
big stone like that. Our whole lifestyle just wasn't right for it. And we
wouldn't be comfortable living in a grander style, not even for the most
magnificent aquamarine. 'No', I said slowly, still looking at the stone
against Suse's skin. 'No, I'm sorry. We really can't afford it.'

The Indian smiled a melancholy smile. He shoved the stone back
into the paper cone with the flat of his hand. We watched him as he
did so, and then the radiant glow was gone. 'You will be sorry!' said
the gem dealer with a shrug. 'A stone like that – and there may never
be another one like it. Three thousand marks I give away – and only
because it is madam!' He smiled and walked away. I have sometimes
regretted not buying it, but not very much. Not much later I did buy
my wife a pendant with an aquamarine from a mine in South America.
It isn't half as big, and perhaps doesn't quite have the fiery glow of that
stone, even though it didn't cost that much less. But the stone suits us
better somehow; it is beautiful, but people don't stare at it all the time.
(And I do sometimes wonder if our melancholy Indian gem salesman
was a crook, who was out to con people with fake stones. The beautiful
big aquamarine really was amazingly cheap. In which case, my dislike of
ostentation saved me from making a prize fool of myself.) Of the other
guests who stopped off at this caravanserai I will just briefly mention a
genuine Indian rajah,[55] a fat man who appeared at the guesthouse for a
few days with several women and a large number of dark-skinned children. We saw little of them, apart from the children; they spent most
of the time sitting in their rooms, and they didn't eat with us either.
The children sometimes romped about in the corridors, as children of

every nationality doubtless romp about in long, echoing corridors the whole world over. But the man I often observed with admiration was the cook, who had appeared as part of the rajah's retinue. For religious reasons the rajah could not eat any of our food, and so this cook had turned up with his own saucepans and skillets and little bowls, all made of copper, and was busy at the stove alongside our fine German cook. He was a huge man, very fat, with not particularly dark skin, wearing a grubby turban, and to go with it an equally grubby-looking capacious white gown, like a kaftan. As the kitchen wasn't very large, and all the available space was really needed to prepare the food for the other guests, the giant cook had been given the window sill next to the stove – which was fairly wide, it's true – as his kitchen work surface. So there he stood, mixing and stirring and sprinkling coloured powders from little silver shakers over sauces and rice, while we, father and son, watched with bated breath. He had a true Oriental serenity about him, seemingly quite unaware of our shameless gawping, and he never once looked at us. One day, though, he held a dish under our noses with a little splodge of something reddish, and another little splodge of something yellow. The giant gestured invitingly, and for a moment I looked around for my spoon, but then I thought: 'Let's pretend we're dining with a rajah!'

I exchanged glances with my son, who preferred the red stuff, and we both knew what to do: we reached into the dish with our fingers, took some of the mush and put it in our mouths.

Dear God in heaven, it was as if I had swallowed fire itself, my throat felt cauterized and burnt, and suddenly I was gasping for air! But I had no time at all to worry about my own sensations, thanks to the ear-splitting howl which my son now let out. Without the least regard for good manners he spat the food out and screamed like a banshee. The cook, meanwhile, was back at his window sill, sprinkling powders from his little shakers with serene Oriental composure. He was not a bit interested in the victims of his culinary arts. We never watched the nasty man at work again – not that we know for certain that he really was nasty. Perhaps he was just unfamiliar with the European palate.

We were actually the only Germans staying in the guesthouse now, apart from a certain Professor Nathansohn,[56] although according to the thinking that was gaining currency at the time he was not a German at all, but at best a 'German Jew'. And he did look the part, a fine figure of a man, portly and well-fed, with a splendid hooked nose[57] and very full, very red lips, well-mannered, affable and well-endowed with that self-irony in which the Jews so excel. I gathered that Professor Nathansohn was a very famous man, though I had never heard of him myself. He was the inventor of 'Wistra', a fibre that could be used to make the most wonderful silk fabrics. But that had not stopped the Nazis kicking him out as soon as they had seized power. Prof. Nathansohn wasn't too bothered: he had probably moved his money out of the country by then, as a successful inventor he could find work anywhere, and so he had happily moved to London without a moment's regret. Meanwhile the Nazis had discovered that 'Wistra' was not quite working out as planned, and nobody else could sort out the problems, so they had lured Prof. Nathansohn back from England with lots of money and fine promises. So now he was working on official government orders in a large laboratory made available for his personal use, getting 'Wistra' back on track, and was meanwhile busily inventing 'Wollstra' too. I must admit that I often looked upon the Professor with lively pleasure, as living proof of the fact that the Nazis never hesitated to dump the sainted Party program the moment that something else seemed more important to them. And I must also admit that I would not look upon the good Professor with the same pleasure today. I did not succumb, like most of my fellow countrymen, to the endlessly repeated propaganda claiming that all the ills of the world stem from the Jews, and that the Jew is the Devil incarnate. Up until 1933 I suppose I was what people today call a 'philosemite'; that is to say, my circle of friends and acquaintances was an entirely random mix of Aryans and Jews. I made no distinction, and had never given it any thought. The anti-Semitic propaganda of the day (see 'Hangman' Streicher's *Stürmer*!) had always sickened me. But now, in 1933, after the Nazis had seized power, I made one or two observations that did give me pause. When I saw this Prof. Nathansohn, for example, sitting there in all his affability and dining off roast goose at the expense of the German Reich, I couldn't help thinking that if I had been thrown out in such ignominious fashion I would not have come back to Germany and racked my brains to invent things for the benefit of the Nazis, no matter how much money they paid me. We also had a Jewish lady friend,[58] the one who so cleverly managed to evade detection by dodging from one room to the next when the SA came to the house to arrest me. One of her daughters was living in London, another in Copenhagen – both daughters were married and both were comfortably off. Having asked their mother many times to leave Berlin and come and live with one of them, they finally begged her to leave, so that she wouldn't have to put up with the humiliations and persecutions of the Nazis any longer; but the mother stayed on year after year, holding out until it was almost too late to leave. And why did she hold out? She was getting a very modest pension from her husband, who had died many years previously, less than a hundred marks a month, and as she said indignantly: 'I'm not going to hand over the money to that gang of crooks! They'll never transfer the money to London, never! No, I'm going to get every last mark out of them!' So what I discovered was that the Jews have a different attitude to money than I do, and it was an attitude that I didn't care for personally, in fact one that I found quite repugnant. One of them came back for the sake of money, the other one wouldn't leave for the sake of money: but both of them allowed themselves to be humiliated for the sake of money, consciously and by their own choice.[59]

And then I had another experience that really shocked me. At my publishers we had an editor in the office, Paulchen Mayer,[60] a little Jew from Cologne, with tiny hands and feet, one of those products of endless inbreeding, with the fragility of porcelain, where the body hardly seems capable of supporting life. But what a head he had on him, this little man! Not a handsome head, not at all, but it was fizzing with ideas and passion! Our Paulchen had read everything, he knew everything, he thought about everything. Inside that neat, deep-browed skull blossomed a life eternal . . . And he was quite incorruptible.

Rowohlt was a big, powerful man, full of vitality; you contradicted him at your peril, even when he was in a good mood. He would immediately explode like an erupting volcano. But Paulchen contradicted him anyway, Paulchen didn't care if he was about to be engulfed in lava flows, and Paulchen was forever telling Rowohlt that the Rathenau novel by Mr von Salomon,[61] beautifully written as it was, was a piece of unprincipled opportunism unworthy of the Rowohlt imprint. Rowohlt could slam doors as much as he liked, and shout down Paulchen, pitting his mighty 110 kilos against Paulchen's puny 35; Paulchen just put the tips of his fingers together, and from every finger he extracted an incontrovertible proof. In the end Paulchen always won – in theory, at least, because in practice Rowohlt didn't care about the opinions of his editor, but simply published the books that he wanted to. So in the end the vanquished Rowohlt would scoop up Paulchen in his arms and parade the little fellow through the office, nuzzling him and horsing around. So that was Paulchen Mayer, our editor, the conscience of the Rowohlt publishing house, friend and adviser to us all, incorruptible, faithful and true: nothing but a little, degenerate Jew weighing barely 35 kilos, and grotesquely ugly.

And then we had a second Jewish employee in the office, although he was not really an employee as such, he was a trainee clerk or a partner, as you preferred. Or as he preferred. Leopold Ullstein[62] was a scion of the famous Ullstein publishing house, the largest in Germany at the time – and didn't he know it! In actual fact he was only the grandson. The old generation, which had built up the vast enterprise, was now living out of sight in back rooms, quietly pulling the strings behind the scenes. They were the generation that had acquired the business. Their sons had followed on after them, smart and capable businessmen, not especially brilliant, but choosing the right staff and paying them generously: they were the generation that sustained the business. And they in turn were followed by the grandchildren, the generation that squandered the business, spendthrifts and wastrels. They were already working in the office, in so far as they were prepared to work at all, and they were the subject of amusing and not-so-amusing stories. But the worst of all these grandchildren was this Leopold Ullstein. He was so awful that not even the efforts of his powerful father or the intercession of his all-powerful grandfather had been able to obtain a position for him in their own large enterprise. But these wealthy people had a financial stake in the Rowohlt publishing house, and they used their influence as shareholders for the sole purpose of securing a cushy job for their wayward offspring. So now we were stuck with him – and we soon realized what we had let ourselves in for. A more arrogant, boorish and unpleasant person it would be hard to imagine. It was lucky for us that he took a casual approach to office hours, often not appearing much before noon, when he would condescend to glance through a few papers, dash off an opinion that was not clouded by the slightest knowledge of the subject in hand, and then disappear again. And if we could not stand this Mr Ullstein, he and our Paulchen positively loathed each other. How could it be otherwise: they were polar opposites, this shallow hedonist with loutish manners, and the fastidious, intellectual little Jew.

And then came the time when the new regime seized power, and everything changed. Now Paulchen and Leopold Ullstein were always in a huddle, they always had something to discuss, and whenever somebody else came into the room they stopped talking. They were the Jews, and we were the gentiles, they belonged together, and we were the outsiders. During those weeks I came to understand that in the hour of danger a Jew feels closer to another Jew, however much they disagree and differ, than to his truest friend of non-Jewish blood. I realized that the Jews themselves are the ones who have erected this barrier between themselves and other nations, which we refused to believe when the Nazis claimed as much; and that it is the Jews themselves who feel the difference in blood, and insist on it, when we had always smiled at the notion. This realization did not make me an anti-Semite. But I did come to see the Jews in a different light. I'm sorry, but that's just how it is. I really hate to say it: but I can't alter the fact.[63]

As soon as we were in Berlin, of course, I tried to sort out this business with the Sponars. I was not minded just to roll over and accept

their outrageous demands. I had agreed to make the payments only on
one specific condition, namely that they consented to the foreclosure,
and since they now refused to give their consent, I was no longer
bound by the agreement. The objection that I was taking advantage of
the plight of a fellow German national in order to acquire a house was
simply ludicrous. The house did not belong to the man any more, and
I was actually trying to alleviate his present plight! It seemed to me that
the law was all on my side, and that they didn't have a leg to stand on;
so I went at once to see the big lawyer who had got me out of protective
custody so quickly. But the reception I got there was not at all what I
had expected. After I had given a brief and unadorned account of my
recent differences with my landlords and the local SA, the big lawyer[64]
launched into a furious rant: 'You idiot! And to think I got a schmuck
like you out of protective custody! You should have just stayed nice
and quiet, not said a word – and now the idiot is trying to stir things
up again! Get out of my office, now! I should have let you rot in jail!
I don't want to see you again! Get out!' I was already out of the door.
I was outraged at this man's behaviour. I still hadn't read the signs of
the times. So one wasn't allowed to defend one's rights, simply because
a local Party branch leader happened to be a friend of the landlord?
Well, we'd soon see about that! There were other lawyers in Berlin,
after all! And I went to see them. But the strange thing I found was that
none of them was willing to take on my case. Most of them gave me
a dusty answer, whether they were Party members or not. The polite
ones agreed that I definitely had the law on my side. But in these times,
they suggested, it was not advisable to go up against the Party, even for
one's legal right. People had put the Party in the wrong for so long that
one must now make allowances if it went a little too far . . . By way of
redressing the balance, so to speak . . . I should wait until quieter times
returned – that was the message I heard wherever I went. My dear old
father had been a judge himself, and now I understood him better. In
my youthful arrogance I had sometimes mocked him for his pedantic
insistence on sticking to the exact letter of the law as it was written
down. He would give me a long look with his gentle, intelligent eyes,

before replying: 'Know this, Hans my son: the law is a sacred thing. The judge must see to it that no jot or tittle of the law is harmed. If the smallest hole is opened up, the whole dyke will be swept away!'

But now they tore down the dyke themselves from the outside, and created a new law, or rather one law for the Party and one for those who were not in the Party. Finally, during the war, when any real sense of the law and any faith in the law had long since been extinguished, they decided that judges must reach their verdicts solely on the basis of 'the mood of the people'. As they were not Christians, they had never read the passage in the Bible where the people cry 'Crucify him! Crucify him!', whereupon Christ was crucified – in accordance with 'the mood of the people'. And Pilate went forth, washed his hands, and asked: What is truth?

(28.IX.44.) So as I said, I could find no-one whose job it was to help someone like me who was willing to do so. This was not a good time for me; I wasn't getting enough sleep, and I was drinking too much. For the first time in my life I had suffered a patent injustice, I had been blackmailed in the crudest fashion, and I could find no way to put things right. I was consumed with rage and bitterness, and what had been done to me by a handful of brownshirts I now projected onto all the brownshirts, from the Führer down to the smallest Hitler youth, and whenever I saw them with their standards and whenever I heard them singing the songs they had stolen from the SPD and playing the fanfares they had taken from the Communists, I shuddered with disgust. And I still feel the same way today, eleven years later, I still haven't got used to these brown uniforms and the bulldog snouts of the people who wear them. That feeling of disgust will never go away. There is such a thing as a typical Nazi face. A friend once gave me a small cartoon by Honoré Daumier, one of those portraits of parliamentarians that he did by the hundred, with their stupid, sly and brutish faces. The picture is entitled 'Pot-de-Naz'.[65] I have no idea what it means, but in my own mind I translated it simply as 'Nazi mug'. How many times

have I cursed and sworn at this picture! How often, when I was feeling particularly bitter, did I look at this fat face with its bestial chin and cunning little piggy eyes sunk into rolls of fat, and say to myself: That's what they look like, all of them pretty much, the elite of the nation – Messrs Ley, Funk and Streicher.[66] There's a lot of talk these days about the gangster culture that's said to be on the rise again in the States. Well in Germany it's already here – entrenched in the highest offices and positions, and they've certainly picked a right bunch of gangsters for those jobs! Just such a visage, all decked out down below in brown, red and gold, was standing on the rear platform of an electric tram in Berlin, during this present war, when the young conductress went to the aid of a frail old gentleman who wanted to alight. He thanked her, and she replied with a cheery 'Auf Wiedersehen!' She had rung her bell, and the tram had already moved off again, when the Nazi in his fancy uniform remarked sternly: 'You forgot to say "Heil Hitler!", miss!'

The pretty young conductress only half-turned towards him and gave the fat 'Nazi mug' no more than a passing glance. 'And you', she remarked coolly, 'have forgotten to relieve my husband at the front for the past three years!'

At this the brown tub of lard flushed a deep red, but said nothing; and everyone on the rear platform gazed off into the distance, trying to keep a straight face – and likewise saying nothing.

Anyway, I wasn't doing very well at all during these weeks, and my wife wasn't doing very well either. Apart from anything else, she wasn't doing very well on account of the fact that I wasn't doing very well, because I kept on disappearing from the guesthouse for short periods of time on the flimsiest of pretexts (i.e. in order to down a quick schnaps), and because I stretched out every evening into the small hours. It gives a good wife no pleasure when her husband starts to drink heavily, especially when he does it secretly and on his own, which is the very worst sort of drinking. But she could not come with me, because the twins that she was expecting were already giving her a very hard time, and because the strains, worries and agitation of recent times were now really starting to take their toll. So we led a pretty miserable life, and

I really don't know what would have become of us, or at least of me – for I was burying myself more and more in my futile and obsessive fantasies of justice – if a saviour had not appeared in our hour of need, a true, helpful friend, who not only steered our own lives into calmer waters, but who also mustered more courage than all the lawyers in Berlin, and in a series of personal negotiations brought the stalled business of the house in the little village of Berkenbrück to a conclusion that was not excessively costly, at least, and which did in any event end the matter once and for all. This man by the name of Peter Suhrkamp[67] was one of the shadowy figures of our time, with the power to do good things and bad things in equal measure, possessing many brilliant gifts, but obsessed by the deluded ambition of the age to rise high at all costs. He was a tall, very slender man of muscular build, with an almost ashen face that over the years came increasingly to resemble a skull with just a covering of skin. About eight weeks ago, when I was still living in freedom on the outside, I heard that this successful and ultra-cautious man had finally suffered the same fate as so many other Germans: he was arrested for treason. He too had said too much in an unguarded moment, allowed his true feelings to show, revealed something of the hatred that smoulders in each one of us. Perhaps, as I write this, he is no longer alive, or perhaps his superior intellect and presence of mind have enabled him to cope with the Gestapo's interrogation methods. I sincerely hope so. We went our separate ways in life a long time ago, we were just too different; it is years now since I heard from him directly.

Peter Suhrkamp was the only son of a farmer from Oldenburg, and they are a tough, taciturn, gnarled breed of men. As a boy he fell out with his father, who wanted his son to take over the small farm when he retired. But the son felt destined for different, higher things than running a small, impoverished moorland farm; whenever he tended the sheep, he heard a voice in his heart that told him he was destined to be a writer. He owned a little book that contained the *Tales from the Calendar* of Johann Peter Hebel, and these plain moral tales, so beautifully told, determined the direction his ambition would take: he resolved to become a writer of folk tales, plain, unvarnished stories about the simple life, but written for a whole nation. Such were his dreams as he tended his sheep. When he reached the age of fourteen and left the one-class village school, and when his father flatly refused his request to continue his education and tried to make him his farm boy instead, he ran away from home. The father still had legal authority over his son and could have had him brought back again, but he was just as stubborn as his son: he simply erased him from his life, as though he had never existed. He never spoke to him again, he never spoke about him again, and he forbade the boy's mother ever to mention her son: they had never had a son, and now they were a childless and ageing couple.

At the age of fourteen the son did not find things easy in the nearby little town in Oldenburg, where he had taken refuge. He was tough as nails, and needed very little to live on; but little as it was, he had a hard time scraping it together. He worked all day and studied half the night: for now he wanted to become a teacher – and after that the way ahead would become clear. He often went without food, but he became as hard as an old oak tree, and impervious to everything. From time to time his mother would secretly send him some bread and milk, and sometimes she saw him too, and wept tears of grief over the prodigal son. But tears would not come to him, and he was never able to cry for the rest of his life, so hardened had he become. He had set himself the goal of becoming a great popular writer, and for that no price was too high to pay!

He had already begun to discover world literature, and in the library of this little Oldenburg town the world was revealed to him in all its vastness and splendour! Stretching out beyond the plain calendar tales of the Swabian poet was the immense pandemonium of books, and he avidly consumed as many as he could get. A kind of fever had come upon him, an insatiable craving had seized hold of him: he wanted to discover everything, know everything, savour everything that the world had to offer – and only then would he start to write!

When the First World War broke out he returned to his father's farm, still very much a boy, and ran the farm for his mother, who was now left alone at home – his father was away at the war. Barely sixteen, the boy sat on the grass mower and read his books whenever he took a break, insensible to the wind that blew in his face, deaf to the larks that wheeled in the blue skies above his head.

When his father was killed at Hartmannsweilerkopf, he sold the farm, bought a life annuity for his mother from the sale proceeds, and used the rest of the money to advance his studies. He became a teacher, and got a teaching job in a small village school. But what did that signify? Was it for this that he had worked so hard and sacrificed so much? He was already nineteen – and still hadn't achieved anything! In his time off he studied for his university entrance exam, passed it, gave up his teaching job, and went to university to study, now short of money again. Again he went hungry, froze in cold rooms and laboured for money – hard labour for little money, tamping tarmac on the roads by day, scanning Homer's hexameters to the thudding beat of the heavy iron tamper. Did he ever pause and look back at his life? Did he perhaps remember the small boy who had tended the sheep on his father's moorland farm, carrying a small, dog-eared copy of *Tales from the Calendar* in his pocket and dreams of becoming a writer in his heart? I don't know. Years later, in a moment of intimacy, he showed me a few pages he had written, ten or twelve perhaps. They were covered with microscopically small and incredibly neat handwriting. 'The beginning of my novel', he said in a curiously abrupt and throw-away manner. 'I've been working on it for years, I'm constantly re-writing it. It's so difficult. There's so much that I still don't know. Do you remember, somebody once said that if you want to write a good book you need to have read all the books in the world once in your life, and then forgotten them all again? And then there's Flaubert. He was working on his *Salambo* for years, you know, and on his *Tentation* for years, and on *Bovary* for years.[68] It's never finished . . .!' He hastily gathered up the loose pages again, as if fearful that I might read a line, a word that he had written. Everything buried, everything from his fair youth forgotten and buried – and he didn't even realize it!

He became a teacher again, he taught at a grammar school, at a woodland school – but none of it was what he really wanted. Once again he burned all his bridges behind him, heading off once again, virtually penniless, to the big city, to Berlin. Here he discovered the misery of waiting for long hours in the outer offices of editorial departments, chasing commissions, churning out the lines, and the despicable behaviour of those who had made it, resolutely boycotting a man they suspected of real talent. And all he had to show for it were a few paltry articles – nobody ever gave him a break. He went hungrier than ever, his best suit was becoming shabby, the soles of his shoes were letting in water.

And then his luck turned, and he saw it as a real stroke of luck: he got a foot on the bottom rung of the ladder, and became the assistant editor of a big magazine. Magazines, let's remember, were for a time very fashionable in Germany, the latest big thing from America. There were all sorts of them at all sorts of prices, magazines for little girls and magazines for elegant ladies, but what they all had in common was that they started with a lengthy and usually rather racy love story, before descending into snobbery and more or less veiled eroticism in the later sections. And all of them had lots of pictures, beautiful landscapes and beautiful girls, the latter more or less undressed (usually more rather than less).

Such was the good fortune that came his way, to become assistant editor at one of these magazines, after twenty years of struggle, hunger and study. At least it was the one publication in Germany that was trying to raise the tone of these magazines: they didn't rely on sex and smut to sell copies, but published good, exciting short stories by well-known writers, preferred to be amusing rather than smutty, and gave only as much space to snobbery as was necessary to keep the readership loyal. It was during these years of his editorship that I got to know Peter Suhrkamp. He had written me a letter and gave me a commission. It was just around the time I was starting to become known, I was still fresh and hungry for work, and I was interested in every new proposal. The first commissioned piece was well received, and many more followed. I became a permanent staff member at the magazine, and some of my best short stories – a form that doesn't really suit me, because I need a broader canvas – were published there.[69] Some things worked, some things didn't. As an editor he was still a teacher at heart, and he had a matter-of-fact way of pointing out the weaknesses in my stories without ever giving offence. It was always as if the teacher was handing back a German essay that he had marked. The relationship between us remained like this: he was the teacher, I was the pupil. He was always in the dominant position, and that emerged even more clearly when he became our helper and adviser in the business with the Sponars. I'll come on later to the story of how he sorted that out, but for now I'd like to continue with the account of this man's remarkable life. My wife of course had also got to know him – and like him – during this period, and sometimes he would come and see us of an evening in our exotic caravanserai, or more often we would go to him. He lived in a bachelor flat on the sixth floor of a large apartment block way out in the west end of Berlin; from his balcony we often looked out across the city, sparkling with light, while the nearby radio mast threw out its beams of light, like outstretched arms, into the night sky. Today it is all just a vast expanse of rubble, misery and ash, just as our friendship has been reduced to ash – be still, o heart of mine! But back then we chatted away merrily and laughed, the world was our oyster, we were just starting out, we were on the way up, life's possibilities seemed endless. We smoked countless cigarettes, we drank wine or whisky (he just became ashen-faced and colder when he drank, I've never seen the least sign of drunkenness in him, and his body was like a burned-out shell from years of privation, all leather and bones), we yelled at each other: 'Have you read this? And this?' We would leap up and grab a book from the shelves, scouring it for a particular passage . . . By that time Peter Suhrkamp had also discovered women, the second great discovery of his life, but far less important than the first one. When I first met him he had already been married once, I think, and was now divorced, but I'm not exactly sure. At the time he was living with an attractive, leggy, vivacious woman, a correspondent for some newspaper, and a lively participant in our discussions. And she was no mean drinker either, whereas my dear wife never quite managed to overcome an innate – as I supposed – aversion to alcohol, no matter how good the wine. Like the rest of us, Mrs Schubring[70] was a fanatical Nazi-hater, though later on she chose a different path. She left her boyfriend Peter Suhrkamp and married a much younger man, a man with very different ideas, who wrote books so rooted in the soil of the fatherland that you could actually smell the earth . . . He was highly esteemed by the Nazis, the sort of person that the actor Emil Jannings[71] (of whom more later) liked to call 'a Nazi hack'. Under the influence of this man Mrs Schubring, now a high-born countess, cast down all the idols she had once worshipped and became a fervent Nazi herself, persecuting her former friends, and especially their achievements, with implacable fury, eternally jealous because her husband enjoyed only meagre success.

But at the time, thank God, she was not yet that woman, and I was often entranced by her vivacity and intelligence, but also by her affectionate and deferential manner towards her man – not to mention by her really remarkably fine legs, which she knew how to use to captivating effect. While Peter Suhrkamp did indeed have his foot on the bottom rung of the ladder now as assistant editor of a big magazine, and money worries as such were a thing of the past, his future was by no means secure, because there was of course another editor above him, on whose goodwill he was entirely dependent. The senior editor in question, a Mr Kroner,[72] was a fair-haired Jew, always immaculately turned out, and as it happens one of the most serious nutcases ever to occupy an editorial chair. The fact that half of his editor's inner sanctum was completely taken over by an electric railway layout on seven or eight levels was only the half of it. This model railway, complete with electric points, mountain scenery, stations, tunnels, level crossings, sidings and dozens of trains, was something Mr Kroner liked to play with during editorial meetings. He made the trains stop and go, changed the electric points by remote control, prevented collisions by a hair's breadth, made the trains go faster and slower, and all the while was explaining to his somewhat irritated listener exactly what he had in mind for the next issue of the magazine. Mr Kroner always had something in mind, but the actual work was then done by his assistant editor Peter Suhrkamp. As I say, this thing with the trains was only the half of it, doubtless just a pose or affectation, designed to make him look important. But Mr Kroner had other strange habits besides this. For example, he asked me why I looked so depressed. I told him I had had a spot of bother, not to say serious worries. To which Mr Kroner replied: 'Worries? What are you on about? It's all in your imagination! Go and get a haircut, this very day, and see how you feel then! You won't even think about your worries then!'

Or else he would insist on my accompanying him to a men's outfitters on Leipziger Strasse, where he would make me buy a new tie that I disliked intensely. I had to put it on right there in the shop. 'You can chuck your other ties away! With a tie like that you'll never write a decent short story. You can take my word for it! But with this tie, you can't put a foot wrong!'

It is not hard to see that two so utterly different characters as Mr Kroner and his assistant editor Peter Suhrkamp were bound to come to blows one day. Mr Kroner had one of his ideas – totally mad, I imagine – but this time not relating to the attire of his contributors, but to the magazine itself. This idea had to be acted upon, and Peter Suhrkamp refused to do so. He still refused after he had been threatened with instant dismissal. So he was fired. Once again he was out on the street, and of course he had not put any money by. Whisky, women and books – and the pay of an assistant editor has never been very high. But he was in luck again. A highly respected book publisher, one of the biggest and most respected in Germany, published a weighty monthly magazine containing a mix of fiction and essays on contemporary themes. Many leading authors had had their first work published here. In earlier times, decades previously, this magazine had been young and full of youthful vigour, but gradually it had entered the more mature years of its manhood, and now the mellow sheen of old age had sometimes lain across its pages; in short, and despite the high regard in which it was still held, it had become just a little bit boring. So the decision had been made to give it an infusion of fresh blood with a new chief editor, and my friend Peter Suhrkamp was the candidate of choice. It really was a great stroke of good fortune, because a job like that attracted hundreds of applicants. So he was at least six or ten rungs up the ladder already! Yesterday the assistant editor of a dodgy lightweight magazine, today the chief editor of a publication that picked its contributors from among the leading lights of the nation and felt free to approach any government minister for an article. It was just a few months before the Nazis came to power that Peter Suhrkamp started in his new job. I was really pleased for him. Now at last he had an opportunity to realize his own writing ambitions. I thought about the ten or twelve pages that he had briefly shown me once – he'd be able to publish a fragment such as this in his own magazine, his name would become known, I was already jealous of his fame. But what then appeared many months later, when we had already drifted apart, were cautious, tentative essays by a man who was seeking to accommodate himself to National Socialism. You could tell from the writing that this was a man doing his best to see the good side of something that was fundamentally bad, a man who was forcing himself to think in ways that were alien to him. What a change was here! What had happened to him? I have it on good authority from people who were around him all the time in those days: he had seen his great opportunity, and was determined to make the most of it, case-hardened as he was. The founder, owner and still the head of the big publishing house[73] was an old Jew, a clever old man with that deep instinct for quality that so many Jews have. He had discovered many young talents, encouraging, developing and nurturing them, and he had also persuaded them to stay with him after they found fame, which is the greatest achievement of all for a publisher. As a result, his publishing business had grown very large, and the small, ageing and ailing Jew was still sitting there in his great publishing house, still pulling all the strings. Better than anybody else who worked for him, he had known everything from the very beginning; he knew better than anyone the foibles of his authors that had to be handled with care, their vanities and conceits, he knew the ones who could be trusted with large sums of money, and the other ones, of whom there were many, who had to be fobbed off all the time with small instalment payments. In this manner he had shrewdly and wisely steered the fortunes of his great publishing house – until the day the Nazis seized power, which changed everything. For now there entered into the life of the old man something that he could not understand. National Socialism: he'd heard of it of course, his magazine had published essays about it, a political party, one of twelve, one of thirty-six. And anti-Semitism, yes, he knew about that too, and had been directly exposed to it himself, the way one is exposed to many things in life, good and bad. But what was coming now, this was something else. These people who now held the reins of power, they did not represent a political party that one could belong to or reject; no, they had it in for the old man, his heart, his life, his whole life's work. They claimed he was an inferior human being, a bad human being from the day he was born; everything he had done had been done for bad reasons, and so it was a service to mankind to exterminate him and his kind. How could the old man understand such a thing? It was simply impossible! 'Look here', he might have said to himself, 'I have a hundred authors in my publishing house, or maybe a hundred and fifty or two hundred – whatever. And not even a quarter of all these authors are Jewish, three-quarters of them are Christian, or as you like to call it today, "Aryan". And among those three-quarters of Aryan authors are the biggest names writing in Germany today. They were young and unsure of themselves when they first came to me, under me they grew up, and I did my little bit to help them grow up. And now everything that I've done over all these years is somehow "bad"? Now I am to be exterminated and all my work spat upon? But this work of mine, these men who grew up under me, you're not spitting on them, them you are honouring, the men who are a part of my work? And me you want to destroy?' Helpless and full of fear, these thoughts were just going round and round in his head. And he was afraid, the old man, physically afraid of being beaten and roughed up. The real world was all around him, after all, the telephone rang in his office and someone was on the line telling him about some new arrest where someone was knocked to the ground and kicked. The old man shook with fear. And if he stood at the window and gazed down into the street, the moment always came when the band struck up, the banners fluttered, the tramp of marching feet was heard, and he saw the brown columns filing past, and gazed once again into these young and oh-so vacuous, so coarse faces, faces quite different from those he had looked upon all his life, hard faces without a trace of pity in them. And when they broke into song, and he heard a line about the blade that must run with Jewish blood, he trembled all over and cried out and tore at the curtain and wrapped himself in it to block out the light, as though he could shut out the new world that was so darkly dawning with a few metres of fabric. And he shouted and raved in his fear, the old Jew, and told them to remove the telephone from his office, he didn't want to hear any more, and it was a real job to calm him down again.

The new employee happened to be in his office during one of these panic attacks. He put his arm around the old man and got him to lie down on a sofa, he sat down with him and showed him how strong he was, he told him he was a farm boy from Oldenburg, whom the country's new masters could not touch, that he was indeed one of those they wanted to have on side. So saying, Peter Suhrkamp calmed the old man down, and when the telephone rang he answered it for the old Jew and spoke for him. There was some tiresome matter to be sorted out with some government department or other, and he dealt with it in his usual efficient and businesslike manner. From then on the old publisher started to call for the chief editor of his monthly magazine, at first only when he was feeling very low, but later on also whenever there were difficult negotiations in hand; for he suddenly felt that he could trust the new arrival more than he could his long-standing colleagues, whom he had known for ages and now disregarded. To begin with he summoned him to his office as and when, but he was on a different floor in another wing of the building, and it was a long way to come; so he set up an office for him right next door to his own. In the end he arranged for all his incoming telephone calls to be routed through his young assistant, who then dealt directly with any difficult or unwelcome matters, and similarly it was Peter Suhrkamp's job to meet and greet all visitors. Eventually he had his newly chosen adviser ride home with him in the big limousine in the evenings after work, and because the villa in its spacious grounds now seemed to him so isolated and exposed, Peter Suhrkamp also had to keep him company there in the evenings and eventually stay overnight. The old man felt easier in his mind: he had found succour, strength for his failing arm and peace for his troubled heart.

But in the editorial offices of the big city they have very keen ears, they can hear more than just the grass growing; and it wasn't long before a modern fairy-tale began to circulate – the tale of the little, unknown, insignificant editor of some footling magazine who overnight became the right-hand man of a wealthy publisher. And not long after that Peter Suhrkamp acquired the malicious nickname that stayed with him for ever: 'the legacy-hunter'. That's what they called him, and that's how he was always known thereafter: 'Peter Suhrkamp the legacy-hunter'.[74]

Now it may very well be that Peter Suhrkamp did all these things with the best of motives to begin with, only wanting to help out, for he was, as I myself had discovered, a helpful person, and a good mate to his friends. But later on he couldn't fail to notice the suspicious looks that people gave him, and the malicious 'legacy-hunter' nickname will surely have got back to him via some gossip-monger or other. I've said it many times before, and I'll say it again now: he was a hard man. Seeing that everybody thought only the worst of him, and that nobody believed in the purity of his intentions, he said to himself: 'All right, if that's what you think, then so be it! Yes, I *will* be the heir, the old man won't fare worse as a result, and nor will the legacy.'

In his dreams – and how different they were from the dreams of his youth! – he saw the great publishing house with its many famous authors entirely under his control, he saw the power that now lay so passively in the weak hands of the ailing old Jew passing into his own strong hands, and he would make greater use of it, he would use it to his own fame and glory! In his imagination the name of the

Jew was removed from the firm's title and his own name put in its place.

It was a prodigious dream that he dreamt: he, the little, unknown, impoverished editor aspired to become the owner and director of one of the largest German publishing houses, with great minds and men of genius at his command. This was indeed, as he proudly said to himself, a thousand times more than the dreams he had dreamt when he was tending his sheep, or reading the homespun *Tales from the Calendar* of old Johann Peter Hebel! If he could achieve that – ! It's a legacy-hunter they want? Well then, he'd soon show them, and have them bowing and scraping before the legacy-hunter!

He had made his decision, and he was just the man to act on it there and then and never look back. He started to write those cautious, clever, if somewhat dull essays, in which a man discovers National Socialism and makes its ideas his own, progressing by degrees from the position of cautious observer to follower and admirer. Hitherto he had stepped in to handle matters with the appropriate Reich and Party authorities only when asked to do so, but now he wanted to be in charge of all such negotiations, and before long he was the public face and voice of the great publishing house, representing it at all important meetings. Of course, this didn't happen without fierce internal struggles, the staff hated this parvenu, this legacy-hunter. 'I'm living among murderers', he once said at the time. But he had what it took to live among murderers, he could kick and bite with the best of them, he could be razor-sharp and brutal, he was not afraid of anyone. And on top of that he had the old man behind him, who needed him, who could not live without him. Once Peter Suhrkamp understood this, once he realized how utterly dependent on him the old Jew was, he exploited his power ruthlessly – not least against the old man himself. There are some really shocking reports, reports of senseless torments, so bad that I don't know what to believe. So many terrible things have happened since then in Germany, and in the last few years we have become so desensitized to horror: anything is possible under such a leadership, which always expects the worst of people.

I can see him sitting there, Peter Suhrkamp, always wearing very fine shirts and dressed in a dark suit, I can see him sitting in his office outside the anxiously guarded inner sanctum of the old Jew. He is in a bad mood, having had to spend the whole day dealing with the intrigues and back-biting of his colleagues – and now the old man has overruled him in some important matter. He reflects for a while, hesitates, and then reaches for the telephone and calls the old Jew. He has disguised his voice, and now barks brusquely at the old Jew, summoning him to Gestapo headquarters for questioning the next day. He quickly replaces the receiver and goes back to studying the papers on his desk. And now the connecting door to the next office is flung open, the old man is standing in the doorway, tearing his hair in a state of total despair, already facing the firing squad in his mind. He begs his young friend to help him, but he is sullen, letting the old man know that he has done him an injustice by overruling him. How he torments him! How he makes this poor, sick creature suffer and groan! And then he gives in, he promises to get the matter sorted out, deferred at least – and pulls off a miracle: the Gestapo, the most implacable and unrelenting agency of the German state, cancels the interrogation!

And this didn't happen just the once, it happened several, many times, until the old man was reduced to a puppet, who said yea and amen to everything. To everything that Peter Suhrkamp wanted. And while this was going on he was consolidating his position, feeling his way forward, speaking with the financial backers; everything else was just a matter of skilful management. And skilful he was: when the old man finally lay dead, free at last from all his tormentors, he was the designated heir. To begin with he was just the acting manager, and then he was formally named as the new head of the company. He acquired shares, he married a wealthy woman (the fact that she was older than him, and drank, didn't trouble him); the years passed, and the day came when the name of the dead Jewish publisher was expunged, and his name was put up in its place: the dream had become reality, the hungry student begging for work had become a powerful man, master of millions. But had he completely forgotten the dream that he had dreamt back then, when he was tending his father's sheep on the moor, with Hebel's homespun *Tales from the Calendar* in his pocket, stories as simple in their message as the lines of the song that begins: 'Be truthful and honest in all that you do . . .'?[75] Had he forgotten all that? The dream had not forgotten him, and now it rose up against him. When all was said and done he was a farm boy from Oldenburg, and made of different stuff than the gentlemen who now ruled the land. He had ingratiated himself with them when it suited his purposes, he'd become a reliable Nazi, because it was the only way to gain advancement; he had purged his publishing house of all Jewish and pro-Jewish authors, and had become a model Nazi. And as a result of all this he had come to hate the Nazis with a passion. He had sat with them and drunk with them and laughed, actually laughed at their witless jokes, their tedious bragging, and had applauded it. With them he had ruined people's lives without a twinge of conscience, and at their behest he had elevated some dreary scribbler into a literary god, arrayed like Apollo himself. But back home, hidden away in a corner, lay ten or twelve pages, covered with tiny, neat handwriting – and they had risen up against him. That he had once aspired to something like this now became more important to him than all the success he had ever achieved. Oh, how he loathed them, how he longed to spit in their stupid, vacuous faces and tell them straight out for once what he really thought of their empty slogans! But he could keep his own counsel: not for nothing did his face resemble a skull, and many things were buried inside that head of his.

So how did it happen that at some point he did let something slip? Perhaps he was drunk, or perhaps even he needed a confidant eventually, someone to whom he could unburden his heart of the hatred he felt inside. And this confidant then reported him to the authorities. I don't know. I just heard that he said too much, that he was arrested for treason, and that for all I know he is already dead as I write. Hanged by the neck. And it was all for nothing: the years of hunger and privation, the long, grey road, the struggles, the shameful treatment of the old Jew – all for nothing! All for nothing the betrayal of his own ambitions – what shall it profit a man,[76] if he shall gain the whole world, and lose his own soul? Oh, if only I were still tending the sheep on my father's moorland!

And this was the same man – just to touch briefly here on this aspect of his character – who came to me shortly after the Nazis took power and said: 'Listen, Bertolt Brecht is hiding out at my place;[77] I've got to get him across the border into Czechoslovakia tonight, and we're collecting money for him. How much can you give? You'll probably never get it back again.' Bertolt Brecht had only escaped arrest by a miracle. It's well known, of course, that the librettist of the *Threepenny Opera* was particularly unpopular with these gentlemen. But like the rest of us, he had no idea how much danger he was already in. He had slept soundly, drunk his breakfast coffee, and had then gone across the street just as he was, without hat and coat, to get a quick shave. When he emerged from the barber's again, there was a car parked outside his apartment building, one of those nice big cars used by the police. And there were sentries posted in front of the building. It was a five-storey apartment block, with multiple occupants, but Bertolt Brecht had the distinct feeling that this early-morning visit had to do with him. He gazed thoughtfully for a moment at the car and the sentries before turning on his heel and walking away, deep in thought, towards a very uncertain future, with no hat or coat and just a handful of coins in his pocket. He finally ended up at Peter Suhrkamp's place – and he was just the man to bring an adventure of this sort to a happy conclusion. He sketched out an itinerary, he collected money, he dug up an old car from somewhere, and he drove off at the wheel with Bertolt Brecht on board. How he managed it, I don't know, but he got him safely across the border. He was risking his job, his future prospects, even his life, in order to help a man to whom he was not personally close, and for whose literary work, given his own predilections, he can't have had much time. That's the sort of man he was, Peter Suhrkamp, the legacy-hunter: no worse than that, but no better either. Much like the rest of us, in fact.

It's probably better that I recount this last commendable deed of Peter Suhrkamp here, before reverting to my account of my own experiences. I'm rather sorry that the flow of the narrative led me to jump ahead and recount the rise of Peter Suhrkamp first. For us, back then, he was our friend and saviour. We admired him, and we put our complete trust in him. And what he did for us was fully deserving of trust and thanks. First of all he got us both out of our elegant guest-house and shipped us off to a small country sanatorium in the Mark of Brandenburg, where we found peace and quiet, sun, and the green out-doors, where our boy could play properly again, and where we didn't just waste our days killing time, but took rest cures in the grounds and swallowed little potions that made us believe we'd acquire nerves of steel. And then, when I was finding it impossible to write during those months of inner turmoil, he set me a specific task: he sent me off to look at villas, cottages and small farms. I was told I should buy something else, a place where I could write and that would give us a project to work on. I protested that I had no more money and that I needed to sort out the business with the Sponars first, but to no avail: he was unrelenting. He insisted that I should buy something, and so in the end I did. I have already written about this in another book.[78] And he took it upon himself to arrange the business with the Sponars, even turning it into a victory of sorts for me. He came up with a very simple idea, which neither I nor any lawyer had thought of: he went and sold on my mortgages to someone else. Yes, I lost money on the deal, and it was not exactly chicken feed either, but at least I was no longer tied to this beastly property. For the Sponars the sale had one very disagree-able consequence. Hitherto, needless to say, they had never had any intention of paying me interest on the mortgages; they had simply pocketed my rent and lived very well on it. And schmuck that I was, I was powerless to do anything about it. But a big bank, even under the Nazi regime, is not powerless: the back interest now had to be paid and the ongoing interest payments had to be kept up, and all the rent money I paid to the Sponars now went to the bank to cover these costs.

Meanwhile the twins had been born, and the younger of the two girls died a few hours after the birth. There was a very specific medical reason for it, which had nothing at all to do with the agitation and stresses suffered during the pregnancy; and yet I was never able to let go completely of the idea that the Sponars were partially responsible for this misfortune, the Sponars and everything that went with them – the hated brownshirts and the protective custody and my wife's long trek through the night to reach the little town of Fürstenwalde. It's unfair to think like this, and I have no evidence to support such a view, but I still say: they are partly responsible. Things would not have worked out this way, and our little girl would still be alive today, if we had been allowed to carry on living in peace and contentment, if this wretched Nazi takeover hadn't occurred!

In the meantime we'd found the house in the country[79] where we wanted to live from now on, a secluded house by the water, and now it was a matter of retrieving our furniture and other things that were still being held by the Sponars as 'security' for their claims. Here too our friend Peter Suhrkamp proved to be our saviour. He boldly drove back to our old village to conduct negotiations, and instead of going to see the poor 'fellow German national' whom I had so wronged, he went straight to the man who really mattered, the building contractor Gröschke. That was a nerve-wracking day for us! We could not relax at all, I for one was pacing up and down the whole time, I couldn't settle to anything, and pestered my tired and sickly wife with a thousand fears and misgivings. I pictured our negotiator already under arrest, and could well imagine the evil and malicious Gröschke, how furious he must be about the sneaky sale of the mortgages! The waiting was agony . . .

Then our friend returned, and as was his wont, he told us nothing at first, but instead made very free with his criticisms, particularly of me. He had already heard from the nurse how restless I had been, how I had been pestering my wife, and also that I'd been drinking alcohol again, and now I really got it in the neck! It was a case of once a teacher, always a teacher with him, and he could be really acerbic and downright scathing when playing that part. Sometimes I fought back, because it really went against the grain, as a forty-year-old man, to be told off like a naughty schoolboy! But on this occasion I kept my mouth firmly shut, since any argument on my part would have just delayed his report on what he had accomplished. And so after we had been hauled over the coals and given a thorough drubbing, he finally got round to telling us what had happened.

(29.IX.44.) It had all gone remarkably well, as it turned out. The sale of the mortgages and the resulting loss of the rent payments had not caused tempers to flare, as I had feared, but had made them pause and reflect. They were prepared to make the best of a bad job and negotiate. And so they had talked money, finally agreeing on a figure that satisfied all outstanding claims from the Sponars and secured the release of my furniture. It was still extortion, it was still an injustice, and it was still a tidy sum; but it was something we could live with, viewing it as the penalty to be paid for an act of great folly.

And then I see before me the bright, sunny summer morning: the stunted pine trees through which my wife once fled through the night are already giving off a subtle scent of resin. The two brightly painted removal vans come to a halt on the brown gravel road in front of the villa. The removal men are carrying the items of furniture out of the house one by one. Inside the packer is going about his business – this is just a removal job like any other for him, with nothing to indicate the story that lies behind it. The Sponars are nowhere to be seen. My presence is completely superfluous, but my friend Peter Suhrkamp insisted that I should be here, that I should show my face here again, for the sake of the removal men, but also for myself. As I said: once a teacher, always a teacher, and one has to do one's homework, however tiresome it might be. My homework was to show my face here again. And now comes the hardest and most hateful part of all! He taps me on the shoulder: 'Right, then. Let's go!'

'Fine', I say, throwing away my half-smoked cigarette and lighting up another one immediately. We start walking. 'Take it easy', says Peter Suhrkamp, 'He won't arrest you a second time!'

'No, no', I reply. 'Of course not.'

We go into the house, the pretentious product of a country builder's fancy. We enter a room that is half parlour, with upholstered seating, and half office, with a roller blind. I am introduced to the tall man with the curiously small, hard head. He greets me pointedly with a 'Heil Hitler!' I return the greeting, cursorily. Mr Gröschke is in his shirtsleeves, the sleeves of his brown shirt. 'Time to count out the cash, Fallada', says Peter Suhrkamp. And to the local Party branch leader: 'Well, it's all turned out a bit differently from what you expected, Mr Gröschke.'

This is a direct challenge, but Gröschke replies matter-of-factly: 'We'll be converting the first floor and the attic into small apartments, and that way the house will cover the interest payments.'

'And you'll get a nice little contract out of it', replies Peter Suhrkamp with a grin. For a moment they both look at each other, and then they both smile. A very knowing smile. 'Oh well', says Mr Gröschke, 'when it's for a friend – !' He quickly counts the banknotes, nods and puts them in a small cashbox. Somewhat surprisingly he then goes on: 'Why shouldn't one do business with a friend occasionally – ?' They smile once more; I am quite certain that the Sponars won't get to see much of my money. But that's the kind of man he was. This was the man at whose bidding I was supposed to be shot 'while trying to escape', who had caused us so much anguish, who had made our lives a misery for a while. That was him. A kind of vulture – with a small, shrivelled head and a long, thin, wrinkly neck. 'Well now, was that so bad?' Peter Suhrkamp asks me, when we are standing outside again on the sunlit street. 'Was it worth staying at home on that account? You'd have felt ashamed of yourself for the rest of your life, Fallada!' I say nothing.

We stay and watch the brightly painted furniture vans start up, the road surface is too soft, they need to be towed off. But then they are on the metalled road to Fürstenwalde, where the contents are to be shipped on to Mahlendorf.[80] The little village of Berkenbrück with the Sponars and its brownshirts is finally behind me. And in Mahlendorf we'll go about things very differently. There we'll get in with the local community leaders and Party bigwigs from day one! (How that turned out we would learn to our cost in due course!)

The months passed and we were now living in Mahlendorf. A year went by, and we were well into the second year, still living in Mahlendorf, happy for the most part . . . We had almost forgotten the little village of Berkenbrück and the Sponars. Sometimes, when I was out walking with the dogs, it seemed almost incredible that we once lived in a house overlooking the Spree, and that river steamers used to sound their horns beneath our windows. Our son had long since forgotten it all. And then we got a reminder. A letter with a black border arrived in the post: an actual obituary notice. 'He has passed away in his 80th year, Emil Sponar', etc., etc. '"Blessed are the peacemakers, for they shall see God." In profound sorrow, Friederike Sponar.'

However, this news did not reach us from the little village of Berkenbrück, it came from Berlin, from the east end of the city, and one of those long, overcrowded streets that are swarming with people like a beehive swarming with bees in the summer. Yes, of course: the safeguard against foreclosure had been abolished, the Sponars were not able to carry on living in a comfortable villa at the expense of their creditors; in their old age they had to move to a place where people lived cheek by jowl. Should we pity them? Do we have to? The card landed in the wastepaper basket – the Sponars meant nothing to us any more. They had hurt us very deeply once, but that was forgotten now. There is so much one has to forget in this life! Rest in peace, old man!

Four more weeks passed, and then another letter with a black border arrived in the post. Could it be that the queen had followed her husband so quickly to the grave? But no, she was still alive, in fact she was writing to us, writing to us in her large, firm handwriting. We had offended her: 'I have waited week after week for a word of condolence for the passing of my dear husband . . . He was a good man, he meant well by you. What he did was his duty, as a loyal follower of the Führer . . .'

'Wastepaper basket, Suse!' I said. 'Why are you getting so worked up? That woman must be mad – remember her eyes! No, not a word, straight into the wastepaper basket!'

The weeks passed, and again we forgot about the Sponars. What reason did we have for thinking about an old, impoverished woman, who was thinking back on her wasted life with hatred and fury? We had enough worries of our own! And then another envelope arrived from her, this time without the black border, and this time with no note or letter, but enclosing a photograph of our eldest son, which Suse had given to the Sponars perhaps, or left behind by mistake when we moved house. Just the photo – so now she was returning our gifts! I looked more closely at the photograph – and saw that she had pricked out the child's eyes with a needle!

I hope my memory doesn't deceive me: Suse never saw this desecrated picture, I was able to burn it behind her back. It's such a long time ago, we've certainly never talked about it: the name Sponar was never spoken between us again. But the strange thing is, I am almost glad, now, that this woman perpetrated this final and supreme act of infamy. For by doing so she justified all the feelings of hatred that I harboured for her and her husband, and she justified in advance the words that I have written about her here. Perhaps she will still be living, a very old woman, when this book is published; I should like to think that she will still be able to read it with all her mental faculties. This is the obituary that I am dedicating to her and her husband. And with that I dismiss the pair of them from my life, a closed chapter as far as I am concerned, way beyond love, hatred and forgiveness!

In the preceding pages I have told the life story, or what I know of it, of my friend Peter Suhrkamp, whom I have not seen for many years. Now I'd like to write something about my esteemed publisher Rowohlt, who has also been a wonderful friend to us. We had to manage without him for many a long, hard year, but at least we do see him now from time to time. He too has been tossed and tumbled by the waves, and like the rest of us he didn't escape the brown tide entirely unscathed. Sometimes it was hard to believe that this man, who always described himself as a survivor who always bounced back, would ever get back on his feet again. But lo, he lives! If my information is correct, he is currently swanning around in the lovely little village of Kampen on the island of Sylt, fanned by glorious sea breezes and doing . . . absolutely nothing for the total war effort.

I've already said that he was just as reckless and just as fearful as I am. But as he met up with at least a dozen people every day, doing business with them, chatting away, sharing news (and what kind of news was there in those early years other than about the Nazis!), it was inevitable that he ran far greater risks than someone like me, living a quiet life out in the country and often seeing nobody for ten days at a time. There are many stories about him from this time, and it's impossible to recount them all. But one of them shows very well how this inveterate gambler, who all his life played every book like a hand of cards, how he also liked to play with fire. In the early days after the seizure of power, when so much had to be overturned and then reorganized again, the Reich Chamber of Literature issued a ruling allowing Jewish authors and Jewish translators to carry on working for the time being, on condition that they had a so-called 'exemption certificate', which was issued by the RCL. This policy was intended as a transitional arrangement, to provide protection against excessive losses for publishers who had many such works in progress at the time. Now we had a Jewish translator in the office called Franz Fein,[81] who was a brilliant translator; nearly all the translations of Sinclair Lewis's works, for example, must have been done by him.[82] Old Rowohlt was a firm believer in loyalty, and he had no intention of getting rid of Franz Fein. So he just let him carry on translating. A week later a warning letter arrived from the RCL, noting that the Rowohlt publishing house was still employing the translator Franz Fein, who had no exemption certificate, and requesting that he no longer be employed in future. Rowohlt put the letter on his 'compost heap', where all the letters that he didn't want to answer ended up, and carried on employing Franz Fein as before. The next letter from the RCL was more threatening in tone: on pain of a fine of so many marks, the Rowohlt publishing house was forbidden to continue employing the Jewish translator Franz Fein, who had no exemption certificate. This letter likewise landed on the compost heap, and Franz Fein carried on working. The final letter from the RCL was a hammer blow: a fine was imposed, and Rowohlt was summoned to appear before the German publishers' court of honour. At this point Rowohlt decided to respond. His reply consisted of a single sentence: 'The translator Franz Fein is permitted to work in accordance with exemption certificate No. 796. Heil Hitler.' The people at the RCL had failed to check their own records properly before writing their letters. Such 'triumphs' were royally celebrated in the office, of course, and we told everybody about them, but in the end they were – like my own aforementioned letter to Dr Goebbels – dearly paid for. Nothing was forgotten, everything was noted down, and the pile of small snowballs grew until it became a huge, crushing avalanche!

There was one time early on when Rowohlt narrowly avoided coming to grief only because of the unwonted urbanity of a Gestapo official. There was another government order requiring anyone who received letters, flyers or suchlike containing seditious material, whether anonymous or signed, to forward the same immediately, together with the envelope, to the RCL or the nearest Gestapo office, and not to show it to anyone. In the early years high-profile authors and publishers did indeed receive quite a few such letters, though later they stopped completely; there was just one man, apparently from southern Germany, who carried on regardless, unleashing a stream of diatribes against Dr Goebbels. In actual fact this worthy was a full-blown Nazi sympathizer; it was just that Dr Goebbels had aroused his particular ire, and he accused him of terrible things, one of which was the wrecking of the German language. But apart from this buffoon the letter-writers eventually realized that their letters were pretty pointless. I'm sure it was all very fine to be sitting in Paris or Prague and exhorting us German writers to engage in active resistance against the Nazis: 'Refuse to obey them! Sabotage their initiatives! Call the people to arms! The fate of Europe lies in your hands, you are the spirit and soul of Europe!' And so on – there was plenty more of this tripe, written from some safe haven. It all sounded fine and dandy, as I say, but to commit suicide cheered on by a bunch of émigrés did seem somewhat pointless to me. So I always bundled up this kind of stuff without the slightest regret and sent it on to the RCL like a good boy. It was such rubbish that I was never even tempted to show it to anyone else. My good friend Rowohlt took a rather more casual view of such letters, but then he received others of more substantial import. One day a gentleman from the Gestapo called to see him. We had moved on from the time when such a visit would throw one into a blind panic. The gentlemen from the Gestapo had already descended upon the publishing house for all kinds of different reasons: to search for Einstein's *Die schlimme Botschaft*[83] in the attic, to confiscate the works of Emil Ludwig, to purge the poems of Joachim Ringelnatz[84] – you name it! So it did not strike terror into the heart any more, but it did still make you a little jumpy, as though you were on your guard: what's up this time? The Gestapo man sat down across from Rowohlt, all very friendly, and asked him if he was aware of the government order stating that anonymous communications containing seditious material, etc., etc. Rowohlt was all cooperation and compliance: of course he knew about the order, and on receipt of any such scurrilous pamphlets he had of course, etc., etc. 'And what about the Pope's Encyclical on the Genetic Health Law, which you received a week ago?' inquired the official softly. Dear old Rowohlt flushed bright red. Thank God he wasn't foolish enough to deny receipt. 'Good Lord!' he cried, 'didn't I send that back? I could have sworn I did! Let me just have a look . . .' He began to rummage in his compost heap. (His consternation was made much worse by the knowledge that this encyclical, for which he was searching so diligently and fruitlessly, was sitting in his breast pocket – it was too good, after all, not to share with one's friends!) 'Or', he went on, 'did I chuck the thing straight into the wastepaper basket in my annoyance?' And he made as if to upend the wastepaper basket. 'Leave it, leave it!' said the official with a wave of his hand, having watched his rummagings with an air of languid inter-est. 'It's just a warning, Mr Rowohlt, a final warning. I would advise you to be very careful.' He smiled at the big, burly publisher, who had gone puce in the face. He added innocently: 'We send these things out ourselves from time to time, just as a test, to separate the sheep from the goats.' And with that he left. 'From now on I'm going to be a sheep and only a sheep!' swore Rowohlt for the hundredth time. 'These fellows are too smart for me!' But that was just him talking. We were both of us incorrigible. So one snowball after another was added to the pile – the avalanche was getting quite sizeable already – and we still had no idea. Well, perhaps that's not entirely true. We *were* surprised that the Rowohlt publishing house had been allowed to carry on, that it had not simply been shut down. Not only pro-Jewish but decidedly anti-Nazi: how much more compromised did the company need to be? What kept it alive, I think, was its high standing abroad. Rowohlt Verlag had always been uncommonly successful with its foreign publishing deals. Its reputation abroad actually stood much higher than its domestic significance warranted. Here it was never ranked among the country's top publishing houses. Its publishing director was far too wayward for that, as I said before, and he didn't follow a clear, straight line in his publishing program, as Dr Kippenberg[85] famously did with his Insel Verlag; instead Rowohlt the gambler looked upon every newly published title as a new card in the game, hoping with excited anticipation that each one would turn out to be a winner.[86] So I really do believe they allowed the company to survive just because they were afraid to kill it off with the eyes of the world watching. (In those early days the Nazi movement still cared about the feelings of the outside world – when less important things were at stake.) And then they thought: 'The business will just die a natural death.' It had been forced to give up most of its authors, including such widely read writers as Emil Ludwig. And the authorities were always making life difficult for the company. It would soon cave in. The obituary would read: 'Died peacefully in its sleep, due to declining physical powers.' It is a tragedy, and particularly so for me, that in the end Rowohlt came to grief not because of his own recklessness, but because of his author Fallada. Since the Nazis came to power I had written a whole string of books. They had not been particularly successful, apart from *Jailbird*, perhaps, which might have become a sales success if they had not banned its reprinting. In the Third Reich it was not permitted to think and write about convicted offenders with compassion. But then I wrote *Wolf among Wolves*,[87] fired by the old fervour again, I wrote without looking up from the desk, I wrote without looking to left or to right. This was a story, and these were characters, that absorbed all my attention for months!

I remember very well the discussions we had prior to the book's publication. The big question in our minds was this: 'Can we dare to publish this novel, or should we not risk it?' In the Third Reich the situation was that there was no pre-publication censorship as such. Anything could be published, but the author and publisher answered with their heads for the book's reception. But whether it would be well received or badly received was totally unpredictable. There were so many authorities involved, and it all depended on which of these authorities pronounced first. If the first review appeared in the *Völkischer Beobachter*, and it was negative, then it didn't matter how positively the officials at the Propaganda Ministry – or as we called it, the 'Propami' – thought about it: the negative Party line was now firmly established, and nothing could change it.

But nobody could predict how the Party top brass would react to mention of the Black Reichswehr[88] and the portrayal of so many dubious characters,[89] including a sex murderer.

We dithered for ages, and in the end the matter was decided by a report written by a courageous man, an editor by the name of Friedo Lampe,[90] and a worthy successor to Paulchen. In his report he wrote: 'If the Rowohlt publishing house is brought down because of this book, then it will have been brought down by something that is worth being brought down for!' *Wolf among Wolves* duly appeared, and it was a great success, not least in the Party press. Once again, the outcome was entirely unexpected. But for Rowohlt Verlag this very success proved a disaster. All those gentlemen who had waited for far too long to see the company's demise suddenly saw its survival assured. But this was unacceptable to them. The real reason, the success of *Wolf*, could not be spelled out, so some pretext had to be found to get rid of this inde-structible Rowohlt, who just kept on bouncing back . . . They actually came up with two pretexts. Rowohlt had published a biography of Stifter[91] by a certain Urban Roedl, an Austrian with an impeccably Aryan name. Now it was claimed that this Urban Roedl was in fact a closet Jew, and that Rowohlt had known about it all along. Rowohlt denied it all vehemently, of course, and it would have been difficult to prove that he'd known about it in secret. But then they brought up the other matter, and here there was no room for denials or cover-ups, whatever the extenuating human circumstances. But then no Nazi agency ever had much time for humanity. There had long been a ruling that excluded Jews from the management and curation of our 'German cultural heritage' – a ruling so elastic that they even invoked it to kick the Jews out of the antiques business. All publishing houses had accordingly been instructed to fire their Jewish employees. Rowohlt too had been forced to do so. Now for many years we had had an older Jewish woman in the office, known as 'Plosch' for short,[92] whose salary was her only income and who also used some of it to help out some impoverished relatives of hers. Rowohlt had to let Plosch go, which he did, but then he did something that was classic Rowohlt: he continued to find work for the sacked employee as an anonymous temp in a little back office. But then someone informed on her, as someone always did, Rowohlt received a formal warning, and the temporary job came to an end too. At the time Plosch was in a terrible situation: her brother, in despair at the plight of the Jews in Germany, had committed suicide. Taking away the woman's job and source of income at a time like this was tantamount to condemning her to the same fate. Rowohlt found a way round this by dictating letters to her in the evenings after the office closed and on Sundays. But no matter how secretly they went about their business, the Nazi spy had been even more secretive. My publisher was hauled before the court of honour and expelled from the German publishing profession in disgrace. The right to have charge of our 'German cultural heritage' was denied to him in perpetuity. 'You have besmirched the honour of the German publishing profession!' Thus wrote that swine Dr Goebbels in the letter confirming his expulsion – the same Dr Goebbels who never thought twice about besmirching the

honour of any man or any woman if it suited his purposes or appetites!
But now I had lost my truest friend and adviser. Yes, I found other
good publishers in time, and I'll have occasion to talk about them later.
But never again will I open letters from publishers with the same pleas-
urable anticipation as I did back then, when they came from dear old
Rowohlt. You could hear the man himself in every line he wrote, with
his boundless energy, his indestructible optimism and his irrepressible
audacity! His sense of fun, his compassion, his ready wit – all that was
gone from our lives, gone forever. We had grown older, we weren't
making any new friends, and the old ones were gradually crumbling
away – how many we were destined to lose over the next few years! In
this way too, life under the Nazis became progressively more impoverished. Oh, how they bled us dry! How they robbed us of every joy
and happiness, every smile, every friendship! And then they plunged
us into this most disastrous of all wars, they conducted their victorious *Blitzkriege* (Hitler's latest work: 'Thirty years of *Blitzkrieg*'), they
destroyed our cities, destroyed our families – yes indeed, these were
and are the true guardians of our 'German cultural heritage'. Even after
this devastating verdict there was of course no actual need for Rowohlt
to leave Germany. He could do whatever he wanted, just as long as he
did not lay a finger on our 'German cultural heritage'. He could sell
flour if he wanted, or elephants, or even paper, or else he could simply
retire on a private income. And I'm sure he planned to do one or
other of these things. But then there was his wife – and then came the
Reich Day of Broken Glass. Rowohlt's wife, his own third Reich, was
a German-Brazilian by birth, and most of her family were still living
over in Brazil. She was the lady who, after the Nazis had seized power,
had over-compensated for the bad impression made by her husband
by giving an enthusiastic Hitler salute to everyone she met – until her
little daughter so thoroughly embarrassed her in public. But it was not
long before the mother herself tired of giving the salute; she was no
actress, and 'that gang', whose deeds she heard about every day from
her husband, just made her sick, as she put it. She was afflicted with an
anti-Nazi sickness of a very acute type. She simply could not stand or

stomach those people any more. She sometimes yelled at her husband that it was shameful the way he let these bastards walk all over him; she insisted that they call it a day and emigrate to Brazil, to a decent country with decent swamps and decent pigs and monkeys! She had these outbursts from time to time – a tiny little woman who turned the scales at 50 kilos. But incorruptible with it! And then came the Reich Day of Broken Glass.[93] Among the many outbreaks of 'spontaneous popular disapproval' that were such a feature of the Third Reich, this one is perhaps already half forgotten. The Party high-ups felt – and the people then of course also felt – that the Jews were still being treated far too leniently, that things were not progressing nearly fast enough with the Jews. Perhaps they wanted to show the outside world what the German people thought of the Jews: and so one fine Sunday tens of thousands of windows in Jewish shops and homes were smashed: the Reich Day of Broken Glass! It really was a beautifully orchestrated out-burst of popular anger, and it was just a shame that the Jews had known about it for a week beforehand. The publishing house's former legal adviser, for instance, felt that his home in the west end of the city was too much at risk, so he lowered the shutters and took himself off with his wife and child to a Jewish friend in Nikolassee, who owned a villa there in a quiet street surrounded by solidly Aryan villas. He thought he would be safer there. But sadly it was a case of out of the frying pan and into the fire. His home in the old western part of the city escaped unscathed, but the Jewish villa in Nikolassee had curiosity value: as just one of relatively few in the area, it not only had its windows smashed, but suffered a bit of light looting as well, and its occupants were hauled off to police headquarters on Alexanderplatz[94] as 'conspirators', where they were held for a considerable time before being allowed to return home.

The Rowohlts also lived on the outskirts, but in the east end of Berlin, in another street lined with big villas, and here the seething populace did not stop at breaking glass or looting, but tried to set the houses on fire as well, so that everyone got to enjoy a free firework display. Dear old Rowohlt, who in addition to all his other virtues was someone who liked to be where the action is, had been quite unable to stay at home, and had felt compelled to at least join the crowd of onlookers. And that's how it came about that the diminutive Mrs Rowohlt could no longer conceal her outrage at these shameful acts, and in the middle of the assembled crowd she had declared in no uncertain terms what she thought of all this wanton destruction and arson. Rowohlt had quickly dragged his wife away; the crowd had merely gazed at her in silence, but there were too many witnesses to her outburst of hatred: back then in Germany, wherever three people were gathered together, one of them was bound to be an informer. That same night they began to pack. It was high time: the concentration camp beckoned. In fact it was more than high time, because the very next morning a couple of Party officials called on him, asking various questions, but this time they went away again. The next time they would not be so easily deterred. Rowohlt went into Berlin, but they planned to leave for Switzerland that very evening, and they had already taken the precaution of getting a passport. And now comes a most touching episode, a real act of friendship which I must now relate – adding one more page of glory to the annals of this unique publisher's life. In all the rush and bustle of their travel preparations, in fear of his own life, with a wife and two children to look after, just eight hours before heading off into such an uncertain future, old Rowohlt found time to think about his author Fallada, who was still in need of a new publisher! Rowohlt couldn't leave Germany yet, he needed to sort something out first, he was not yet free to travel. In Berlin he located the man he thought would be the right publisher for me,[95] put him into a car and drove with him out to our place in Mahlendorf. I had no idea what was going on, but the two men were sitting there in my house. The new contract was discussed, and clever old Rowohlt made sure that it was a lot more favourable than the old one: he wasn't the one, after all, who would be shelling out this time round. I pressed the gentlemen to stay for supper. Rowohlt shrugged his shoulders: 'I'm afraid I can't, my dear Fallada. I'm leaving for Switzerland on the ten o'clock train, with my wife and children – perhaps never to return!' And in a few brief words he told me what had happened.

We took our leave of each other, my wife was crying, and I too had tears in my eyes. The tail lights of the car lit up one more time, and then they were gone. I said: 'He'll be in time for his train, I'm sure.' And Suse added: 'Hopefully they'll make it across the border all right.' We went back into the house. The coffee cups were still there, the folder with the contracts lay open on the table; it was all there, from the first novel I sent to Rowohlt back in 1918 – now lost[96] – to *Wolf*. And all signed 'Ernst Rowohlt'. But now the truest of the true had walked out of our lives, the latest contract on top of the pile bore a different signature: lost and gone for ever!

So what further news of him? We had a postcard from Switzerland, very cheery in tone, and then another card from Switzerland. 'He's taking his time', we said. 'Perhaps they won't get as far as Brazil, perhaps they'll wait out the thousand years in Switzerland.' But later on we heard that he was in Brazil after all, living with his wife's brother, and then we heard nothing more from him. The years passed, and we talked about him from time to time. The new publisher is fine, I've nothing bad to say about him, in fact there's a lot to be said in his favour; but I miss the old green letters,[97] and I miss my old friend. He had such a gift for putting heart into one, eternal optimist that he was! But people like him don't come along twice in a lifetime! Lost and gone!

The war came, and we celebrated the first Christmas of the war, the Christmas of 1939,[98] with an abundance of presents still. Then the telephone rang, cutting through the din of the excited children. Who could be so insensitive as to phone on business when the family is at home celebrating Christmas?! 'You have a call from Bremen . . .' 'Suse! A call from Bremen! Be quiet, you lot! Who can possibly be calling me from Bremen? I don't know anyone in Bremen!'

I hear a disguised voice speaking down the line. 'Guess who's on the phone?' For a moment I am thrown, and then I roar: 'Rowohlt! Rowohlt my old friend, is that you? But how's that possible? Aren't you in Brazil? Rowohlt, it's so great to hear you! You must come and see us straight away, we've got some serious celebrating to do! I still can't believe it's you!'

'Blockade runner', he said. 'Got into Bordeaux the day before yester-day. I'll be with you next week or thereabouts. Got to report for duty first, of course. I'll call you again!'

It turned into a very weird Christmas, Suse and I still couldn't quite believe it. To think that he had risked coming back, after fleeing Germany and going into exile! And to think that he had actually wanted to, wanted to take part in this war after they had dragged his name through the mud in Germany! It made no sense to us. And it didn't make any more sense when he came to see us. He was deeply suntanned, but otherwise still the same old Rowohlt, the gambler, the adventurer, who always had to be where the action was. 'Of course Germany is going to lose this war', he said again. 'But I've been through this before, 1914 to 1918. And I can't just sit on my backside in bongo-bongo land while my old comrades are fighting for their lives here. It caused a terrific row with my wife, of course, and she just didn't want to let me come; she hates the Nazis even more than she did before, if such a thing is possible. I expect there'll be a divorce, and after that comes the fourth Reich!' Indestructible, irrepressible, the same old vitality and unquenchable love of life, a life that is always wonderful, even if one gets the occasional thrashing. But at least one is still alive.

And then he told us about the sea crossing. How he had begged his way onto a German ship in Rio as a seaman, finally succeeding after several rounds of drinks with the captain, and how he adopted the title of 'seaman' only as a cover for the benefit of the port authorities. And how they then, one day out from Rio, handed him a can of paint, and to his surprise had him actually doing the work of a seaman for the entire crossing, for eighteen hours a day and sometimes even longer. How they then disguised the ship to look like an English vessel, and then spent two days cruising around on the high seas looking for a German commerce raider until they found her and transferred their entire cargo of oil, coal and food, while taking on a new cargo in exchange: over 300 captured crew members from enemy ships sunk by the raider. How they then set course for Europe by a circuitous route, with over three hundred defiant prisoners on board, and the entire crew

numbering no more than 35! How they had to be on duty day and
night, only ever allowing six men up on deck at one time. I can picture
him so clearly, the huge figure of Rowohlt, bellowing down into the
dark ship's hold: 'Sing up, my hearties, sing up, and there'll be bigger
portions for lunch today!' And how they then approached Bordeaux,
having made the crossing safely and without incident, and waited for
the pilot vessel that would guide them through the mine barrier. Their
arrival had been radioed ahead, but with a favourable wind they had
got there sooner than expected. So they sat outside the mine barrier,
in sight of the English coast, and the prisoners were getting more and
more restive, and gradually, having steadfastly got through the most
difficult weeks, they began to lose their nerve. Ten hours passed, and
no pilot vessel appeared, fifteen hours passed, and still they were lying
in plain sight of the English coast, at any moment the English could
discover them. Finally the German captain said: 'If they don't come in
the next three hours, I'll take the ship through the minefields without a
pilot, and if we are blown to kingdom come, then so be it!' Everyone's
nerves were stretched to breaking point. But then a German plane flew
overhead, and a short time later, led through the mine barrier by a pilot
vessel, they lay at anchor in the port of Bordeaux, three days before
Christmas. 'And now I've got fourteen days' leave', said the old bucca-
neer. 'And I've come just at the right time to collect a little inheritance
that was waiting for me. So now I shall live it up for a bit, and then it's
off to join my unit, as a lieutenant from the First World War!'

They even made him a captain, and he fought with the army in
Crimea . . . But none of it made any difference at all. He had supposed
that by coming back in wartime and volunteering to fight, he would be
absolved of his former sins; but he had reckoned without the implacable malice of his enemies.

(30.IX.44.) I had repeatedly encountered people in Berlin who viewed
his return to Germany as an act of unbelievable effrontery. These
people seemed to have no conception of the courage, and also of the

capacity to forgive and forget, which that return betokened. When I
pointed this out to them (and these were people who were just kicking
around in civvy street at home, of course), they replied: 'Rubbish, the
old rogue just wants to start up his old business again after the war!'
– something that Rowohlt the army combatant was not even thinking
about at the time, I'm sure. These enemies, who for the most part had
permanent or casual jobs in the book world, knew that Rowohlt now
had a powerful protector in the Wehrmacht, and the kind of feeble
charges they had used to bring him before the court of honour and get
him expelled from the publishing profession just wouldn't wash now.
In the First World War Rowohlt had ended up as an aircraft observer,
and he still had some courageous friends from that time – especially at
the Air Ministry, among them General Udet.[99] But it turned out that
General Udet suffered the fate of so many prominent figures in this
war: he died in a 'plane crash'. And it turned out further that Rowohlt's
enemies, digging away in the dark like the rats they were, unearthed
a petition from 1922,[100] requesting that the death sentence for Max
Hölz[101] be commuted to imprisonment. Max Hölz had been leader of a
Communist gang, who demanded money with menaces from Saxony's
industrialists in 1921/22, and set fire to their villas if they refused to
pay up. The petition to spare this man's life was dug up by Rowohlt's
enemies; it was nearly 20 years old, but still, there was Rowohlt's
name at the bottom. Such a thing was unthinkable for the German
Wehrmacht: the name of a German army captain on a petition in
support of a murderous Communist arsonist! These same enemies were
not at all bothered by the fact that other names were also on this petition, names of people who today occupy the highest offices in the land,
and who are quite secure in those high offices despite having signed the
petition. People like Professor Carl Froelich,[102] who at one time had
even been a fully paid-up member of the Communist Party, who had
signed his name to this petition, and yet had risen to become President
of the Reich Chamber of Film. One of the most baffling mysteries
about the Nazi leadership has always been where they chose to exercise
forgiveness and where not. With most people everything was weighed

in the balance down to the last scruple, while in some cases they just turned a blind eye. Or, as Göring is once supposed to have said: '*I decide who is a Jew!*' Whereupon he went and made the Jewish officer Milch[103] a German air-force general. In Rowohlt's case certainly they weighed every last scruple in the balance, and he was dismissed just like that, without formality or ceremony, receiving the princely sum of 50 marks in redundancy money!

It was a heavy blow for him. Had he come back all the way from Brazil, leaving behind his wife, his children and his security, just to be brought down over some trivial matter dragged up from the distant past? But he would not give up yet; he drove to the Air Ministry instead. Udet was dead, but he had other friends there, perhaps not quite so influential, but they could still be useful to him. And they were willing to help, saying to him: 'My dear Rowohlt, of course we'll get this business sorted out. It's disgraceful, the way they have treated you! But this time we'll make sure the bastards can't touch you again. Get all your papers together, the originals of course, those from the First World War and those from now. The day after tomorrow one of our colleagues is flying out to the Führer's headquarters. He'll see to it that none of these little whippersnappers dares to shit on you again. Just you wait and see – the Major is still looking out for you!'

Rowohlt did as he was asked, the aircraft took off, with his original papers on board, and all his hopes, and Rowohlt waited. And then came the news: the aircraft had crashed and burned, everyone on board was dead, the irreplaceable papers were lost in the fire, his hopes were dashed for ever!

As I have already mentioned, Rowohlt is now taking the air on the island of Sylt, fanned by sea breezes. I hardly hear from him now – well, not at all, in fact. It's as if he is in waiting, in a foreign land; if he were in Brazil he could not be further removed from me. The great optimist, the perennial Mr Hopeful, is now living in the great land of hopelessness. Or is he perhaps still hoping for something after all? I think he probably is, I think he is hoping for what we are all hoping for, in this final autumn of the war, in the year 1944!

And there is another man from our circle of friends who has now gone – was it really two years ago? We got to know him relatively late, but we became very fond of him, a tall man with clever, laughing eyes behind large, dark horn-rimmed glasses, and with a mop of brown hair that he combed all the way back from his lofty and elegantly formed brow. Sas,[104] that's what we always called him, just Sas, he never had a first name, even for his closest lady friend. Sas came from the Sudetenland, and his relatives still own a bakery there to this day. But he was a teacher himself, a primary school teacher in some town in Saxony, one of those densely populated industrial towns where hunger and hardship have taken up their abode. He discovered Communism early on, he was a Communist in mind and heart, and his heart drew him to the poor of this earth; his profound, primal sense of compassion hid all their faults from his eyes with the cloak of suffering. I can see him now, sitting on the floor in my big study, surrounded by a group of young people from the Hitler Youth and the *Bund Deutscher Mädel*, discussing the party program of the NSDAP. And how cleverly he went about it, how he ignited the flame of independent thought in these young heads, which had systematically been broken of the habit of thinking for themselves and filled, day in, day out, with glib slogans; how he carefully fanned the spark of doubt, how the eyes of the youngsters lit up with joy at things they thought they had discovered for themselves, how they suddenly saw a light, a way forward – it was just wonderful to behold! He was always a child, and never happier than when surrounded by children, from the very youngest to those who are fully grown up, and can never grow old; I loved to sit on the carpet with him, quietly watching him and observing with sweet joy the light that shone in his eyes, the light that only pure intellect can kindle. His party had earmarked him for the post of education minister, but then the Nazis came to power, and instead of that he became a forced labourer in a concentration camp. They held him there for a long time, but he survived, and returned to the outside world unbroken in mind and body. What should he do now? He wasn't allowed to practise his profession any more; anyone who had once embraced

Communism was forever unfit to be a teacher of the nation's youth. He went to Berlin, he had always had a great love of music, and now he planned to give children piano and singing lessons and instruct them in the rudiments of dance. But would he be allowed to? It all seemed so difficult – and then it worked out after all, for some mysterious reason they turned a blind eye and allowed him to become a member of the Reich Chamber of Music. He had plenty of pupils, he met a woman[105] and fell in love, he led a busy and fulfilled life. He shut himself off from all the evil that was going on around him. He had learned during the bitter years in the concentration camp how pointless it was to rebel openly, because all that did was to make things worse for oneself. It was better to keep one's head down, to hold oneself together – for the day that must surely dawn sometime. But he didn't live to see that day; a small thing led to his downfall, a moment of thoughtlessness, a careless lapse that could have happened to anyone. On the street in Berlin he bumped into a man he had known many years previously, when they were both members of the same party. They greeted each other, asked each other how they were doing . . . Now the other man, he was just the same as ever, still working clandestinely for the old party, and boasting that they wouldn't catch him so easily! And what about him, Sas? He couldn't believe that Sas, one of the staunchest of the party faithful, had thrown in the towel and given up the fight! But Sas was on his guard, as everyone in Germany has learned to be. Anyone could be a spy, and fratricide stalks the land. No, he explained, he was no longer an activist, he was a music teacher now, teaching children. It gave him a lot of pleasure, and he wasn't interested in all that other stuff any more. The former party comrade was disappointed, and fixed him with a steady gaze: so much for loyalty to the cause! To hell with them all, then! He hesitated a moment, they were about to part, and then he said: 'Well look, we can still be friends – you go your way and I'll go mine! But could you do me a favour? I've got this great heavy suitcase here. I'll be back in Berlin in two days, and I'll pick it up from you then. Could you hang on to it for me until then?' And Sas, always friendly and ready to oblige, took the suitcase, carried it home, put it down somewhere and forgot about it. Weeks went by, and he suddenly noticed the suitcase again because it was in the way. 'Well fancy that!', he thought. 'The good comrade didn't come back for it in the end – maybe the old fox has been snared by his enemies after all?' The suitcase really was in the way, and so he put it up in the attic. Then he forgot about it completely.

Life goes on, his time is taken up with piano lessons, teaching simple songs, going through easy dance steps. The children are his delight – the invincible life force, the power and the glory, the pure light of the stars, fetched down from the heavens to this defiled earth! Being around them, you can almost forget about the increasingly ugly world we live in. And then there is the love of a good woman, love and comradeship, yes, comrade, we live from hand to mouth, not knowing what tomorrow will bring. In this Third Reich of ours nobody's life is safe any more. But we are still alive! So let us go forward together, towards the sun that will surely rise again one day!

And then one day he was arrested without warning; his former comrade had indeed been caught, and now the wretched man had named no fewer than thirty-five people, men, women and girls, with whom he was allegedly in contact. One of them was Sas – and this was his revenge on the former party comrade who had abandoned the fight! His lady friend, who wasn't living with him, heard about the arrest immediately; she still had time to search her friend's apartment for anything incriminating before the Gestapo got there. She found nothing, he had always been so careful, living only for his music. She didn't think of looking in the attic: she knew nothing about the suitcase. (How she tormented herself later with terrible, agonizing self-reproaches!) The suitcase was discovered, inside was a portable printing press, which had been used to produce Communist pamphlets. A few printed copies were also in the case. But even now all was not lost, the evidence against him was not that damning – despite having been denounced by his former party comrade. As the Gestapo men who searched the house themselves noted, the case was covered with the dust of many years, and the oil in the mechanism had gone thick, meaning it had not been used for a very long time. Sas's explanation had the ring of truth about it: the examining magistrate refused to issue an arrest warrant, and Sas was released from jail. So all was well? All was not well! It was very far indeed from being well. Because of course we now have two governments in Germany, two top-to-bottom systems co-existing side by side: the state, and the Party. Sas was released by the judicial authority of the Reich, but at the gates of the police headquarters he was arrested by Himmler's hellhounds. He was taken back to the same cell where he had just been held as a prisoner of the judiciary, but now he was a prisoner of the SS, removed from the jurisdiction of any judge, deprived of all rights, abandoned to a completely uncertain fate. But the officials who interrogated him had words of consolation for his lady friend: a couple of years in a concentration camp, perhaps – how bad is that? In today's Germany, where tens of thousands are living in the camps? The main thing is not to lose heart, because he hasn't really done anything! Or nothing much at least, nothing that can't be put right with a couple of years of concentration camp! Of course, he should have reported the meeting with his old Communist acquaintance immediately to the Gestapo, and he should have handed the suitcase in rather than storing it up in the attic! But a couple of years in a concentration camp would soon put that right; it was a criminal act, of course, but even in the German Reich it was not considered any more serious than that! Sometimes she was allowed to visit her friend for a few minutes. She saw him behind bars, hollow-eyed, unshaven, his blue prison uniform hanging off him. They were allowed to exchange a few inconsequential words, but every time she went home feeling strengthened again: his spirit was unbroken, the old love was stronger than ever, she had now become the purpose and object of his life, all his thoughts revolved around his lady friend. She was not permitted to do anything for him, the food in the prison was terrible and completely inadequate, but she was not permitted to bring him anything to eat. Or do anything else that could have made his life easier. Except for one thing: she was allowed to wash his underwear, in the interests not of the prisoner but of the prison authorities, who saved on soap, linen and work.

And then she was not allowed to visit him for long weeks on end; she learned that an epidemic of typhus had swept through the prison, carrying off victims in their hundreds. All the better – it saved a lot of work, a process leading quickly to death, all the better! And in this time of fear and trembling, of deep faith and fondest love, she got a phone call from a completely unknown lawyer: could she come and see him at once, it's about her friend!

She hurried to the lawyer's office, from the sign on the door she saw that the lawyer belonged to the National Socialist 'League of Guardians of the Law', and the man standing before her a few minutes later was wearing a Party membership badge. The lawyer informed her in a few brief words that her friend could be released the following Friday if she paid him 5000 marks within 48 hours. She was not allowed to ask any questions. With that she was dismissed and out on the street again, her heart pounding with emotion. She did not trouble herself about the morality of such an arrangement. She had after all been living in the German Reich for many years now, and she had heard too much and seen too much to be surprised or outraged by any dirty dealings. But what was she to do now, from a purely practical point of view? What was she to do? She earned a living by giving lessons, she was not wealthy, and she could never hope to scrape together 5000 marks from her own resources. But she had friends, and Sas had friends; it was possible to come up with that sum of money. But should she do it? Wouldn't they just take her money and keep him in prison anyway? How could she place any trust in the honesty of a lawyer who made such a proposal? What was she to do? Would she not blame herself bitterly one day if she did not hand over the money, and her friend remained in prison for years on end? Would she not always be saying to herself: perhaps they would have let him out? And that 'perhaps' decided her. She approached us too, and I must confess that I was hard-nosed enough to say 'No'. I didn't want to give my money to these criminals. I was convinced that it was all lies, a con trick designed to take advantage of a woman in distress. She managed to get the money together without me, and took it to the lawyer's office. The Friday

came, by early morning she was already waiting outside the gates of
the building on Alexanderplatz, doubt giving way to despair and then
again to hope, a crazy little spark of hope in her heart that the enemy
might, just this once, do the decent thing. And the gate opened and
her friend came out. Her joy knew no bounds, she was ready to bless
her enemies. She spent just one day with him in Berlin, so that he
could freshen himself up a bit, and then she travelled with him to his
little home village in the Sudetenland, to stay with his baker relatives,
where the half-starved man could feed himself up again. But when they
arrived in the village Sas was re-arrested by the SS. They were men of
honour: for 5000 marks they had kept their word. He had been released
on the Friday – for how long, that was never said. She never saw him
again. He was taken straight back to Berlin, in a cramped prison van,
and then shipped on to the Oranienburg concentration camp. There
he was put to work. Month after month he worked as a bricklayer, his
musician's hands were ruined for good. But she was allowed to write
to him once a month, and from time to time she was allowed to send
him a food parcel, saved from her own meagre rations. But at least she
was allowed to hope . . . The day must come . . . And then she heard
that he was back in Berlin. He had been removed from the custody of
the SS and was now to stand trial in a court of law, despite the fact that
the examining magistrate had previously refused to issue a warrant for
his arrest. Now he was to appear before the notorious 'People's Court'.
The Communist whom Sas had met in the street that time was being
put on trial, along with 35 co-defendants, including Sas. The defence
lawyer was expecting a relatively short prison sentence. So her hopes
rose again. This was better than the concentration camp; here he would
be sentenced for a specific period of time, which would come to an
end, whereas the concentration camp was indeterminate, open-ended;
it could be a life sentence, or he could be let out after three months –
the worst part was the agonizing uncertainty! No, the People's Court
was better. And it really was very good, this instrument of Himmler's
functioned beautifully, and all the accused were sentenced to death! In
the name of the German people! Found guilty of carrying a suitcase

and keeping it in his house . . . sentenced to death by hanging . . . in the name of the German people! So not over yet? Not yet finished, this litany of torment and suffering, this everyday story of German life during the glorious days of the Third Reich, under the aegis of our beloved Führer, who is so fond of children, and so sensitive that he has passed a law for the protection of animals containing dozens of provisions for the humane slaughter of animals, but who in the process has quite forgotten to observe just a smidgen of humanity when it comes to slaughtering human beings? No, not over yet – not by a long chalk! In the 'Plötze', the prison by the Plötzensee lake, there are dozens, perhaps hundreds, who have been sentenced to death, and who are now privileged to await their death. Sometimes the jangle of keys is heard at a certain hour in the morning, and then all the prisoners in their cells know that one more of their number is being led to the hangman – and to freedom. But there are many days when the jangle of keys is not heard. There's no hurry, for these men sentenced to die; they should be pleased that they have been granted another day, another week, even another month, and then another after that. Meanwhile their relatives are running back and forth with petitions and appeals, demeaning themselves before Party bigwigs, having abuse heaped upon them because only persons of degenerate character could possibly care about the fate of a convicted traitor. They run back and forth, they plead and implore, and yet in their heart of hearts they know that these Party high-ups do not hear them, do not want to hear them, that every last spark of humanity died in them a long time ago: and yet they dare not cease from running and pleading! Perhaps there is still a chance . . .! There must be a reason, after all, why the death sentence has not been carried out yet? Surely they will pardon him, even if it is commuted to life imprisonment! Better that than death! And sure enough, a doctor discovers that Sas suffered a head wound in the First World War. It must have caused him problems ever since, he must have been mad when he took the suitcase and kept it in his house – they can't hang him, they'll have to put him in a mental asylum! Cue more petitions, more running around, more begging and pleading!

And then the deed is done – and one last letter from him is all she gets. Her heart is filled with a solemn stillness. So peace comes to her at last, as it has come to him. Here is the letter that he wrote, in the fourth year of the war, under threat of death, under the leadership of Adolf Hitler. It reads as follows:[106] . . . But that's not all. This is just one of the few, there are others whose stories I could tell. We have witnessed all this, been through it all together, and we have had to fear every hour for the lives of our loved ones and our own lives – for eleven long years now. Eleven years without respite or peace! And meanwhile these fools are sitting comfortably abroad,[107] not in any kind of danger, denouncing us as opportunists, as Nazi hirelings – blaming us for being weak, for doing nothing, for failing to resist! But we have stuck it out, and they have not; we have lived with fear every single day, and they have not; we have done our work, tilled our acre of land, brought up our children, our lives constantly under threat, and we have spoken a word here, a word there, giving each other strength and support, we have endured, even though we were often afraid – and they have not!

And something else. Here is a man whom everyone has heard of, the illustrator E.O. Plauen,[108] real name Ohser, who came from the Saxon town of Plauen, renowned for its many weaving looms. He was a man like a child, an elephant who could walk a tightrope, who was perhaps best known for his savage cartoons in the weekly *Das Reich*, but who remains unforgettable for children and parents alike for his 'Father and Son' comic strip stories. Here we see the man himself, big and heavily built, but with such a wonderfully childlike laugh, and his son, his only son, a wily, weasel-faced creature full of laughter. (When writing about Plauen one is constantly using the word 'laughter'; laughter was his natural element, laughter was as natural to him as breathing, and I don't believe there was a single day in his life when he didn't laugh.) A wonderful man, because he was like a child, still holding on to the paradise world of childhood. I got to know him relatively late. My publisher wanted to put a cartoon of me on the cover of my book of memoirs, *Our Home Today*, and Plauen was given the commission. I went to see him in his studio on Budapesterstrasse, with a clear view over the trees in the Zoological Gardens. We hit it off immediately. He was a wonderful host, fetched water straightaway and brewed up a splendid pot of real coffee – in the middle of the war, when coffee beans were like gold dust. He quickly discovered my fondness for strong liquor, and conjured up a little bottle of vodka, just enough to make me animated, but not so much that I became tipsy. He had amazingly good cigarettes. We chatted away, we were immediately of one mind. In those days you could soon sniff out a kindred spirit, and with Plauen you just knew that this man was no informer, that he was completely genuine. I asked him how he, hating the Nazis as much as I did, and with the same absolute conviction that this war could never be won by them, because at the end of the day evil cannot prevail, how he could bring himself to draw political cartoons every week for the magazine put out by Dr Goebbels.[109] He smiled, and told me: 'But they *are* our enemies, when all is said and done, your Churchills and your Roosevelts and your Stalins – and there's no shame in fighting your enemies. I'm only doing to them what they do to us. But one thing I won't do: I will never draw an anti-Semitic cartoon, and I'm not going to play that filthy game.' One day, however, his wife told me the deeper reason behind his drawing, why he felt compelled to draw and to keep on drawing. It was during the time of the worst air raids on Berlin, when the Americans were stepping up their campaign of carpet bombing. Mrs Plauen said: 'When Berlin has been reduced to rubble he'll be sitting on the ruins and drawing, the last survivor – because drawing is what he has to do!' That 'has to' is the key here – he could not do otherwise: *Das Reich* gave him an opportunity, and he took it.

I duly admired the collection of kitsch items in his studio, which was a constant delight to him: wonderful postcards of lovers kissing, harmless images that you had to hold up to the light to discover the naughty bits, a seashell with silver-limbed nymphs painted on its mother-of-pearl lining – all the delights of bourgeois desires unchained. Such things gave him much pleasure, and made him roar with laughter. Later on I was able to send him another item for his collection from Paris, which I acquired one night in the Metro, a big-bosomed lady dressed in green with long, brown stockings; it was almost as if you caught a glimpse of the mysterious darkness into which these brown stockings disappeared . . .

All that's left today is a scene of devastation, the house in Budapesterstrasse has been reduced to a pile of rubble, and Plauen's little collection of saucy kitsch is lost and gone forever. Also lost are the sketchbooks, endless numbers of them, which this tireless worker filled with . . . female nudes. His political cartoons did not demand a lot of effort. He churned them out with efficient regularity, like doing school homework. He didn't fret or worry about inspiration beforehand. One day he would browse through the newspapers, looking for ideas, and the next day he would draw the cartoons, usually five or six at a time, sometimes even seven. You really needed to see the originals, carefully drawn with a pen, often on a colour wash background – the newsprint reproduction gives only a feeble impression of the real thing. But it was just a sideline for him. His real interest lay in his female nudes. He dragged women and girls in off the street, plucked them from cafés and parties, and drew them in all manner of poses and contortions. 'I never tire', he said, 'of looking at the female body and drawing it.' He wasn't interested in beauty, only in truth. He went into minute detail, and many of his nudes are verging on the disgusting, while others, with the soft curves of their seated bottoms, are ravishingly beautiful. What fluidity of form in repose! How one thing flowed into another in a seamless transition, a cosmos within the cosmos! But he was always the cartoonist, even when drawing his nudes. He would put the head of a resentful, envious old maid on a magnificent body. He would draw a naked woman down on all fours like an animal, the ends of her shrivelled and impossibly elongated tits scraping the floor! He had drawn a Leda whose swan had his head emerging from her mouth, cackling in agitation! In short, he was an impossible person, as impossible as every unspoilt artist, living life to the full, bursting with vitality. In addition he was virtually deaf. You had to speak quite loudly to make yourself understood, and he often spoke very loudly himself: like many deaf people, he had no sense of the volume at which he spoke. Which was not without its dangers, given the things we talked about. It would not have done to have a spy lurking behind the door. Plauen was full of jokes and witticisms about the Nazi regime, his own and other people's. He tossed them out as they occurred to him, as carefree as you like, and nobody enjoyed his jokes more than he did. He laughed like a drain. And then thought of another one. He bustled around his studio, this elephant of a man was like a cat in his movements, soft-footed and watchful. In fact, for all his merry laughter there was something quiet and melancholy about him, a sense of deep-seated sorrow – only fools could be blithely cheerful in these times, everyone else felt a deep undercurrent of sorrow in their hearts.

And then he started drawing me. He suddenly became quite still, his face was tense, and I had to be still too. He screwed up his eyes, studied me closely, now very serious: a stranger who was feeling his way to the bottom of my soul. His first attempts were unsuccessful, failing to get beyond the physical externals. The nose, a little exaggerated in the way it stuck out, perhaps, but that wasn't what he was after. So he set to work again, the pen making a frightful scratching noise on the paper. I started to say something. 'Not now, you have to be quiet', he said sternly, and carried on drawing. And then he suddenly said: 'Finished!' And looked at me, the smile had returned to his face. I looked at the cartoon[110] – and I was looking at myself. I was thrilled with it. It was amazing, it was magic, what he had done there. It was me, in fact I didn't even think of it as a cartoon in that sense: not at all, that was the real me, that was how I really looked, with the squashed roll-up hanging from my expressive and yet rather limp mouth. Needless to say, the publishers decided not to use the cartoon for my book. They thought it was very good, really quite wonderful, but perhaps just a touch too daring? For the present times, that is? Instead they put a cosy little cottage with a little tree on the cover, which would have been much more appropriate for Marlitt.[111] But before that they commissioned Plauen to do a 'serious', 'academic' portrait of me. I was delighted, as it gave me an excuse to spend more time with him! But the serious portrait didn't work out either: 'It's no good, I can only draw cartoons!' he cried in despair, having struggled with it for hours. We met up with him a few more times, and he also came out to see me in Mahlendorf. We had a lot of laughs. He was full of new ideas, as ever. 'When Berlin has been reduced to rubble, Plauen will still be sitting on the ruins and doing his little drawings.'

I was in Berlin this spring, and standing on the tram with a friend. We were travelling through the bombed-out streets of the city, heading somewhere where we could still get something decent to eat. The friend said to me: 'Have you heard – ?' and broke off again. 'Heard what – ?' I asked. 'No, I'd better not tell you, it'll just upset you . . .' 'Look, Max, just tell me! After the ten years we've been through, I doubt if anything much can upset me!' He looked me in the face. 'Plauen shot himself. Two weeks ago now . . .' I was wrong: I could still get upset, even after the ten years we'd been through. Plauen? Shot himself? It was not possible, this man who was full of life and laughter, this irrepressible jester – shot himself? Impossible! 'It's not possible!' I said out loud. 'A man like Plauen would never shoot himself!' And yet he had done it. His studio had been bombed out, as I have already described, so he took his family down to southern Germany and then found temporary accommodation for himself in Fürstenwalde, the same Fürstenwalde where I had once been kept in protective custody. He needed to be fairly close to the editorial offices of *Das Reich*, where he had to deliver his cartoons every week. He shared his new quarters with a friend, and when the two of them were talking and laughing together in the evening, their landlord was sitting next door[112] and taking down every word in shorthand! Plauen's deafness meant that every word could be clearly heard. This vile creature kept it up for six months, then went and handed all the material over to the Gestapo. I doubt if he was paid for his pains; he probably dished the dirt out of pure, high-minded devotion to his beloved Führer. What a dung heap they have turned Germany into! And just look at the plants that have grown on this dung heap – unspeakable!

The material was just too incriminating, even Goebbels could not have saved his pet cartoonist. But they did do something for him; they

placed a revolver in his cell, and left it to him to anticipate the verdict.
Which he did. I wish I knew if he died laughing. It's entirely possible,
I'm tempted to think so – in fact, I firmly believe it. He was a cartoonist
and a caricaturist from the day he was born, and I doubt if he saw the
world any other way – he just had to smile about it. And so died E.O.
Plauen, real name Ohser, born in the Saxon town of Plauen. May he
rest in peace!

I must interrupt myself at this point. This is a separate entry,[113] inserted
into these notes I am making. You'll recall that I am writing these lines
in the autumn of the year of the war 1944, in the asylum at Strelitz,
where I have been sent for observation by the public prosecutor, doubtless as a 'dangerous lunatic'. (There are various ways of getting rid of
undesirable writers; this is one area where the German Reich is not
short of ideas.) I was given permission to occupy myself by doing some
writing. I wrote a few short stories to start with, followed by a little
novel. And then it suddenly occurred to me: this was the place, inside
these four walls, under constant guard and surveillance, where I had
to make a start on these notes. I've been carrying it all around in my
head for so long now. I've just got to get it down on paper. And I know
that I am crazy. I'm risking not only my own life, I'm also risking, as
I increasingly realize as I go on, the lives of many of the people I am
writing about. I don't have a drawer or cupboard with a lock on it.
All my things are freely accessible to anyone. I'm writing in a cell they
allocated to me, where other prisoners are constantly passing through,
police guards are looking in on me all the time, smoking a cigarette and
asking stupid questions about what a writer does. They admire my tiny
handwriting, the only protection I have against spies and nosy parkers.
I know that every letter, every line I write here has to be censored by
the public prosecutor's office before it leaves here. I haven't the faintest idea how I am going to evade this censorship, how I am going to
smuggle the MS out. Am I just being reckless? Or am I acting under
an irresistible compulsion? All these thoughts plague me day and night,

and make me forget my own fate here in this house of the dead: it's only when I am sitting writing these notes that these thoughts cease to torment me! And yesterday something else happened that worries me even more. One of the police guards took me to the director's office, and they showed me a letter, with everything carefully masked apart from the sender's name. 'Who's this?' 'Küthers',[114] I replied, 'a young soldier, an admirer of my books, who sometimes writes to me from the field. We've never actually met.'

'Well, I am obliged to inform you that the Prosecutor General has confiscated this letter. Constable, take this man away again!'

That was all, and it isn't hard for me to guess what's in the letter. Küthers, the poor boy – he spent a year and a half in a field hospital, and in his last letter he told me that he would probably have to go back to the front again soon. This will have been his first letter sent from the front, and no doubt it didn't sound particularly enthusiastic, this letter from a young man whom they'd been patching up for a year and a half in order to make him fit for more slaughter. He will doubtless have expressed the hope that this 'shitty war' would soon be over – an old campaigner just knows instinctively that he can speak his mind freely with someone like Fallada. But what this young man couldn't know was that his letters were no longer reaching Fallada directly, but were being censored first by the public prosecutor's office – to whom one cannot afford to speak one's mind at all freely. Poor boy: they will probably court-martial you now because of your ever so slightly disgruntled remarks. In Germany, you see, one has to remain enthusiastic about a lost war even when the world is collapsing about your ears! Poor boy – my hands are tied, I can do nothing to help you. You have made your bed, and now you will have to lie in it!

But will I not find myself lying in the same bed? Won't the recipient of such remarks come under the same suspicion as their writer? Won't they go through all my post at home? Won't they suddenly haul me off somewhere else to be cross-examined about defeatism, before I've had chance to destroy this MS? Won't they pounce upon these pages, and will not even the tiniest handwriting fail to save me, once they have deciphered a single sentence? Wouldn't it be better to tear up everything I have written in the last few days and flush it down the toilet? I don't know. I'm struggling with myself. Now night is falling. Soon they'll be bringing our bowl of gruel with a few cabbage leaves in it, and then at half past seven we have to go to bed, in the cramped cell that I am sharing with a schizophrenic murderer, a mentally deficient and castrated sex offender and another mental defective locked up for attempted rape and murder. My three companions always sleep very soundly, but I don't sleep so well. I have a long night ahead of me to reflect on my many problems. Shall I carry on writing tomorrow? I'd be mad to do it!

(1.X.44.) Swenda – A Dream Fragment, or My Troubles.[115] I must have known Swenda from earlier, but my memories of her are unclear, they are like the shadows of clouds that sometimes fall upon our lakes even on sunny days. The first thing I know about her for certain is that I am climbing up a broad, antiquated staircase with lovely shallow oak treads, which leads straight up to a set of big, double doors with panels of transparent mirror glass instead of wood. The doors are like the ones that lead to the garden in my own home, except that they are much larger and not so handsome as the doors at home, having ugly decorative trims of brass and coloured glass in the corners of the frame. Through the clear mirror glass panes I can see Swenda standing there, her dark tresses tumbling to her shoulders, looking straight at me. For a moment I stand still on the landing outside the doors, we gaze at each other in silence for a long time. Then I reach for the handle of the door. Swenda shakes her head. And suddenly I remember what I had forgotten, that I may not enter here ever again, that I proposed to Swenda and was rejected, that terrible things happened here which I can only dimly remember, they are like the shadows of clouds that sometimes fall upon the lakes at home on sunny days.

I turn and slowly go back down the stairs. I walk through the streets of the city, I leave the city behind and find myself in open country. I walk slowly onwards. I come to a railway track, the level crossing barrier is just being lowered, the monotonous sound of the bell announces the approach of a train. On the far side, raised up on a mound of earth, stands the crossing-attendant's cottage. I lean on the top pole of the barrier and look across at the cottage, nestling in a profusion of yellow and pink hollyhocks. A young girl emerges from the door, the red signal flag in her hand. Her dark tresses fall to her shoulders, it could be Swenda, but I know that it is not Swenda. I know this girl's name, but I cannot remember it. And as the passing train rattles and lurches between us, I remember that I was rejected here too. I slowly turn round and walk back into the city, whose towers, shimmering in the sun, rise up from the fields as I approach.

I am standing in a large, unevenly paved market square, where I have just bought three horses. They are incredibly big. 'How on earth am I going to feed them?' is the thought that goes through my head. Then I recognize them: these are the ancient nags belonging to our drunken innkeeper. And there is the man himself, greeting me with a laugh, the corners of his mouth are stained brown with tobacco juice, he is unshaven and dirty, as always. I leave the market square and head into the city, the horses, which are unharnessed, follow me readily, one of them has my cigarette case hanging from its hindquarters on a strap. One of the horses is especially affectionate to me, pushing its head under my arm and nuzzling me as I walk on; I walk slightly to one side, I'm afraid the horse might tread on my painful right foot with its broad hooves.

I stop in front of a large house. I go up and inquire if Mrs Stössinger is there. No, she is away at the moment – but a room has been prepared for me. I go upstairs, thinking to spruce myself up a little, but I have to come and eat straight away. I sit down at a long table, opposite me is a general. He is wearing a white linen suit, but I know that he is a general. He is mentally ill, and he hates me. He has a small, very red head and he watches me silently through bloodshot eyes. The food is served very quickly, and the plates are not changed between courses. There's poached white turbot, pike tails in a watery aspic, shellfish with mustard butter. No meat – they show me the huge menu, and I note that today is a meatless day. Finally a large, white, marbled ice-cream bombe is served. I take a large portion and put it on my plate, which is already full to overflowing. The ice cream immediately collapses and melts, spilling out over the edge of the plate, the whole plate now overflows. I spread my legs to let the cascading food drip down onto the floor between them. I look round quickly: the bloodshot eyes of the mad general are firmly fixed on me, everyone at the table is looking at me in earnest silence. Between my legs the overflow from my plate is still trickling steadily onto the floor.

I suddenly remember that I have forgotten to retrieve my cigarette case from the horse, I have no cigarettes on me. I go to the window and open it. The horses have disappeared, and I know I shall never see them again. Now I have nothing to smoke. I look out onto the square around the Kaiser Wilhelm Memorial Church. The church is burnt out, the houses around it are in ruins, the streets are buried under deep piles of rubble. There is nobody to be seen. 'There is a war on', I say to myself. 'Berlin lies in ruins.' The house from whose third-floor window I am now looking out has also been burned out by an incendiary bomb and blown apart by an aerial mine: I myself saw it lying in ruins that time when I was in Berlin on business. I am my own ghost, I think to myself.

Then I discover a cigarette machine on the wall. I fiddle about with it, trying to get a pack of cigarettes out of it. 'There's a war on', somebody says behind me. 'Those are all empty packs, just there for show.' But at the top I discover a compartment with a flat door that I can open just like that. This compartment is also completely filled with empty cigarette packs, but right at the back I find four packs of tobacco. The tax stickers have been torn off. 'That's good, that I've found some tobacco', I think to myself, remembering that I've probably still got plenty of cigarettes with senior nurse Holst,[116] but only half a pack of tobacco. I leave two marks in the compartment for a pack of tobacco.

By now it is dark, the arc lamps are burning in the deserted stations, no trains are running any more, I'm running away from my father. He is dead, I know, but he has come back to call me to account for what I did to my mother. There's nothing frightening about him as such, my father, he looks fresh, the little goatee beard, which was white when I knew him, is now brown, he is walking quickly and easily along the street next to the railway line, intent on pursuing me. I run along the railway tracks ahead of him, trying to escape. The line has been bombed, but they have laid out large quantities of long, white roofing battens, over which I am running very fast, half flying in fact. My father has long since dropped out of sight, and as the batten-covered stretch of track starts to climb steeply I know that I must turn off, and then my father will never find me.

I enter a house and ring the bell at a door in a very dark courtyard. The door is opened by a white-haired lady in a black dress with a narrow, white ruff at the neck, who welcomes me as the representative of the owner, who has gone away. I ask for two rooms to be prepared for me to work in downstairs, and another for my secretary, but she firmly refuses my request: I must make do with the rooms upstairs. My secretary is waiting for me in the large room downstairs, with its upholstered chairs covered in a yellow cretonne patterned with little reddish flowers. I hired her in a bar, a very attractive, very tall woman, just a touch taller than me. At the time she was wearing a lot of face powder, but the powder has washed off in the meantime, revealing two little anchors, blue ship's anchors, tattooed on her pale cheeks. This woman could almost be my wife, so closely does she resemble her; she is even wearing my wife's baggy blue trousers with the embroidered anchor, and her face is the spitting image of my wife's – except that she has these two little anchors tattooed on her cheekbones. I am very disappointed. But at least I can dictate my work to her, at long last!

Once again I am climbing the broad, easy-going oak staircase leading to the glazed double doors behind which Swenda was standing. I feel very sad, I know that there is no hope for me any more. My feet are dragging, my heart is heavy. When I look up, I see Swenda looking at me through the glass in the door. I go through the door and stand before her. She just looks at me; there is nothing in her eyes, neither rejection nor entreaty, no fear and no questioning.

I take her in my arms and carry her into the back of the apartment. The doors open soundlessly before me as I advance with the woman lying inert in my arms. A pale, unearthly light, which does not come from outside, fills the rooms. I'm standing in front of a big, wide ceremonial bed, surmounted by a massive baldachin with dark, pleated drapes. The bed itself, however, looks white and cold. As I go to lay Swenda down on it, her clothes peel away and tumble to the floor, like the petals of a yellow rose falling softly and silently to the ground. I lay Swenda down naked on the cold, white bed, there she lies, her body is whiter than the sheets, and her tresses lie black upon the pillow. She gazes fixedly at me, without love and without anger. I knew her in another time, I was turned away, terrible things happened, my memories of all this are unclear, like the shadows of many a cloud that fall upon the lakes at home. I bend over Swend . . .

In 1937 I was commissioned by Tobis[117] to write the screenplay of a film for Emil Jannings. At the time Jannings was struggling somewhat. He was used to appearing in a couple of films a year, but recently things had not been working out too well for him, simply because he was not being offered the right material. Now all they had lined up for him was the Virchow role, and he said to me at our first meeting that the part filled him with dread: 'They'll just have me looking down a microscope the whole time, and that's not acting, that's just looking! I want a proper part to play!' (People might recall that Emil Jannings did subsequently play the Virchow role,[118] because 'our' film project fell through, for reasons that will appear later. And nobody who has seen this film about the research scientist will ever forget the moment when Jannings-Virchow caught his first glimpse of the tuberculosis pathogen through the microscope. Your heart stood still, you held your breath. This peerless actor had managed to make something as simple as 'looking' into a tremendous feat of acting, or rather of human empathy!) Jannings, who tended to lapse into Berlin dialect when telling his stories, went on: 'And the best thing in old Virchow's life, these fellows won't even show it!' Jannings shot an accusing glance at his production manager, the film director Froelich[119] from Tobis. He was Jannings' full-time minder – you never really saw Emil without him. Jannings was something of a problem child for the film company: his every mood was anxiously observed, and everything was done, every whim satisfied, just in order to keep him sweet-tempered. 'The thing is', Jannings went on, 'old Virchow played around a good bit well into his old age. The old boy was a pillar of society, an Excellency and all the rest of it, but at night he would go out chasing skirt. He picked up some woman in some dive on Elsässerstrasse, or somewhere around there, a *chanteuse* or whatever they call it, and they really hit it off – big time. And then he married her, just like old Professor Unrat and his Marlene – no, hang on, she called herself Molene. But you know what I mean, Fallada! So that's the story, and the best thing about Virchow, and these fellows won't show it, they won't let me do that!' And Jannings, fat and not very tall, with his sallow complexion and soft, fleshy face, pointed an accusing finger at Froelich. 'My dear Jannings', said the latter reproachfully, 'why do you keep on going over the same old ground?! We've told you a dozen times that this former *chanteuse*, who now really is the widow of an Excellency, is still alive, and she would object immediately if we tried to portray her on screen.'

'Object, my arse!' said Jannings irritably. 'You're just too tight, that's all it is! Just throw money at the old dragon, shut her up with half a million, a million for all I care – I'll earn it all back for you! Any film I'm in, it doesn't matter how much it costs to make, I always earn it all back! Fallada, I must show you the telegrams I've received from Budapest, they're about to premiere my *Broken Jug*[120] there. People are climbing over each other to get tickets. The theatre is already booked out two weeks ahead.' And he showed me the telegrams. I knew enough about the film business, however, to know that these were the standard telegrams that every film company sends to its star, either directly or indirectly, to keep him happy – and Emil Jannings really ought to have known this himself. But he was a big child, for whom fame (even when manufactured to order) was the breath of life, and so he preferred to believe that these bits of paper were both spontaneous and genuine.

Jannings went over to the window and raised a threatening fist. This conversation took place in the Hotel Kaiserhof,[121] which of course is just across from the Propaganda Ministry; Jannings always stayed at the Kaiserhof when he was in Berlin, and always took a suite of rooms on the top floor. 'That's terrific, Mr Jannings!' I had said in response to the telegrams. 'You see!' he cried, and shook his fist at the Ministry building. 'You see! I could be the greatest actor in the world, but him over there, that little spastic,[122] he begrudges me my fame! I only need to get a couple of telegrams like these and he's eaten up with jealousy! He begrudges me everything. The little creep is worried sick that I might become more famous than he is. He frets about it day and night!' Froelich and I exchanged a quick, knowing glance behind the back of the ranting thespian, and grinned. Jannings ploughed on: 'But that other fellow, Göring – now he's something else! If I could only work under him – ! Then I'd be the greatest actor in the world! What does this fellow do, this Göring? His state company of actors is on tour in Kiel, and not a soul turns up to the performance. So what does he do? He gets into his yacht, sails up there and parks himself in the royal box. Well, from then on, of course, the theatre is packed – now that's the man for me! But as for that jealous little prick – !' And he shook his fist again. 'But look here, Jannings', said Froelich soothingly, 'just calm down a bit, will you! Why get yourself so worked up? Now you've got Fallada writing a marvellous screenplay for you about Iron Gustav[123] . . .' Such was indeed my allotted task. But there wasn't a lot of material to work with. There was an ancient cab driver in Berlin who was nicknamed 'Iron Gustav', because he clung with iron determination to his horse-drawn cab and refused to switch to a motorized taxi. After the Great War, in 1928, this indomitable old man had the idea of trotting off to Paris with his horse-drawn cab, at a time when the French were not exactly well disposed towards the Germans. The experiment had proved unexpectedly successful, and the old man had been lionized by the Parisians. Then he had returned home again and was forgotten.

He had long since given up his cab, and 'Iron Gustav' was now selling postcards with his portrait on them at some railway station. He was said to have taken to drink in a serious way.

So not a lot of material to work with, and the story of his life prior to the Paris trip would all have to be made up – but that would not be a problem. 'Fallada', Jannings implored me, 'you're the only man who can do it. You must write me a German *Cavalcade*.[124] A chronicle of everyday life in Germany from 1900 or so to the Paris trip. The bourgeoisie, the world war – everything. You know what I mean!' I knew very well. The call for a German *Cavalcade* was one I had heard before, the ambition to make such a film burned in the heart of every German film producer. I told Jannings I would see what I could do. I asked when it had to be finished. I got the usual film producer's answer: 'By yesterday!' In the film business, everything is needed in a hurry. Any idea that is not acted upon immediately is effectively useless. 'How much time do you need, then?' In my mind's eye I pictured a weighty tome – the entire Hackendahl family, with all the sons and relatives, life before the war . . . 'Three months at least', I said. They squealed a good deal, but I would not budge. I can work incredibly fast, I can get a move on like nobody else, but what I can't do is miracles. And I don't have the gift for writing brief film synopses. I can only make up a story if I can describe things properly and go into detail. In effect, I had to write these people a fully fledged novel, which would then have to be boiled down by their own script department. It was a somewhat cumbersome procedure, but given the nature of my talent, it was the only option.

So this was the task I had been set, and since I had never seen the film *Cavalcade*, I could set about my work with no previous baggage. Of course I had to get a move on, and of course I had taken on far too much again, and of course my dear wife watched me embark on this with somewhat anxious eyes and feared I would suffer a total breakdown; but I managed it, and on schedule – in fact I delivered the text with two days to spare. In the meantime there had been another of those typical film industry crises. Rowohlt called me and told me the director, Froelich, had lost his job.[125] That would probably have consequences for my film project, he opined, and suggested that I ease off and take my time. Thank heavens I didn't listen to the voice of temptation, and sure enough, two or three days later Froelich called me in person and inquired anxiously how my work was going. In response to my surprised question – surely he had lost his job? – he replied with a laugh: yes, indeed he had, but now he was back at his desk again! I never heard anything more about this palace revolution at Tobis – not that I really wanted to. In the film business, even more than in the literary world and the theatre, everything can just change overnight! Anyone who has just reached the top is already on his way down: eagerly pursued projects are junked: everything's in constant motion, just like the movies themselves.

So I had delivered the goods, and now waited for the outcome – the schoolboy was keen to know what mark he'd got. I didn't have long to wait. First came a telegram from Emil Jannings, who just thanked me effusively for creating such a splendid character for him to play, then came a letter from Tobis, which said much the same thing in its own quieter way. (I mention this not to enhance my own reputation, but simply to throw more light on the events that followed.) My job as such was now finished, but when is anything ever really finished in the film-making business? They wanted me to attend various meetings with the film's director, so I travelled to Berlin and sat in. The meetings were boring, but they gave me an opportunity to get to know Emil Jannings a little better as a person, and that was a real delight! He was a mass of contradictions, was Jannings. For example: he was generous to a fault with his personality, he gave freely of himself in conversation, and was never too lazy to tell a story and amuse his guests. But in money matters he was just plain stingy. I have never seen him offer his guests anything, not even a cigarette. That just didn't happen with him. I am a passionate smoker myself, I actually can't think unless I am smoking, and there we were, five or six of us at a script conference, all sitting around rather morosely, while the sentences dripped haltingly from the mouths of the assembled men, because none of us was smoking. In the end I couldn't stand it any longer, I took my cigarettes out of my pocket and said to Jannings: 'Do you mind if I smoke, Mr Jannings?', and lit up regardless. 'But of course, my dear Fallada!' replied Jannings. 'I shall join you!' – and promptly lit a cigarette himself. A sigh of relief went round the table, everybody reached into their pockets and lit up, and now the words flowed more freely, the thoughts came more easily! And it was always the same: Jannings would ring for service, and when the waiter came (we were meeting in the Hotel Kaiserhof) he would order a bottle of mineral water and ask: 'Would anyone else like to order something?'

We would, we did, and we paid ourselves. All well and good, and perhaps just as it should be; perhaps a man like Jannings cannot be expected to pay for everyone at these meetings all the time. But then something surprising happened, something completely at odds with the picture I have just painted. In the middle of one of these meetings the door opened and Jannings' manservant Ernst came in. My gaze followed him as he passed through the illustrious gathering and went up to the desk where Jannings was sitting. 'He'll have a message for his master', I said to myself. But Jannings merely glanced quickly at Ernst and carried on talking. Now Ernst was not, as one might suppose from what came next, an aged, grey-haired manservant with years of honourable service behind him, who now enjoyed special privileges. On the contrary: he was a young man of about thirty. Now he was standing at the desk, and he opened up the cigar box that was sitting there and took out a cigar. Taking a knife from the pen dish, he cut off the tip of the cigar and lit it with the ornate gold lighter that was also on the desk. The manservant Ernst then walked off with a relaxed air, inhaling deeply and pleasurably on his master's cigar, bought solely for Jannings and himself. What a strange and contradictory world we live in, how mysteriously labyrinthine is the human heart, for ever impenetrable to the inquiring mind! It has also happened that I have been with Jannings in the evening, chatting away, when all of a sudden he had to go out, and rang for his manservant Ernst: 'Ernst, get me my coat and my hat! – Good, Ernst, and now I need money!' The manservant reached into his pocket and placed two banknotes into his master's hand. Jannings

looked at them, and shook his head: 'That's not enough, Ernst. I'm off
to see the women tonight!'

'Mr Jannings – !' The manservant's tone was reproachful, his eye-
brows raised.

'It's no use, Ernst, I'm off to see the women! I need more money,
Ernst!'

'Then I'll have to open the safe, Mr Jannings', still in a beseeching
tone of voice. 'Then do it, Ernst, my boy. I'll wait.' And he launched
into a conversation with me, which I had great difficulty in keeping
up, so stunned was I by what I had just witnessed. In the end Ernst
came back and placed five hundred-mark notes in his master's hand,
not without reproach. 'That should be enough, Ernst, and if it isn't, I'll
have to ring and get you out of bed!' Whereupon Jannings bade me a
hasty farewell. I was completely taken aback by this bizarre domestic
set-up, and this master-servant relationship, and it occurs to me only
now, nearly ten years later, as I am writing all this down, that the veteran
actor was perhaps just play-acting and putting on a little improvisation
for his screenwriter. The fact is he never stopped being an actor. One
of my most delicious memories is the time he acted out for my benefit
a visit that 'his' Minister, Dr Goebbels, paid him when he was staying
by the lake at St. Wolfgang. Much of the charm gets lost in the telling,
of course. You really had to be there and see how Jannings acted out
the various parts, how this fat, sallow man was suddenly transformed
into Councillor Schmidt, or Dr Goebbels, or some Bavarian village
cartwright. But I'll attempt it nonetheless, not least because this little
story so beautifully illustrates Jannings' relationship with 'his' Minister,
the man who was the focus of all our thoughts at that time. I'll let
Jannings tell the story in his own words, just as he told it to me at the
time, in his characteristic Berlin dialect: 'Look here, Fallada, you know
I have this little house by the lake at St. Wolfgang. So there I am, still
in bed, shortly before nine one morning this spring, still feeling nice
and woozy, because we'd had a few the night before at the White Horse
Inn. Suddenly, there's somebody standing in the room. "What's up?"
I ask, pretty annoyed, because I hate being disturbed in the night.

Ernst says to me, in his doleful voice – you know what he's like: "Mr Jannings, there's a man from the Gestapo downstairs who would like to speak to you."

"Oh Lord, Emil", I say to myself, "what on earth did you say last night when you were pissed out of your mind! I've said it before, and I'll say it again, Emil: one of these days you'll talk your head right off your shoulders!" But there was nothing for it, I had to bite the bullet; I threw on a dressing gown and knocked on Gussy's door. You know, don't you, Fallada, that I'm married to Gussy Holl?'[126] I nodded. "'Gussy", I say to her, "you see me now, but in a little while you won't be seeing me any more. The Gestapo are downstairs. Say goodbye to your Emil, woman." I go downstairs, and there's this fellow all kitted out in Bavarian gear, the works, with *lederhosen* and a loden hat with a great shaving brush sticking out the top, some type from Berlin. Complete with glasses and legs like matchsticks. "Jannings", I say, to introduce myself, and he introduces himself as "Councillor Schmidt". And then we stare steadily into each other's eyes. I think to myself, if you want something from me, then just spit it out. And we carry on staring, neither of us wanting to speak first. In the end the whole thing just feels silly, so I say to him: "So what can I do for you, Councillor?"

"Well", says he, and my heart is trembling like a blancmange. "Well, Mr Jannings, the Minister wishes to pay you a visit today. That is a great honour, Mr Jannings, because generally speaking the Minister doesn't visit people in their homes. I have already carried out an inspection of your property. On one side is the lake, on the other side there's a stream, on the third side is a wire fence, so now we'll have to post the sentries on the side facing the road in order to secure the property." And the man did his job thoroughly, I will say that: you couldn't find a bush to pee in without stepping on some Gestapo lad, all togged up for the great outdoors, with *lederhosen* and a hat with a shaving brush, which was thicker or thinner, depending on rank and seniority.

"Gussy", I then say to my old lady, "we are highly honoured, the Minister is visiting me today. Now listen, Gussy, you're a clever woman, and I need your advice. The morning and the lunch, we'll manage that somehow. But what are we going to do then? You know what it's like: if I spend two hours with the man, we end up arguing, he's got his ideas and I've got mine. He can't stand being contradicted – and I'm even worse. So what am I going to do with the Minister all afternoon?"

"That's easy, Emil", says Gussy, showing that she really is a clever woman, "there's the lake and you've got a motorboat. Take the Minister out in the boat and show him the sights from the lake – the engine makes so much noise that you won't be able to have a proper conversation anyway!"

"Perfect, Gussy", says I, "you've got it sussed again. But there is one little problem. You know that the Minister has a physical deformity – dot and carry one, you know what I mean – and it's pretty awkward climbing into the boat. How are we going to swing that, I wonder?"

"Oh Emil", says Gussy, "that's simple, that is! You just nip into the village, see the cartwright, and get him to make you a little stepladder. You can make up some excuse, if the Minister's visit is supposed to be secret." So off I go into the village to the cartwright's place. "Master Cartwright", says I, "I want to go out in my motorboat today, and I've just twisted my ankle. Would you be so good as to make me up a little wooden stepladder quickly, so that I can get into the boat more easily?"

"We know all about it", says the cartwright, and laughs. "I'll get it done right away – on account of Mr Dot and Carry One!"

So, the Minister turns up, and everything goes swimmingly. And after lunch I say to him: "Dr Goebbels, would you like me to show you the sights around the lake – ?" He's very happy to go along with that, so we walk down to the boathouse together. And as we're standing there chatting away, while my bosun fires up the engine, I see the Minister glance at the stepladder, and he sees straightaway that the ladder is new, and I know he just can't stand being reminded of his little physical deformity. "How's this going to end?" I think to myself, and before I've finished thinking the thought the Minister suddenly squats down on his haunches and bam! he's jumped into the boat, and didn't even look at the ladder. "That's good", I think to myself, "that's pretty smart!" And then we set off. I explain all the sights to him, the engine makes such a racket that we have to bellow into each other's ears, but it all goes well. And the whole time we're on the water I'm thinking: "Okay, he's in the boat now, but how's he going to get out again? He's never going to use the ladder!" And what can I tell you, Fallada: we'd hardly tied up before the Minister squats down again, gives a great heave and shoots almost straight up in the air, and before you know it he's standing on the jetty! He made it! And I said to myself, Fallada: "The guy's got what it takes, the guy's pretty smart, the guy's all right! Anyone who's as switched on as he is, is fine by me. He's a poisonous, jealous little bastard, but he's all right just the same!"' With these words Jannings ended his tale of the Minister's visit – showing just how ambivalent were his feelings towards the man who now held the fate of our film in his hands.

(2.X.44.) 'How will the Minister react to the plan?' – that was the big question that was exercising us all. 'How do we tell the children?' – that was the hardest part. In my view it was all very easy: you gave the Minister my novel to read, and since he was clearly not stupid he would see immediately that the book really did chronicle the fortunes of a German man from 1900 to 1928, and more to the point, that it offered a splendid role for Emil Jannings. But the old film hands just shook their heads at such naive suggestions, saying that the Minister should not read this novel, because it contained far too many things that a Nazi government minister should not know. And there were lots of things missing – as I was soon to discover. So the film bosses spent a lot of money, a lot more money than they had already paid me, and got a whole series of writers on the job, writers whom Emil Jannings dismissed as 'Nazi hacks', in other words established screenwriters favoured by the Party. These gentlemen fell upon my novel, excerpted, condensed and abstracted it for all they were worth, twisted the plot, cut out some figures and invented new ones, skewed characters so that a villain suddenly became a noble-hearted hero, while a virtuous girl

now committed some act of infamy – and justified all these abomina-
tions with the 'requirements of film', which apparently obeys different
laws from those that govern the theatre, the novel, life in general – and
indeed the entire universe. As all these people beavered away, it soon
became clear that I had once again delivered too much 'product' for
the money they paid me: they could have made five or even ten films
out of the material I had supplied. Deciding what to use became a
real problem. In the end they agreed to make a two-part film on an
epic scale, which would be shown over two evenings. To sugar the
pill for the Minister they designated this beast a 'classic German film',
and manfully suppressed – in my presence at least – any impulse to
address the question of just what the Minister would say to a 'classic
German film' involving the undesirable author Fallada.[127] In the end
they commissioned a well-known German woman writer[128] with a lot
of film experience to work up the draft prepared by the Nazi hacks and
give the thing a bit of artistic polish. This woman – Jannings called her
'the old film tart', as he called all women working in the film industry
'old film tarts' – actually managed to pull it off, restoring some life
and lustre to the poor butterfly that had long since had all the bloom
rubbed off its wings by repeated handling: the screenplay that was sent
to the Minister now had a number of decent scenes and one very fine
one.

I've told the story at some length in order to give the reader some
idea of how, under the National Socialist regime, every artistic activity
was inhibited and rendered almost impossible by the need to defer to
the tastes and prejudices of senior government figures. The issue was
never: how do I make a good film? The issue was not even: how do I
make a film that will please the public? Instead it was all about the one
issue: how do I make this film project palatable to my Minister? Every
artistic consideration and every question of taste took second place to
this one overriding issue.

Thank heavens, I was not directly involved in any of this, and my
feeble protests were met with a patient smile, like the objections of
a child who knows nothing of the world. But like everyone else I

couldn't wait to find out what Dr Goebbels would say to the draft screenplay. The script was returned, and I can testify under oath to the fact that Goebbels had really read it. On every page we were taken to task for something we had all forgotten, I more than anyone, and on every page one word had been heavily scrawled in pencil, followed by one, two or three exclamation marks and sometimes by a question mark as well: 'Jews!!!?'

Yes indeed: we had all forgotten, of course, that the Jews were to blame for everything bad that had happened in Germany since there were Germans on the planet, and that no classic German film could possibly be complete unless they were given major leading roles. But strangely enough this ministerial criticism never assumed any practical relevance – yet another of the wonderful mysteries of film: the screenplay had apparently been approved in its present form, despite the missing Jews. The Jews were merely a ministerial flourish, a poor mark handed out to inattentive schoolboys. Better yet: the film project had secured the Minister's glowing approval, including the plan to show the film over two evenings, and as the production costs were going to be very high, the Minister had even deigned to make one and a half million Reichsmarks available for the film from a special fund. Everyone was cheering for joy, everyone heaved a huge sigh of relief, everyone threw himself into the practical work that could now begin; the only one who was weeping was the author. Jannings and the director Froelich took him to one side and passed on a special message from the Minister for the author, Hans Fallada, stating that it was of course absurd to have the film end with the trip to Paris! There was – of course – only one possible way for the film to end, and that was with the seizure of power by the National Socialists! So the stories of the individual characters would have to be continued up until the seizure of power, especially in the case of old Hackendahl, 'Iron Gustav', who had to be shown developing into an ardent Nazi in the years between the trip to Paris and the seizure of power.

I listened to these comments in dumbfounded silence. I had no idea this was coming. Had I foreseen such a thing, I would never have accepted the commission. I had set out to create a character for the actor Emil Jannings to play; helping the Party's propaganda effort was emphatically not part of the plan!

But this is not what I said to my two listeners. I reminded them how unpopular the author Fallada was with the Party, how he had almost been banned completely once before as a result of *Jailbird*.[129] To continue the story in the way the Minister was proposing, I would inevitably have to introduce characters who were Party members, show SA men fighting in the streets, depict the workings of Party organizations and incorporate debates between Communists and Nazis. Now if an undesirable author such as Fallada were to write this story, describing Party figures and extolling their struggles, that would unleash a storm of protest from the entire Party that would not only sweep me away, but also kill off the entire film project. I reminded Jannings of the hordes of 'Nazi hacks' waiting in the wings, who were far better qualified than I to write such a story, and who undoubtedly had a lot more personal experience than I did as veterans of many a roughhouse and many a Party meeting. Both Jannings and the director Froelich could see the sense of what I was saying, and Jannings promised to try and get an early meeting with the Minister. He mentioned that Dr Goebbels had expressed a wish to make my personal acquaintance, and asked me if I wouldn't like to come along to the meeting and put my objections in person. I declined with a shudder. I could cope with living under a shadow and being an undesirable author; but to fly so close to the sun of Dr Goebbels' favour seemed to me to be inviting the fate of Icarus.

The answer that Emil Jannings brought back to Fallada, the Minister's answer to his objections, was short and to the point, leaving no room for misunderstanding: if Fallada still doesn't know where he stands on the Party, then the Party knows where it stands on Fallada!

I'm not given to grand gestures before the thrones of tyrants, and it's not my style to get myself killed for no reason, when it doesn't help anyone and merely harms my children. So after three minutes' reflection I agreed to do the additional work. How I squared this with my conscience in private, that's another story. The month I spent writing this Nazi sequel is outlined in black ink on my calendar, I hated every minute of it – and I hated myself even more.

But the day came when I was finished, and I delivered the manuscript. I had fully expected that this dog's breakfast would be greeted with some indignation, but instead it was greeted with a tentative squawk of satisfaction, tentative because first of all the Minister had to squawk. The Minister duly squawked, the Minister gave the go-ahead, the Minister finally allocated the one and a half million. Work on the film began, the first sketches were made, studio space was rented, actors were hired, and 800,000 marks had already been blown – when events took a new turn: Minister Rosenberg had declared[130] that a classic German film with the name Fallada on the billing was not acceptable. Fallada should be regarded as a 'cultural Bolshevist', and was therefore a prime candidate for eradication!

And then it all vanished in a puff of smoke, like a conjuring trick. The preparations for filming were halted, the actors disappeared, the scripts were buried at the bottom of the dustiest drawers. Once again director Froelich's future was in question, and once again he survived: now he had to quickly prepare the Virchow film for Emil Jannings, so that the actor would have a new role waiting for him. Three days after the celebrated Rosenberg *diktat* nobody in the film studios, in the entire city of Berlin, knew that a film called 'Iron Gustav' had ever been planned, nobody had ever worked on a film project of that name, nobody knew the first thing about it! Except of course for one man, who could not hide behind feigned ignorance: and that was the author Fallada. His novel *Iron Gustav* had already appeared in the bookshops, so the unfortunate author's name was already out there. Up until then the book had sold quite nicely and without the slightest murmur of objection, and Fallada's readers had even swallowed the Nazi sequel without protest – which further eroded my belief in the good judgement of my readers. But now all hell broke loose. Everything I had predicted now happened: I was reviled because I had dared to portray Party figures, I was excommunicated, ostracized and outlawed. Just as they had after the publication of *Jailbird*, the SA and SS now took to the streets and forced booksellers to remove my books from their window displays, and indeed from their shelves; from now on Fallada was only sold under the counter by courageous booksellers to customers who had specially requested a copy. I was looking at the end of my writing career.

But what about the gentlemen who had commissioned me to write this stuff, who had showered my work with the highest praise in telegrams, letters and personal exchanges – how did they react? Where were Mr Froelich, the set directors, the gentlemen from the script department and the Nazi hacks involved in the rewrites? There was not a peep from any of them, nobody put their hand up, and in a way I can't really blame them. Kicking up a fuss would not have helped me, and would only have got them into trouble.

The only exception was Emil Jannings himself, who wrote me a letter and asked me to come and see him so that he could explain everything. But at the time I was too 'stupid', I was sick of the whole business and didn't want to hear another word. So I didn't go and see Jannings, I didn't get to hear the explanation, the facts as I was seeing them and living them on a daily basis were quite enough for me. I have not seen Emil Jannings again since.

But while I could understand why everyone kept quiet, and never reproached them for distancing themselves from our joint endeavour, the entire burden of which they now left me to shoulder, there was one man who should have spoken up for me, the man who had known about and approved this project, who had backed it with a grant of one and a half million, and who in the face of all the author's legitimate objections had forced him to write the Nazi ending with the threatening words: 'If Fallada still doesn't know where he stands on the Party, then the Party knows where it stands on Fallada!' I refer to Minister Goebbels. Minister Goebbels was a powerful man, he didn't need to grovel, he didn't need to fear for his own and his family's safety, he could have come out openly in support of his plans, he could have fought his corner with his colleague Rosenberg; he could have taken his cue from something his Party comrade Göring had said, and boldly declared: '*I* decide who is a cultural Bolshevist!' But Minister Goebbels did none of this. He kept quiet just like everybody else, suddenly he too didn't know a thing about it. But why was that? He really didn't need to, surely? Well, yes, he did. Once again he could not afford to play the strong man, he was in no position to fight, this loyal henchman of the Führer, because now he was tainted, because yet another of his dirty deeds stank to high heaven. He could not fight back against his colleague Rosenberg, although he was actually the stronger man, because at this moment he was in a weak position – not least with his beloved Führer. Minister Goebbels, who is a great admirer of other men's wives, had been talking a little too loudly and a little too often about how such and such an actress has the loveliest navel in the world, and something had happened that was completely unheard of in the Nazi Reich: an actor who was not even a Party member, who regarded himself as engaged to the actress in question, had slapped the Minister's face.[131] And the Minister had to make the best of it, while the whole of Berlin, indeed the whole of Germany, had a good laugh at his expense. One person who was not laughing was the Minister's wife, who had already had to put up with a great deal, and there's always one last straw that breaks the camel's back: so she had wanted a divorce and was planning to go and live in Switzerland with the children. But of course that had not been allowed; government ministers can get up to all the dirty tricks they like, but the public interest bars their wives from taking appropriate action in response. The Führer himself intervened: the wife had to stay with her husband (and continue to bear him children in a model German marriage), but the husband was sidelined for a while. At that point Minister Goebbels could no longer afford to fight for his own plans and challenge his colleagues, which is why the author Fallada had to carry the can alone – and was nearly finished as a result.

Oh, he's a dangerous man, this Dr Goebbels, and maybe more dangerous to his friends than he is to his enemies. Take the case of the actor Mathias Wieman,[132] which I witnessed at first hand. Mathias Wieman was a friend of Dr Goebbels, and something of a pampered favourite. The two of us, me and this tall, almost scraggy figure, a native of Westphalia, a strong man, and a 'biter and kicker', as he likes to describe himself, who is most at home playing slightly sickly, morbid male characters, had been brought together by *Wolf among Wolves*. Following a long period of complete despondency and creative drought, I had written this long novel in one go; the passion for writing, the rush I get from creating characters and developing them, seem to be indestructible in me. One evening we heard a voice on the radio, it was the voice of Mathias Wieman, reviewing *Wolf among Wolves*. He did a wonderful job, speaking about my book in that beautiful, measured voice of his, which is made for speaking the verse of Goethe or Hölderlin. He didn't review my book so much as describe a profound personal experience: here was a man talking about something that had moved him deeply.

I too was touched and deeply moved, but perhaps less by what he said than by the fact that here, for the first time since 1933, someone was publicly speaking out for the writer Fallada. Since 1932 the name Fallada had never been mentioned on the radio, here too I had been proscribed and banned. And now Wieman was speaking on a personal note, like an old friend . . . I admired the courage he showed in breaking through the ring of silence that surrounded me. It nearly cost him and me dear. Minister Rosenberg, the same man who had called me a cultural Bolshevist and blocked the production of my film, naturally heard about Wieman's public endorsement of Fallada, and felt it was high time these two gentlemen were consigned to the place where they belonged, namely the void. And a suitable opportunity for putting them in their place now presented itself: Rosenberg had to give a speech at the University of Halle,[133] and as he planned to talk about German culture, he could also use the occasion to talk about the enemies of German culture, in other words the Bolsheviks – including Wieman and Fallada. Such was the plan, and so it would have come to pass, meaning that for the last six years or so I would have written no more books, and Wieman would have done no more acting, had it not been for the fact that Mr Rosenberg's plans encountered a little obstacle – and one, moreover, put in their way by his own people. In the world at large people know, or perhaps they don't, that Reichsleiter Rosenberg edits the *Völkischer Beobachter*, the official Party organ, which he favours from time to time with leading articles that are as abstruse and high-flown as his *Myth of the Twentieth Century*.[134] And just as Mr Rosenberg was preparing to deal a crushing blow to me and my *Wolf*, as well as the actor Mathias Wieman, events took an unfortunate turn when the Reichsleiter's own newspaper printed a glowing review of the selfsame *Wolf* – and this on the very eve of his speech in Halle! So what was Reichsleiter Rosenberg to do? He could fire this rogue journalist on the spot, and this he duly did. But he could not discredit himself: he had to stand by what was written in his own newspaper, or at the very least he had to keep his mouth shut, if he did not wish to become a general laughing-stock. So he kept quiet. I was saved once again – but by such gossamer threads does the fate of an author hang in the Third Reich!

Mathias Wieman was less fortunate. Minister Goebbels developed an affection for this big, strong actor, and made him his friend. He had a strange way of relating to his friends, the Minister, he treated them like lovers. He would ring up in the morning and inquire eagerly how his dear friend had slept, later on he would send flowers and chocolates. Wieman had to visit him daily, and they would have a drink and talk about everything under the sun, and always they were of one mind. Until the day came when they were not of one mind; they fell out over something or other of no great importance in itself. But a Minister is a Minister, which is to say, someone very high up, while an actor is a much lesser personage, who cannot ever win an argument with a Minister. But Mathias Wieman couldn't see this. Whereupon the Minister turned very frosty, sending his friend away under a cloud, and there were no more telephone calls, no more flowers or chocolates.

But even a Minister cannot nurse a grudge for ever, and one day Mathias Wieman received another telephone call, the flowers and chocolates started coming again, and a fresh invitation was issued. They were friends again, just like the old days – until the Minister asked: 'About our recent little disagreement, Wieman. I'm sure you've

thought about the matter again in the meantime, and can see now that
I was right?'

Yes indeed, he had thought the matter over, replied the actor, more
brave than he was smart, and he was now more convinced than ever
that the Minister was wrong. Powerful men are all the same, whether
living in the German Reich or under the Sun King: opposition, and
obdurate opposition at that, is a thing they cannot abide, and it leads
to a spectacular fall from grace. Wieman was sent packing under a
cloud – this time for good. He bore it with composure, and indeed
was privately glad, perhaps; this friendship between the actor and the
Minister had never been a wholly edifying affair. The weeks passed, and
Wieman noticed a change in the atmosphere around him. To begin
with it was just a slight *froideur*, but then it felt more like the cold
shoulder. People became very short with him, nobody seemed to want
to know him any more, bookings that had been firmly promised to him
now fell through, and offers of parts that he thought were already his
were now withdrawn. 'Please don't take this the wrong way, Wieman,
but we really do think this role is better suited to P. than to you. But
there's always a next time!' Except that the next time never seemed to
come now.

Eventually Wieman learned that there had been a meeting of the film
board at the Propaganda Ministry, and that at this meeting Minister
Goebbels himself had recommended that the actor Wieman only be
employed with extreme caution. The Führer, he said, had just watched
the film *On Higher Orders*,[135] in which Wieman played the part of a
Prussian officer, and had commented: 'No Prussian officer conducts
himself like this actor! I don't want to see this man in uniform again!'

When Wieman heard about this he felt utterly crushed; if the
Führer had judged him in these terms, then his artistic career was over.
But had the Führer really said that? It was certainly possible. But a
tiny doubt remained in his mind. Wieman had been a friend of the
Minister, but had fallen from grace – could it be that the Minister had
now become his enemy, a malevolent enemy intent on destroying his
former friend? Perhaps, perhaps: but even a man like Goebbels would

surely not dare to misrepresent something the Führer had said, or even make it up completely?

Wieman had a lady friend[136] who was an occasional guest in the house of Reich Field Marshal Göring. He told her the gist of the story, and asked her to make inquiries when she saw Göring. She did so at the first available opportunity: after a dinner she asked the Reich Minister: 'So what's the problem with Wieman, the actor?'

Göring returned the question: 'What problem would there be? Wieman is a sound man and a fine actor, I've heard nothing bad about him.' The lady then told him what the Führer had allegedly said. Göring said: 'That's possible, the Führer is very particular in such matters. I've heard nothing about it, but I'll make inquiries and get back to you.' In such matters Göring can be relied on absolutely, and the anxiously awaited report duly came back: the whole thing was pure invention, the Führer had not even seen the film *On Higher Orders*. According to Göring, Wieman had nothing to worry about.

But Wieman worried all the same. His former friend Goebbels had now been unmasked in all his pitiful nastiness. In vain did he tell the film producers that there was not a word of truth in the whole thing; they simply shrugged their shoulders and said: 'It makes no difference, Wieman. If Goebbels says we should employ you with caution, that means we shouldn't employ you at all – and we have to comply. The reasons Goebbels gives are neither here nor there, and it wouldn't matter if he claimed that an angel of the Lord had instructed him in person.'

Mathias Wieman saw himself facing a long dry spell, in which he would get no engagements and earn no money. He was in the same situation as most of us: he had been earning good money, but it had melted away like butter in the sun, and although he had enough to live on for a while, it was only for a while. Thank heavens he had no children, but he had a wife, who stood by him through thick and thin. He moved with her to a little village by the sea, and disappeared from view, the unknown victim of a ministerial friendship.

He lived there in banishment for two years, and then he was

gradually allowed back into circulation, starting with a theatre engage-
ment in Hamburg. Today he is free to perform in films again. But
Minister Goebbels recently declared triumphantly that in future he
would treat more actors the way he had treated Mathias Wieman. Film
took a heavy toll on acting talent, he claimed. So it was good for them
if a 'creative break' was imposed on them from above. Whereupon
the Minister went and sidelined three young actors whom he couldn't
stand.

There are many stories about Joseph Goebbels, but none perhaps
that better illustrates the dangerous, two-faced character of the man
than the following. In Berlin a reunion was held for holders of the
order *Pour le mérite* from the World War. 'The Doctor' had been
invited to give the address, and he had spoken about the person of the
Führer in his usual rousing and trenchant style. Afterwards Goebbels
was standing talking to a group of older officers when a general came
up to him and thanked him in emotional terms for the speech he had
just given. The Minister, who had possibly had a little too much wine,
screwed up his eyes and said that perhaps he and they could spend a
little private time together afterwards? Because he had a very special
surprise for them. And so it transpired, and the Minister, the Führer's
most loyal henchman, stood up and gave another, much more rousing
and impassioned speech about the person of the Kaiser, a speech that
just sent these old generals into raptures and moved them to tears.

But that is Goebbels as he really is: two-faced, not a genuine fibre
in his whole body! He can talk about anything in vivid, down-to-earth
language, and if need be he would speak about Bolshevism tomorrow
in exactly the same way he speaks about Nazism today. Within the
group of hysterics, psychopaths, monomaniacs and sadists who make
up our 'people's government' today, he is the embodiment of pure evil,
Beelzebub in person – and all the Jews in the world will never be able
to hold a candle to him.

I have never felt at home with my new publisher the way I did with
old Rowohlt, as I have probably already said. The assets of Rowohlt
Verlag, which continued to trade under the old name, had been trans-

ferred to a large publishing company based in southern Germany,[137] an enterprise of many parts that had been built up by a capable man with extremely diverse tastes, with some authors whom I could not abide, and others who excited me very much. The thing that united me with the head of this large publishing house was our shared hatred of Nazism. His voice would shake when he spoke of these 'criminals', and his face turned white. His whole life and work were now focused increasingly on fighting for authors who had made themselves unpopular with the regime for one reason or another, and for whom he sought to make it possible to carry on working. Amongst his authors was one very good man,[138] who was also highly esteemed by the Party, who had written a fine novel about the father of Frederick the Great. But this man had committed the crime of marrying a Jewish woman, and now persisted in the much worse offence of standing by her, despite all the threats he received. The head of the publishing house fought long and hard to ensure that this man was able to carry on working. He succeeded in holding on to this author, but when he himself was ousted,[139] the author soon followed him – and then shot himself.

There was also a female author, widely renowned in the German-speaking world, and a sensitive, cultivated woman,[140] but this woman had committed the crime of writing an entire novel about a priest, and a favourable portrait at that, when any mention of priests in novels was prohibited. Admittedly this novel had been written prior to the prohibition, just as that other author had married his Jewish wife prior to January 1933, but it didn't make any difference, or mitigate the crime in any way. Such were the battles that took up the entire time of a publisher in those days . . . That reminds me of a nice story that happened to me when my dear old Rowohlt was still in charge, which beautifully illustrates these senseless battles that had to be fought by publishers when they rubbed up against the regime in those days. I had written *Sparrow Farm*,[141] a fairy-tale after the style of E.T.A. Hoffmann, with some added Fallada-esque touches. For reasons that I can no longer remember, the manuscript had ended up on somebody's desk in the Propaganda Ministry, where it was vetted, despite the fact that we had no pre-publication censorship as such. Right at the beginning of this book there is a scene where the wealthy farmer Tamm[142] distributes alms to the village poor in his own peculiar way: across his farmyard he hides whatever he's got left in the way of smoked meats from the previous year – bacon, sausages, hams – and invites the village poor to search for it, like children looking for hidden Easter eggs. It so happens that an ancient little woman discovers a ham concealed on top of a tall stack of logs. She quickly fetches a wheelbarrow to stand on and, reaching and stretching, tries to winkle out the pork hindquarter. A young lad from the village, who is watching this jolly game of hide-and-seek, calls out to the old woman: 'Hey, Trina, I've seen your box!' And the old woman comes back to him as quick as a flash: 'My boy, it would have given you more pleasure fifty years ago than it does today!' And that was all. My publisher now had to talk on the telephone to some undersecretary at the Propaganda Ministry, who had serious reservations about the publication of this innocuous fairy-tale. In particular, he could not get past the scene I have just described. For a start, the way this farmer chose to distribute his hand-outs to the poor was quite contrary to all National Socialist thinking. It was quite repellent, the way these old people in the story were made an object of ridicule for the entire village. Rowohlt had a hard job convincing this high-ranking official that there is a huge difference between merry laughter and serious mockery, and Rowohlt ventured to remind him, with all due respect, of certain Dutch paintings of village life, in which such scenes were depicted to the general merriment of all . . . In the end the undersecretary relented, though not entirely convinced. 'However', he said in a sharper and more emphatic tone of voice, 'that vile obscenity must be removed from Fallada's book!' Rowohlt could not believe his ears. A vile obscenity – in this innocuous fairy-tale?! 'But Mr Undersecretary', he asked, utterly bewildered, 'I really can't recall . . . what obscenity do you mean – ?'

'You know very well what I mean!' cried the undersecretary on the other end of the line, now quite furious. 'Don't play the innocent with me! You know exactly what I mean!'

'I really don't know, on my word of honour, Mr Undersecretary – !'

'In that case you have lost all sense of what constitutes obscenity . . . I am referring to the passage where the wretched village boy looks up the skirts of an old woman, and I am referring to the shameless exchange that ensues – !' Whereupon dear old Rowohlt ran out of patience once again and said with brutal directness: 'If that is a vile obscenity, then please explain to me, Mr Undersecretary, how exactly babies are made in the Third Reich!'

He hung up, and nothing happened. The book appeared, complete with vile obscenity, and again nothing happened. But this was an exception: generally speaking something always happened, and it was never anything pleasant.

So publishers, whom a German reading public imagines as spending their time reading manuscripts, publishing books, bagging hopeful young authors in happy hunting expeditions, actually had to perform very different tasks in the Third Reich: making accusations and defending both themselves and others, preparing written submissions, compiling statistics and attending conferences, where self-important guardians of the nation's culture issued new guidelines for the realignment of the cultural front – decreeing, for example, that the historical novel must henceforth take second place to the romantic novel. That a greater emphasis on sex would not go amiss in future. That more works of fiction dealing with the lives and work of primary school teachers need to be published as soon as possible – presenting teachers in a very favourable light, of course, since there is a shortage of good people entering the teaching profession. And more such 'cultural' drivel in the same vein.

It may be that I judged my publisher unfairly during these years. Rowohlt Verlag continued to trade as R.V.,[143] despite the fact that it had been bought up by this large publishing house in southern Germany, and it even had its own publishing director, a man whom Rowohlt himself had trained up for the job and appointed as heir to his tradition. Unfortunately Rowohlt hadn't been a great teacher, and he had hammered away at this young man – who had probably never been that tough in the first place – for so long that all traces of self-will and courage had been beaten out of him. I have often complained bitterly about this spineless management regime, that never took any risks and was always looking anxiously over its shoulder. I have always firmly believed that self-abasement gets you nowhere with the Nazis, and the best tactic is just to carry on with what you are doing – but avoiding direct confrontations, of course. It is never sensible to enter a field carrying a big red flag when you know perfectly well that there's a raging bull in there. But nor is it any good just to crawl into a mouse hole and never come out again. So there were a good many differences of opinion, but they were always settled by the exercise of good will on both sides. I'd been with Rowohlt Verlag for so many years that I didn't want to change to a different publisher; I hate change, anything new – I like it best when everything carries on in the same old way. Now the year 1943 was drawing closer, the year in which I became 50, and also the year in which I looked back on 25 years as an author with Rowohlt Verlag; I had submitted the MS of my first novel to Rowohlt in 1918. It's a strange kind of anniversary, for sure, 25 years as an author with the same publishing house. I think that is not a bad testimony either to the publisher or to the author! I was determined to celebrate my 50th birthday quietly at home in Mahlendorf, and contrary to possible expectation I was not bitterly disappointed when the press were instructed by the Propaganda Ministry to ignore Fallada's 50th birthday. That suited me just fine. (By the way, I should point out that there were decent men here too. Despite the explicit instruction from the Propaganda Ministry, a number of newspapers did mark my birthday, most notably the *Münchner Illustrierte Presse*, which even published my picture.) It was all the more gratifying to receive birthday greetings from well-wishers and readers all over the world, especially from young soldiers at the front, who touchingly even sent me little presents: the cigarettes I so loved, envelopes (now in short supply), and even cheese! I lacked for nothing, it was a lovely day, and my Rowohlt Verlag had even sent me a splendid Kubin drawing[144] as a birthday present. But just a few weeks later I received a letter from my publisher telling me R.V. had been closed. Such closures were a feature of the wartime economy; in order to free up manpower for the armed forces and the munitions factories, businesses that were deemed non-essential were shut down for the duration of the war, and contracts entered into with these businesses were 'put on hold'. Just a few days later another letter arrived, correcting the information given in the first one: now it seemed that the publishing house had not been closed down to help the war effort, but had been wound up following its transfer into new ownership – more details would follow in due course. I found it all rather mystifying, but since there was nothing I could do but wait and see, that's what I did. Soon afterwards I received a telegram, announcing a visit from the management at Rowohlt Verlag – the very man whom the old master himself, Rowohlt, had trained up and appointed as his successor. What I learned from him now was anything but reassuring. Inside the big south German publishing house that now owned Rowohlt Verlag, a fierce power struggle had been going on, and the founder of the business, the Nazi-hater I talked about earlier,[145] had been gradually forced out from one position after another; in the eyes of the Reich Chamber of Literature and the Propaganda Ministry, the man couldn't do anything right. In the end they had undermined his authority within the company, made it impossible for him to exert any influence or continue his work, so that eventually he had no choice but to sell the business to the buyer who had been waiting in the wings for a long time, namely Eher Verlag in Munich, the Party's own publishing house. In effect he was selling out to Mr Rosenberg, Mr Hitler, or the German Reich – the choice of name really doesn't matter, since they all amount to the same thing anyway: the imposition of Nazi influence within this hitherto private business. When the big publishing house was bought up, ownership of the little Rowohlt Verlag was of course transferred to Eher Verlag along with it, and it was a foregone conclusion that the hated name of Rowohlt must be dropped immediately. The big publishing house was required to take on the desirable authors from the Rowohlt stable, while the undesirables were left to fend for themselves. That was the situation in brief, as I gradually managed to winkle it out of Mr Ledig, the managing director, and I need hardly add that I was the most undesirable of all the undesirable authors, given that the new publishing organization was operating under the aegis of Mr Alfred Rosenberg! I told Mr Ledig that in this respect our wishes coincided, as I had no desire myself to be an author in the pay of a Party publishing house. However, I pointed out that there were a number of contracts still in force between us: a general publishing agreement relating to all my works published to date, and three individual contracts for novels that had already been completed.[146] Eher Verlag was of course responsible for these contracts now, as the legal successor to Rowohlt Verlag – so how was the company thinking to fulfil its various obligations under these contracts?

That's easy, I was told, we'll just cancel them! I was such a famous author, I would have no difficulty in finding a new publisher!

I gave a thin smile and said I thought that was probably so. But looking for a new publisher would take time, and once I'd found him he would then have to submit new applications for paper supplies to be allocated for my books, so that for nine months, or maybe a year, nothing of mine could be published, and Eher Verlag would have to compensate me for that period of lost time. To cut a long story short: after some discussion the managing director and I came to an agreement which included a very cheap compensation payment for me, and with that he travelled back to southern Germany. I then promptly received a telegram telling me the managing director was not authorized to conduct negotiations with me, and that therefore the agreement was null and void. So why did you send the man to see me in the first place, I wondered, fuming, and hired a lawyer to carry on the negotiations on my behalf. For my part I wanted nothing more to do with these gentlemen, and I resolutely resisted all the siren calls that sought to entice me to Berlin to negotiate in person. It was my lawyer's job to conduct the negotiations, and as I knew him to be a very canny operator, and I had the law on my side (the contracts were there in black and white, had a long time to run, and could not be terminated unilaterally without notice), I did not doubt the outcome of the matter. I was certain of victory. At the same time I went around in a constant state of distress and anger, of course, as anyone can well imagine. Twenty-five years as an author with the same publishing house, to which I had stayed loyal through thick and thin – and now to be turned out on the street in this manner: I was having none of it!

But then it got even better, and I found myself on the receiving end of the same methods that had been used against me when I bought the villa in the little village of Berkenbrück. Except that then I was dealing with a simple little failed businessman and an equally deadbeat building contractor, whereas now I was facing an encounter with the Party high-ups! What my lawyer now told me was as outrageous as it was devastating. I was expected to agree to the immediate, unconditional termination of the contracts without compensation, in return for which they would pay me very generously for the remaining stocks of my books as a consideration! I said 'No!', a furious 'No!', and I repeated it many times, instructing my lawyer to sue Eher Verlag for performance of the contracts. He advised me against it, telling me that no lawyer in Germany, himself included, would file such a lawsuit for me; Eher Verlag was effectively the Party, and you don't bring a lawsuit against the Party! So there I was, up against a brick wall, just as I had been before. And now the wall was even higher, even more insurmountable, and even more brazenly barring the road to any form of justice. The lawyer kept on trying to persuade me; I really should drop the idea of causing any trouble for these people; they had made it abundantly clear that if I did, they would cause trouble for me: then I could expect to be banned from writing altogether. The same old blackmail tactics: these people just keep on playing the same old tune! It doesn't matter what it is, whether they want to grab the Sudetenland or get rid of the Danzig Corridor, whether they want to steal a nice house or break a few contracts: in large things as in small, they are as uninventive as they are brutal.

I travelled back to Mahlendorf without giving my answer. I fought long and hard with myself. I made myself ill with anger and worry. But in the end I said 'Yes' after all. There was not the slightest possibility of a 'No' anyway – a 'No' would have achieved absolutely nothing. The practical consequence of a 'No' would have been to ensure that the RCL banned me from working as a writer, so that all my contracts would have lapsed anyway, and all I would have accomplished would have been to put an end to my writing career.

So I said 'Yes' – and as I started to feel better I went in search of a new publisher.[147] I found him – and now began a season of surprises. We wanted to draw up a general agreement like the one I had before, and Eher Verlag had previously told my lawyer that they would do what they could to help (you were not allowed to enter into general agreements during the war). But now Eher Verlag was saying that it couldn't see the need for a general agreement; I could simply sign an agreement for each individual book once the necessary paper supply had been allocated. So my publisher applied to the Propaganda Ministry for a paper allowance, and was told that there was no more paper for Fallada for the time being – maybe in a year or two years' time . . . So I sat down and wrote to Eher Verlag, asking them to send over their remaining stocks of my books to my new publisher on the 'generous terms' they had promised. I got a reply stating that unfortunately not a single book of mine remained in stock. Those bastards had sold all the copies of my books in the meantime and then pocketed the proceeds themselves. I had fallen into the hands of crooks and thieves, but these crooks and thieves traded under the name Eher Verlag – and they had the backing of the German Reich. So that, in brief, is the story of what happened to a minor German author, and I'm sure I don't need to spell out what he thought and felt about all this, or how it fuelled his animosity towards the ruling regime. But now I'm sitting here with a good publisher and several unprinted manuscripts,[148] but no paper and no prospect of paper and no books – only the few remaining foreign rights are still yielding a trickle. But Eher Verlag continues to milk that too, if someone has not remembered to stop the payments, and it takes its nice little cut, even though it is not entitled to, now that it is no longer my publisher. And there's a sequel to it all as well, another piece of blackmail by an even higher authority. I'm tired of relating all this dirty business, and I expect the reader feels much the same. So I'll keep it very short, omitting all the details. The Propaganda Ministry itself commissioned me to write an anti-Semitic novel,[149] specifically for distribution abroad; the prospect of paper supplies was the carrot, and the threat of disbarment as a writer was the stick. So now the author Fallada is writing an anti-Semitic novel. But it's a huge topic, and the novel will run to some 1800 printed pages – so it's a race between me and the war: which will be finished first, the novel or the war – ?

(3.X.44.) When we moved to Mahlendorf[150] in the autumn of 1933 we were determined, after the bad experiences we had had, to get off on the right foot this time with the local government officials and Party leaders – come what may. We had had enough of fighting these losing battles, which, as people without rights, we could never win.

We found that things were very different in Mahlendorf, and the local mayor was an elderly salt-of-the-earth small farmer, a wonderfully forthright and dependable character. He was not a member of the Party himself, and it was soon apparent that he was not particularly well-disposed towards it. So we had nothing at all to fear from him. As he had lived in the village all his life, he knew from personal experience who the informers and malicious gossips were, and was completely impervious to their tittle-tattle and tale-telling. Life in the village was peaceful, in so far as it can be peaceful in a village that sits on a peninsula, with no through road to bring in new life from outside. Everyone was related by blood or marriage, everyone knew everyone else, and everyone else's weaknesses, so it was a fertile breeding-ground for those family feuds we've all heard about, which were often perpetuated from one generation to the next. But these feuds, vicious as they were, were not political in any way, they had nothing to do with changing party allegiances, and outlasted all of them: they were not our business. The second important person in the village was the schoolmaster, an older man, who was also not a Party member, and who at the time of our arrival in the village had more than enough troubles of his own: some sort of charge had been brought against him following accusations that he had seduced female pupils. The girls had testified against him, and he was fighting desperately to clear his name. So we had nothing at all to fear from this man either.

There were very few actual Party members in the village, which somehow had never taken much interest in politics. And these few Party members were barely active. There were a few elderly farmers, a fishmonger, an innkeeper, a painter and decorator . . . but they all had their own worries. Times were hard, a lot of people in the village were unemployed, the parish was poor. The stony, sandy soil and the uneven terrain had never yielded big harvests, and in recent years the harvests had been particularly bad, as nobody had the money to buy good-quality seed stock and fertilizers.

Our arrival was greeted not just with curiosity, but soon afterwards with outright joy, when it turned out that I was in a position to relieve the village of many of its cares and burdens. I needed building work done, I needed a lot of work doing in the garden, digging out boulders, creating new features, planting fruit trees, putting up fences – in short, there was always work to be had at my place, and money to be earned. I threw myself with such energy into the work of tidying up the property that it was as if I had to make up for decades of neglect in just one year. Six to eight men were working for me almost the whole time, as well as three or four women in the garden. The local farmers carted loads of timber, stones and other materials for me. In Mahlendorf I had solved the unemployment problem before Mr Hitler got round to it, and the village was grateful to me, especially its thoroughly decent old mayor, who was thereby relieved of many worries. In those early days I made good friends among the ordinary people of the village, the masons, the carpenters, the forestry workers, friends who have remained true to me to this day, and who never mind giving up a free Sunday if they can help me in some way. But the local bigwigs, the farmers, have long since forgotten that time, and for them I am once again the unwelcome outsider, who doesn't belong in the village.

At the time, though, I lived in peace with everyone, and felt completely safe and secure. The first tumultuous months after the seizure of power seemed a long way off. We only learned about what was going on from the newspapers delivered to our house. We savoured the peace and quiet with profound thankfulness, we felt restored, and I was working again. This peace and quiet had an unfortunate consequence, however, which at first we failed to notice, but which in time would have serious repercussions: I grew reckless again – particularly in what I said. It wasn't very long before my workmen were telling a new arrival to their ranks, who greeted me with 'Heil Hitler!': 'You don't need to say Heil Hitler here, mate, the boss isn't one of those!'

Fool that I was, I was still flattered by my rapidly acquired reputation as no friend of the Nazis, and I never stopped to think that this reputation of mine would now spread from farm to farm, beyond the village to our local small town, from here to the county town and all the way up to the district council office, where it would be set in stone for all time – regardless of what I did. Indeed, in this initial period, when I thought I was safe, I did everything possible to justify and cement my reputation as a black sheep; and by the time Mahlendorf was being run by men of a very different stripe, it was much too late to be careful. I'd been careless for far too long. This mixture of unthinking recklessness and sudden bouts of caution was a typical feature of those very early days. I suddenly hit upon the idea that I should give some sort of house-warming party in the village, to publicly celebrate my moving in to the community – that would do wonders for my good reputation. Excited by this notion, I contacted the village innkeeper, who was pleased at my suggestion, since it was obviously going to be a nice little earner for him. He also told me about someone who would act as my 'master of ceremonies', the manager of a local estate, and I happily accepted the suggestion – the man was a staunch Stahlhelm supporter, and a sworn enemy of the Nazis. (Note the unfailing Fallada knack for making perfectly sure that everything goes spectacularly wrong!) After a few discussions the two of us agreed to stage a 'German Evening', so that's what we did. What was specifically 'German' about the evening,

I can't remember any more. Perhaps a few poems were recited, but anyway, the dancing, drinking and smoking went on into the early hours – and all at my expense. The whole village was able to treat itself, and the dance hall was packed, with a local brass band up at one end playing dance music at deafening volume. But the local dignitaries and farmers had stayed away, or else they just looked in briefly. The evening was a resounding success – for the innkeeper, certainly. I stayed until the very end, and my wife fetched me home in person in the not-so-early morning – my wife and my secretary at the time,[151] a very striking Jewish girl of Hungarian origin, who opened a restaurant in Tel Aviv two years later. Such was my debut in Mahlendorf, and as usual when I have just made a big mistake, I was pretty pleased with myself.

The first decisive change in our quiet village circumstances occurred when the elderly schoolmaster was transferred – doubtless they wanted to put some distance between him and his young accusers. Incidentally, he was able to clear himself of all charges in due course: as often happens, the fourteen-year-old girls had made up all kinds of stories about their teacher, whom they liked well enough.

His replacement was a Mr Ritzner, a very tall, powerful man of about thirty, who always went around in a brown shirt and full-length boots, was a Party member, and even held some position in the SA. It was only a minor post, but generally speaking – and invariably with this party – the little tyrants are more dangerous than the big ones. We feared that this would be the end of our quiet life in the village, especially as Mr Ritzner was immediately appointed to various official positions: chairman of the local agricultural cooperative and village electricity cooperative. He was also put in charge of the fire brigade – and the post of mayor seemed certain to go to him, especially as it was already against the rules, in fact, for a non-Party member like our old small farmer to hold the office of mayor. But for the moment it didn't come to that . . . I said to my wife: 'From now on we must be very careful and mind our p's and q's', not realizing that the verdict on me had already been delivered.

It soon became apparent that the new schoolmaster was seeking out our company. It began with occasional little chats in the village street, and this was followed by a formal invitation to afternoon coffee and cakes, which is something I absolutely cannot abide, but on this occasion I accepted, thinking it was all in a good cause. We spent several hours in the Ritzners' home, which was furnished in a somewhat surprising style: alongside ancient furniture that was falling apart were some contemporary chairs covered in the most hideous fabric and with that garishly grained wood that spread like a rash across German domestic interiors during those years. There was also a huge, brand-new wireless set of the latest design, and a truly enormous standard lamp with an orange conical shade, which stood all on its own amongst the ancient detritus. We sat and chatted, first of all about the weather and the prospects for the harvest, as country-dwellers do. Then the women got into a conversation about gardening, and about the difficulties of finding a decent washerwoman in the village, while Mr Ritzner talked about his wife's many illnesses and operations, and the substantial costs involved. It was a very pleasant afternoon, and on the way home I said to my wife: 'This time it'll be all right! We'll get along very well with the man. He won't make trouble for us.'

So then it was our turn to issue the next invitation to coffee – that's the thing about invitations to coffee, they always come around in pairs, at the very least. The second afternoon started off in the same perfectly predictable way as the first one: the weather again, the harvest, and a revisiting of Mrs Ritzner's ailments. Then I found myself listening wide-eyed as husband and wife suddenly launched an emotional appeal, going at us for all they were worth, with tears in their eyes: his wife's operations had eaten up so much money, he'd had to pay one bill after another, and on his modest teacher's salary . . . Now he'd exhausted all his resources, the bailiff was paying him daily visits, bringing shame upon him in the eyes of the whole village. I had to help him, I was a wealthy man, etc., etc. This wasn't the first time in my life I had heard this kind of thing, and I have to admit that I didn't like what I heard. Following the success of *Little Man*, when money seemed to flow into our house in a never-ending stream, we had listened to many such requests, and we had lent a lot of money to strangers, acquaintances and friends. And then it had happened that someone who was actually a very good friend of ours had crossed the street to avoid us. In short, we learned the truth of the saying that the quickest way to lose friends is to lend them money. At the time we had vowed never to lend money again. Giving it away was one thing, but lending – never again!

As the entreaties became a little less insistent, I gazed thoughtfully at my host's brown shirt. We had vowed never to do it, but then again – in this special instance . . . In earlier times the Jews had paid protection money, now it was the turn of non-Party members . . . I glanced across at my wife, and it seemed to me she gave me a slight nod. So I said I was by no means a rich man, I lived completely from hand to mouth: but in this case of dire human need I would think about it, and if the sum involved was not too large, it might perhaps be possible. What sort of figure did he have in mind?

Oh well, he said, he didn't have an exact figure to hand, maybe four hundred marks, five hundred at the most! He'd need to go and do the sums first . . . I suggested that he do that, and that he should make a complete list of all his debts, not leaving anything out. If I was going to pay off his debts, then I wanted to be his sole creditor. All this back and forth with the bailiff and these unnecessary costs had to stop. And he needn't worry, I would offer him repayment on favourable terms!

He nodded dutifully in reply and promised to do as I asked. When could he come and see me again?

I said that I would let him know; nothing was decided as yet, and I needed to think it over carefully first.

The coffee party was over, and my wife and I were walking in the garden. Neither of us felt entirely happy about the business. But still, it was worth good money to have peace and quiet and feel safe, and five hundred marks was not such a huge sum – the Sponars had cost me a lot more. I thought I should sleep on it – but would probably decide to go ahead.

The next morning came, and I had a very early visit from Mr and Mrs Ritzner, accompanied by another man with a long face, glasses and a briefcase, who introduced himself as Mr Ritzner's lawyer. He put his briefcase down beside him after taking a few papers out, and made a short, friendly speech. He was delighted that a generous benefactor had turned up who was willing to pay off Mr and Mrs Ritzner's debts on reasonable terms. Their financial circumstances really were in the most deplorable mess. He had brought with him a list of all the Ritzners' debts – and before I could recover from my astonishment and protest, he had pressed two sheets of paper into my hand. It was a very long list; I immediately turned the first page over and looked at the final total on the second page. I put the papers down and said indignantly that this was completely out of the question. I'd been told it was 500 marks at most, but this list came to nearly 2000! No, I was not prepared to do that and I wouldn't be doing it. There was no point in discussing the matter any further.

I handed the papers back to the lawyer, but he wouldn't take them. Instead all three of them began entreating me not to take away their last hope. They begged me not to be the author of their misery! The only way out for them now was a bullet! If the school authorities got wind of these debts, he would lose his job. If Mr Ritzner had initially named a much smaller sum, it was not for any devious reasons, but simply because he had completely lost track of his spending! That surely couldn't make any difference to me . . . While this assault was under way, I took a closer look at the individual items on the list. I now discovered that the famous debts incurred as a result of the wife's illness made up only a tiny fraction of the total. What I found on the list instead were the new wireless set, along with the garishly grained chairs and the standard lamp with the conical shade – despite his debts, the man had simply bought whatever he wanted . . . And next to these I found the smallest items listed: here were five loaves of bread not yet paid for, a moderate shopkeeper's bill not yet settled, ten bottles of beer bought on tick from the innkeeper – this man was just an irresponsible and habitual debtor devoid of conscience! My 'No!' became increasingly emphatic, and all political considerations were now cast aside. In the course of the conversation it slipped out that parents and relatives had already helped them out on two or three occasions, but in no time at all they were back in trouble again. I kept on saying 'No!'. But they wouldn't give up, they just kept on and on. It went on for hours. I rushed from the room in a rage and escaped into the garden, unable to stand their endless talk a moment longer. They just carried on talking to my wife. They were determined not to leave until I had said 'Yes', and I just couldn't get rid of them. Sure enough, they didn't leave until they got what they wanted. They wore me down. They talked me into the ground. And in the end I said 'Yes'. I told them my terms. As far as the repayments were concerned, I was very reasonable: for the first six months they would not have to pay anything, after that he was to repay 50 marks a month out of his salary, and I wouldn't charge interest. But, if Mr and Mrs Ritzner got into debt one more time, then the entire amount of the debt would become repayable at once – no notice, no ifs or buts; and in this event his own lawyer must cease to act for him and act for me instead, doing whatever was necessary to collect the debt.

They agreed to everything, they would have accepted any terms just to get off the treadmill of permanent debt. I wrote out a cheque and handed it to the lawyer. He thanked me with the friendliest of smiles. I repeated my warning one more time: 'But at the first sign of any new debt, you start acting for me!'

'We will never get into debt again', cried schoolmaster Ritzner, and raised his arm in his brown shirt.

In the next few weeks my wife had much to do up in the village. She had set up a proper system of domestic accounting for Mrs Ritzner and went to check daily that everything was being correctly entered. Mrs Ritzner herself turned up out of the blue once and asked in some agitation how she should enter the proceeds from the sale of three eggs. It was all going swimmingly.

And then one day some people in the village told me that Ritzner had bought two pigs to fatten up from the livestock trader – but not cheap piglets like we buy, but a pair of good solid barrows weighing over a hundredweight. Suse and I debated for a long time whether this purchase constituted a breach of our conditions forbidding him to get into debt again. There was no way the Ritzners had paid for these pigs; we knew their financial circumstances too well for that. So they must have bought them on credit, and the question was: was that allowed? Everyone in the countryside needs to keep one or two pigs for slaughter, and if it is too late in the season for piglets to be fattened up in time for slaughter . . . There was a case to be made for them, certainly, and so we decided not to make an issue of it. The strange thing was that from then on my wife no longer felt compelled to go up to the village in the evenings to check on the Ritzners' bookkeeping; and Mrs Ritzner apparently had no more questions for my wife regarding entries in the accounts. We didn't exactly avoid each other, but we only spoke if we happened to meet by chance. And chance didn't bring us together very often.

Then one day the bookkeeper of the village electricity cooperative called on me – a painter and decorator by trade, but not the one I've already mentioned, who was a Party member, but another one who also lived in our village. He wouldn't come straight to the point, but seemed to be sounding me out with various questions – was it true what people were saying, that I had paid off the Ritzners' debts, that they were entirely in my hands, etc., etc. But he finally got round to the thing that was troubling him: Ritzner, who was of course chairman of our village electricity cooperative, had acted in that capacity to buy twenty hundredweight of briquettes in our local small town and charge them to the cooperative's account, and had then had them delivered to his house. The invoice had been sent to the bookkeeper that day, he had driven straight into town to lodge a furious complaint, and that's when he learned of this sequence of events. He took the view that this was actually fraud, since a village electricity cooperative had no need of coals, and what did I now propose to do about it? What indeed? Mr Ritzner moved in mysterious ways. He was no longer running up debts in his own name, but in the name of others – and that was actually much more worrying. I finally made up my mind, went to see his lawyer and told him what had happened. He said this was definitely a breach of our agreement, he was no longer prepared to represent

Ritzner, and he was now at my disposal. He advised me to proceed with caution, however, and counselled against direct legal action. Ritzner was a Party member and a member of the SA, so this was really a matter for the Party to deal with. (Yet again, the special rights enjoyed by Party members!) He advised me to take my case in the first instance to the local Party office in our local small town.

And so I did. There I encountered a young man with pointed features, who was somewhat astonished when I said my name. He had probably not expected to make my acquaintance on Party premises. I explained the matter to him. He said it was probably all just tittle-tattle and gossip. He said he would look into it at some point. I said, somewhat tartly, that since a crime had very likely been committed here, something rather more than looking into it at some point was required. I told him my car was outside, and if he would care to get in and come with me we could clarify the matter in fifteen minutes. He was a very young man; an older and more experienced Party member would have sidestepped my invitation and sorted the matter out on the quiet. But this young man let himself be persuaded and got into the car with me. We drove to the bookkeeper's house and inspected the invoice. Ritzner had been asked to join us. He entered the room and freely admitted to having placed the fraudulent order. He said he was at his wits' end. He had no money in the house – he was being eaten alive by debts. So the wretch was up to his neck in debt again. I became angry and accused him of breaking his word to me. I told him I would do whatever was necessary to get my money back, that I would have his furniture seized and impounded. He replied abjectly that their furniture had been pawned long ago. A teacher's salary was just too meagre, and his wife had had to go to the doctor's again. He cut a pitiful figure, truly the most pitiful that I ever saw in a brown shirt. They were not cowards, as a rule. But this man was a coward. A great strapping fellow, but without an ounce of backbone. The local Party branch leader was just as disgusted as I was, but he still tried to mollify, mediate and talk me round, in the interests of the Party.

Then the door opened and the bookkeeper, who had been out of the room for a while, came back in and said in a loud and agitated voice that the children had just noticed that their school savings moneybox had been broken into, and that thirty marks were missing. Schoolmaster Ritzner turned very pale and said falteringly that he'd had to give the postman thirty marks that morning, but he would put the money back by the evening. And then the wretch began to cry . . . The local Party branch leader asked me and the bookkeeper to leave the room. We were only too glad to do so. We stood for a while chatting outside the door, and imagined the judgment that was now being visited upon the teacher for the sake of the Party, we pictured him hounded from office, disgraced . . . 'He's finished!' we said. In my mind I had written my money off. And the days passed, and turned into weeks, and nothing happened, at least nothing as far as anyone could tell from the outside. Schoolmaster Ritzner continued to teach his pupils – despite the theft of school savings – and remained in post as chairman of the village electricity cooperative – despite the briquettes fraudulently charged to its account. And he carried on wearing his brown shirt; only a party such as this could so brazenly and shamelessly fly in the face of general disapproval. I had instructed my – formerly his – lawyer to write to Ritzner and ask what he could pay back. All I got by way of reply was a consolatory letter saying the schoolmaster's debts would probably be taken over by somebody else, and I would get all my money back. Then one day I received a visit in my study from two more of the Führer's acolytes. It's never what I would call a welcome sight, but on this occasion they were all smiles. They had come to inform me that the National Socialist Teachers' Association had taken on Mr Ritzner's debts in their entirety, and that the sum advanced by me earlier was now available again – that is to say . . . I looked expectantly at the young local Party branch leader, wondering what this last little proviso portended . . . Well yes, he said, still smiling broadly, the thing is, I had only got my money back thanks to the efforts and the intervention of the Party. I was a wealthy man, for whom such a sum was a mere trifle . . . I could see where they were going with this florid oration, the Chancellor's beggars; the Party could never get enough money. But this time I was not prepared to be milked for the Party. I quickly replied that I was not by any means a wealthy man, and that a sum of nearly 2000 marks was anything but a trifle to me, but in view of the unusual circumstances I was prepared to be generous . . . The smile on the face of the local Party branch leader became even broader . . . You gentlemen, I continued, came here by car, so you will have seen for yourselves what a dreadful state the roads in Mahlendorf are in. The parish was poor, and therefore I agreed to make the whole sum available, in its entirety, to the parish of Mahlendorf for road improvement works. The local Party man was taken aback for a moment, but then carried on smiling. He made the best of a bad job and thanked me for my gift. 'But here', he went on, 'is someone else who would like to talk to you, and he has some serious worries . . .' And he pointed to the man from the SA, who had some sort of gold braid as a mark of his seniority. 'Yes', said he. 'My dear Mr Fallada, you know that the Party rally is coming up very soon, our unit is very short of money and needs all kinds of things for the march to Nuremberg. You have given money to many people, so why not be generous to us too, and make a donation to my SA unit? If you do, then my unit will never forget you.' Ingratiating though this last remark was, I couldn't help thinking that it concealed a double meaning. I decided not to bother with a refusal or horsetrading, nor did I ask any questions, but quickly wrote out a cheque for 500 marks. He looked slightly disappointed, but he took what he was given. 'We'll use it to buy knapsacks', he said. They left. I never saw them again, I never heard from them again. I hope they used the 500 marks to buy knapsacks. Shortly afterwards the young local Party branch leader attempted suicide; but his accounts were said to be in order. I don't know the truth of it – it was impossible to get to the bottom of these things. But my efforts to help out a village schoolmaster in a small way after he had got himself into debt ended up costing me a good 2500 marks, including additional costs. But at least – I hear my dear readers ask – the parish of Mahlendorf now has a decent road from the village to the local small town. Well no, dear readers, is my answer to that. The road is as bad as it always was, if anything it has got a little worse since then, if such a thing is possible. When they were ready to start work on the road, and the farmers were supposed to bring in loads of gravel and chippings, as it was winter and their horses were standing idle in their stables, they said: 'What are we doing, improving the road for Mr Fallada? It's all right as it is – it was good enough for our fathers and it's good enough for us!' And rather than lift a finger to improve the road, they left their horses to kick out and break their legs in the stable from too much energy, and went on loading their carts with a third of what they could have carried on a properly made-up road. So I dare say the money is still sitting in the savings bank account of the parish of Mahlendorf, if it hasn't been used in the meantime for other 'more Party-specific' purposes. I never liked to inquire. But what became of schoolmaster Ritzner, the school savings thief whose debts were taken over for the sake of the Party? After a decent interval of time – in case anyone should think it had anything to do with the goings-on related above – he was transferred and given a teaching post in another parish, while his place here was taken by a Mr Stork. Not that Mr Ritzner had been moved on to a lesser position; the new job was actually something of a promotion. But it didn't help him at all, because he was incapable of changing; he remained the same old incorrigible, reckless debtor, beyond all sense and reason. And the day came again when he didn't know where to turn for money, only this time he really couldn't find a single person to bail him out. So he went and hanged himself. His wife, who was just as bad as he was, found him in time and cut him down. The first thing he did, when he was just about able to breathe again, was to slap his wife around the face for saving him. Soon afterwards he lost his teaching job – I don't know what became of him then.

Back in those days I had another visit from the SA, which was just amusing to begin with, but ended up being thoroughly annoying. Anyone who has read my novel *Wolf among Wolves* will perhaps remember the figure of the little bailiff Negermeier, or Black Meier. Well, the portrait of this Black Meier is drawn pretty much from life,[152] apart from all those extra bits of pure invention that we book writers feel we must put in for the sake of effect. He had been a colleague of mine back in those dim distant days when I was still an agronomist myself, and I have to say that for all his eccentricities he was a good and loyal friend. He showed me just how good and loyal he was by remaining my good friend even after reading *Wolf*, not taking the least offence at this highly distorted portrayal. I had not heard from him in ages, when an ancient, open-topped car drove into my yard and five or six SA men got out, one of whom I recognized, to my astonishment, as little Black Meier. In the course of his chequered career he had now became an SA man as well, and therefore, obviously, a dyed-in-the-wool acolyte of the Führer. I invited the party into the house, regaled them with food, drink and cigarettes, and the two of us began by taking a trip down memory lane. 'Do you remember, the old forest ranger – ?'

'And what about the time old Aprilpeter[153] threw you out of the hayloft, and you had to pack your bags on the spot?' 'And that same evening he was downing a bottle of wine with me!' We laughed heartily. Eventually we got round to talking about this trip he was on with his friends, which I couldn't quite fathom. Basically it seemed to be just a joyride in a borrowed car, which had taken them up as far as the island of Rügen. Now they were on their way back to their SA barracks in Brandenburg. On the whole it seemed as if the trip had been a source of endless amusement. They joshed and nudged each other, and some of their shared memories reduced them to helpless mirth. Most of the allusions were obscure to me, not helped, perhaps, by the drinks that I had dispensed so lavishly. What I was seeing now was the other side of the coin. These men were blissfully happy and drunk with a sense of their own power. For the last few years they had been fighting for the cause while their Führer stood on the threshold of power, only to be turned away repeatedly. But now they had become the masters. They felt like little kings. Nothing seemed beyond their reach now. The humble life of an SA man was just a transient state for them; soon the Führer would be handing out jobs to his loyal followers – and they would not go away empty-handed. They would not be slow in coming forward – oh dear me no! They had served their time in punch-ups at political meetings! 'Do you remember the cop who was hitting us right in the face with his rubber truncheon? If we ever see him again, he'll wish he'd never been born! Just you wait!' They laughed again. 'And that time a Communist knocked you off your bike with a soda water bottle filled with sand? I came along just in time, otherwise you'd have been toast!' More laughter. And they blithely told us what an easy time they had of it in their barracks, with no duties at all, a real cushy number! 'When we're lying in our beds in the dormitory at night, nobody can ever be bothered to get out of bed and turn off the light. So we just grab our pistols and fire away until the light bulb's shot out!'

'Then you'll soon be out of light bulbs!' observed my wife drily. 'Us? Never! It's very simple. One of us just goes out and picks up light bulbs for the SA from electrical shops. We go and pick up whatever we need – these days nobody dares to say no to the SA any more!'

I didn't find these stories quite so amusing as these gentlemen, nor would I have wanted to be one of the party on today's jaunt to Rügen. It was all a little too coarse, too crude and too primitive for my liking. Eventually, when it was already dark, I showed them out, explaining that unfortunately I didn't have enough beds to put up such a large company. Someone remarked that the hayloft would have done for them, but I pretended not to hear. Enough is enough, and by now I had had more than enough of the brownshirts and the SA. I said that I had already contacted the best hotel in the local town, and that they were expected there. As they were leaving, little Black Meier took me to one side. There was a look of entreaty in his intelligent, friendly, owlish eyes. The truth was, he said, that they had no money left at all, not for the journey, not for their overnight accommodation, nor for breakfast. I laughed and said I wasn't in the least bit surprised. I rather assumed, I added, that they were not much better provided for when they embarked on their travels. Another case of just picking up light bulbs as and when, perhaps?

Little Black Meier grinned. I pressed a banknote into his hand, and he grinned even more broadly. They piled into their ancient car. They shouted all kinds of goodbyes – though 'Heil Hitler!' did not figure among them. The car leapt forward and disappeared into the night. As it left our driveway it took the sharp left-hand bend on two wheels. 'What are the chances', I said to my wife, 'that they'll get to the hotel in one piece, driving like that? But I expect their luck will hold. Come on, let's go and clean up the worst of the mess in my rooms before we get to bed.' And the night passed and morning came, and I had already been working at my writing for some time when I was summoned to the telephone. It was our fat hotelier calling me. What was the position with the fellows from the SA? Apparently they'd spent all their money on drink yesterday evening, and now had nothing left to pay for their accommodation, their breakfast or the rest of the journey. And none of them had the heart to come to the phone and tell me. What did I think? At first I was inclined to be difficult; I had given Black Meier a big banknote, and they had had plenty to drink at our house, but then I thought that if I refused I would never see the back of them. So I laughed and told the hotelier that I would stump up for the three items he had mentioned, but not for anything else, not a single schnaps, not a single cigarette! Was that clear? Yes indeed, came the reply, and I hung up with a feeling of relief.

Two hours later I was called to the telephone again. No, it's not what you are thinking, dear reader – they were not that predictable. They had not started to drink again, they had left punctually, they were now not far from Brandenburg. This time it was little Black Meier on the phone, and his voice sounded very pathetic and full of entreaty.

What on earth was the problem now? I asked.

Well, they'd had a bit of bad luck, they had driven the car into a closed level crossing gate, and the car had been a bit damaged, nothing too serious, but still, some minor damage . . . So what did that have to do with me? I wasn't a bit interested in their car and their crazy driving! Well, it seems that the car belonged to their doctor, the SA's own doctor, and they absolutely had to get it repaired, otherwise they'd really be in hot water. Could I perhaps . . . the repair costs – ?

I let out a howl of derision and hung up. I was then phoned repeatedly by all the SA men one after the other, then by the owner of a garage, who had already towed the car in. I was foolish enough to ask about the repair costs. When the figure of 250 marks was mentioned, I laughed derisively once more and hung up again. My readers know me by now, and they know that if I am pestered for long enough, I give in. I agreed to cover the repair costs. When I eventually received the bill, it amounted to 378 Reichsmarks – so the damage to the car had not been all that minor after all. To round off the story, I got a letter of thanks from little Black Meier, which was both touching and cheery: he told me he was so happy that I had helped him out of a jam. He had driven the repaired car two kilometres back to the barracks himself, and had been greeted by his friends with a celebratory volley of gunfire; unfortunately he had been wounded, nothing serious, just a bullet in the leg . . . So much for the finer points of social etiquette in the SA following the Nazi seizure of power.

(4.X.44.) I have always held the firm belief that there is some truth to the Latin saying 'nomen est omen'. Names determine what a person is – very often at least – or what they become. People grow into their names, they change in obedience to their laws . . . Somewhere above I said that our new teacher, the successor to the wretched Ritzner, was called Stork. And I have never seen a clearer example of how a name can shape a person's destiny than in the case of this man. He wanted so badly to be a strong man – *ein starker Mann* – but he never quite had what it took, there was always a little something missing; he could never be *stark*, but only ever Stork. The last little bit eluded him. And that's how it was with him in everything. I'm sure he came to us in the village full of the best intentions. No doubt he had learned a thing or two in previous jobs, not all of it good, and he was determined to be both careful and patient. And then of course he had heard that Mahlendorf was a 'difficult' village: the disputes between its residents, the feuds that were passed down from one generation to the next, were renowned throughout the land. You had to take great care not to be drawn into this maelstrom of hatred and malice. A single ill-chosen

word, a visit to the wrong house at the wrong time – these could ruin the standing of a newcomer for all time.

Schoolmaster Stork was on the short side, but broadly built, and he had nimble, slightly twisted legs like a dachshund, a legacy of rickets. His face was pale and wan, with a yellowish tinge, his eyes were dark and deep-set; you quickly became aware that the man could not look anyone straight in the face. He generally looked down when he was talking to you.

The wife of our new schoolmaster was round like a ball, and had a mercurial vivacity about her; but it was not the kind of comforting and contented obesity that comes from enjoying good food, and plenty of it, but rather the kind that stems from a glandular disorder, affecting the pituitary gland, I understand, in the cerebellum. She certainly had the volatile, over-excited manner of someone with glandular problems, alternating unpredictably with sullen moods or downright aggressive behaviour. But generally speaking she was lively, vivacious, full of laughter, and it was not long before she was known to every household in the village, as if she had lived there all her life. She was herself the daughter of a country schoolmaster, so she knew all about village life from an early age, and she knew the teaching profession inside out – better than her husband, so people were soon saying. Rumour had it that she corrected the children's exercise books for him.

He was the son of an agricultural labourer, who had subsequently been promoted to the stewardship of a country manor. The son too had worked his way up from humble beginnings, doubtless enduring all manner of hardships and deprivations along the way – hence the crooked legs, the physique that always looked somehow underdeveloped, the pale, liverish complexion that indicated bad blood.

Schoolmaster Stork's debut in Mahlendorf was not auspicious: in the first week after he moved in, his front door and door handle were smeared with human excrement in the night. The perpetrator or perpetrators were never found, and it remained unclear whether they came from our village, where actually nobody yet had cause to hate him so viciously, or from his previous place of employment. At all events, this outrage, which was universally condemned, became the subject of the first heated quarrel between our old village mayor and the new schoolteacher: Stork demanded that the mayor send someone to clean up his soiled front door, since it was an insult to him as the village schoolmaster. The mayor said it wasn't his responsibility, and he refused. So the village looked on while the unsightly door decoration stayed in place for a couple of days – I don't recall now who removed it in the end. But the incident taught us that the new schoolmaster was a fiery, quarrelsome and self-righteous man, and we resolved to watch our step in future. Furthermore, unlike his predecessor, he was not content to be a member of the Party and the SA in name and uniform only, but was clearly determined to be very active in these capacities. The thing is, he was a 'March Martyr', as we quickly learned, and he was intent on demonstrating his fervour at every turn. He not only took over all the posts held by his predecessor, but was also promptly appointed the 'Political Leader' of the village and the local representative both of the Labour Front and of the NSV.[154] In short, he soon held every official position going, and had also set his sights, so it was claimed, on the job of village mayor, which we felt was in the best possible hands already, the wise old hands of our small farmer. From the very first day schoolmaster Stork let it be known that he was not minded to be content with the quiet life of a village schoolmaster; he was ambitious, he was positively eaten up with ambition and envy. His sole concern was how to get on in the world and ingratiate himself with his superiors, and he didn't care what methods he used to further his career. We only discovered that later. But it was not long before we had seen and heard quite enough of this man to give very little away in our dealings with him. We only had occasional conversations in passing, and when it was strongly hinted that we should get to know each other better over coffee and cakes, we pretended not to hear – for which we were never forgiven.

Meanwhile the time had come when we had to send our six-year-old son to school, and who was going to teach him but schoolmaster Stork? What we saw and heard there, however, went a long way towards reconciling us with Stork. He was not only a good teacher, but he also loved children, knew how to put things across to them, and to win their affection. We were very pleased with the results, our boy really liked going to school – and that was no small thing! Sometimes we stayed behind chatting with the Storks, discussing this and that, and I discovered a certain urbane quality in the man, a great facility for engaging with other people's way of thinking and seeing things from their point of view. In short, schoolmaster Stork was a good conversationalist, who knew how to listen as well as talk. I've always found this very appealing, and one day to my astonishment I found myself having a conversation about politics with Stork in which I no longer made any secret of my anti-Nazi sentiments. We spoke about the Jewish question, and I reminded him of what the Führer had said: that to be a true man you had to keep faith with your friends in their hour of need. The fact was the Jews had been my friends in good times, and I was not about to break faith with them now that times for them were bad. His eyes wandered, but he smiled suavely and said that the Führer had assuredly not intended his remark to be applied to criminals, gypsies, Jews and similar riff-raff. But he wanted to hear what I thought about it . . . I was stupid enough to think he really was interested in my opinion. But I had an uncomfortable feeling about it all the same, I had undoubtedly let down my guard, and my wife, who had listened to our conversation with mounting alarm, said the same thing. But as the weeks went by and nothing happened, I almost forgot about this conversation. I only discovered later that Mr Stork made a habit of initiating compromising conversations of this kind, subsequently reporting what was said either to the Party or to the district council leader, as appropriate. He was constantly gathering material – to incriminate others, and to assist his own advancement. Soon there were growing indications that Mr Stork was not the affable and agreeable man that he liked to appear. I heard from my six-year-old son that his teacher had had the gall to ask him where his father had hung the portrait of Hitler at home, and whether he saluted it morning and evening with a 'Heil Hitler!' Very soon afterwards a big change then took place in our village; our old mayor was ignominiously removed from his post, having faithfully discharged his office for decades, and replaced by the new schoolmaster Stork. The teacher used the handover of administrative and financial responsibilities to humiliate the honourable old man further. He shamelessly raised doubts about the honest conduct of mayoral business, and had the brass neck to say, when his accusations were shown to be groundless, that it was his bounden duty to carry out a scrupulous audit, and anyone who felt insulted by that simply showed that his conscience was not clear. It was quite apparent that he now felt himself to be the lord and master of the entire village, and so in a way he was, since he had the district council leader and the Party behind him, backing up his every move. Stork was determined now to play the strong man, and to use the power that he had. He publicly announced that a wind of change was blowing through Mahlendorf, and that certain lukewarm, not to say subversive elements should tread very warily from now on. Supported by his mercurial wife, he promptly gathered about him all the village gossips of both sexes, nosed into every piece of idle tittle-tattle like a duck foraging in a pool of murky water, diligently wrote up reports, conducted interrogations, agitated and plotted, and managed within a short space of time to re-ignite all the ancient feuds in Mahlendorf that had virtually died out, while simultaneously inciting new ones. From now on the whole village was constantly permeated by a foul miasma of calumny, as every informer now found a willing ear. This was the time when the German population was starting to feel the effects of cutbacks and economies in their daily lives as a result of the government's accelerated program of rearmament, and even the quantity of grain that could be fed to pigs was now rationed. One morning, not long after schoolmaster Stork assumed his duties as mayor, a couple of pitiful dead piglets were found dangling from the war memorial in the churchyard, erected to commemorate the dead of the First World War. Strung between them was a cardboard notice: 'Because you've taken the corn we eat, we lay down our lives at the Fatherland's feet!' This sent our new mayor into a frenzy of rage. The mere fact that his community harboured such a degenerate reflected badly on him and the discharge

of his office. He moved heaven and earth to discover the identity of
the perpetrator, but he was never found. He had better luck in another
case. A farmer who had had too much to drink told people in the pub
that he had a cow in his shed that looked just like Adolf Hitler. The
farmer was taken to court and given a lengthy prison sentence. Later
on he was transferred to a concentration camp, and if he is not already
dead he is probably still living there today. This was an early victory for
Stork's conduct of village affairs, but it was nowhere near enough to
satisfy his vaulting ambition. Many more lukewarm brethren must yet
be sent to their doom. I had long known that he had his eye on me too,
and his confidantes, old women for the most part, had been leaking
information for a long time. He started by going through the records
of his predecessor and claiming that I'd been let off paying some tax bill
or other by mistake. He now demanded payment of the outstanding
amount. I refused; the tax rebate had been correct because my income
had fallen. In the course of our discussions I saw the true character
of the man for the first time: the thin veneer of urbanity vanished in
an instant and a threatening bully now stood before me, consumed
with envy and lust for power, cunning and yet stupid, utterly stupid,
incapable of following a simple argument or understanding a tax document. A dangerous fool, completely incapable of thinking through the
consequences of what he was doing. When I had explained my reason-
ing for the tenth time and saw that my arguments were not making
the slightest impression on him, I gave up and told him to do what he
liked. He threatened me with immediate foreclosure, accusing me and
the old mayor of collusion and corrupt dealings. I slammed the door
and left.

Next morning he asked me to come and see him again, and told
me – all affability now – that he intended to ask the tax office for an
expert opinion on the point at issue. Whether he really did, or whether
his much cleverer, but also much more dangerous wife came to the aid
of his feeble understanding overnight, I don't know. In any event, I
never heard another word about this whole tax business. But he never
forgave me this defeat and quite a few others besides, as I would learn to

my cost in due course. Even so, he was determined to make an example of a few people in this lukewarm neck of the woods, so that everyone would feel a little bit afraid and more ready to submit to his rule. I was first on his list. We already knew that he and his wife were in the habit of trying to glean from our young housemaids, the women who worked in the garden and other workers, what went on in our house and what we talked about. In general I was very lucky in this regard: apart from two exceptions, nobody from our house blabbed in all those years. And there would have been plenty to report; within my own four walls I frequently gave free rein to my loose and impious tongue. . . . But as luck would have it we had just had to fire an older lady who worked for us as a housekeeper, who not only had a son in the SS, but had also – and this was the high point of her life – embroidered a large tablecloth for the Führer himself! She had delivered it in person, and refused to budge until she had placed this work of art, decorated with blue cornflowers and golden ears of wheat, into the hands of the great man himself, and had shaken him by the hand! Following her stormy dismissal without notice, this creature, who certainly wasn't a perfect fit with the kind of home life we led, had spent long hours sitting with our mayor Stork and relating the table talk of the Falladas. The usual reports had then been drawn up and forwarded. Unfortunately – or perhaps fortunately – neither the Gestapo nor the district council leader's office used them to start proceedings against me, because they contained claims so ludicrous that not even an anti-Nazi writer could be supposed capable of such absurdities. Our effusive embroiderer of tablecloths, it seems, had shown herself to be even more stupid than the mayor, and she had got all my little stories mixed up. When she claimed, for example, that I had said that 65 men decorated with the Blood Order[155] had been shot at the time of the Röhm Putsch in our little town (1300 residents), this was such arrant nonsense that not even a moron could possibly have believed it. There was not a single holder of the Blood Order living in the entire place, and there certainly hadn't been any shootings during the Röhm Putsch. So nothing came of it this time round; they were saving me up for later. But schoolmaster Stork called in his brother, also a Nazi, also a member of the SA, and also a 'March Martyr', and the two of them now went around in plain clothes, the *provocateur* and his witness, looking for someone to make an example of. They began by visiting the pharmacist in our little town, a man of nearly seventy, who had once belonged to the Stahlhelm, who had strong nationalist sentiments and up until the Nazi seizure of power had been the king of the little town. They greeted him with a 'Heil Hitler!', and the old pharmacist responded with 'Good day to you'. Our schoolmaster Stork asked him whether he ever said 'Heil Hitler', and the pharmacist, who had never once allowed the hated greeting to pass his lips, replied genially that of course he would greet people with H.H. the moment this form of greeting was prescribed by law. And was there anything else he could do for the gentlemen? Having been suitably dismissed with a flea in their ear by this old bruiser, they now trotted off two doors down to the town's chemist. This chemist, who was likewise an elderly man in his sixties, was something of a sad case, despite the fact that he had succeeded in building up a flourishing business; at one time he had probably thought he was destined for something better than running a country store that typically sold everything from aniseed oil to Harz Mountain cheese, and from rolls of film to spades. The man was a quiet, respectable, educated man, courteous and well-mannered, but every six months or so the madness would come upon him, tormented thoughts of a wasted life, almost put behind him, now overwhelmed him again, and he took to the bottle. He drank for three or four days solid, then staggered home, slept it off, and was once again a respectable, dependable man of business for the next six months. During these bouts of heavy drinking he had the curious habit of quoting from *Faust*, which he knew by heart, reciting Part II with especial relish. The fact that the townspeople ridiculed this proclivity and showed not the slightest appreciation for *Faust* Part II merely confirmed him in his contempt and in his belief that his life had been wasted.

The two Storks who now entered his shop with the intention of tripping him up came upon him at an unfortunate time – unfortunate for the chemist. He'd just started to drink again, but hadn't yet reached the *Faust* stage; he was just in an unusually chatty and affable mood. He greeted the two strangers warmly and could do nothing better than tell them the latest joke going the rounds about the Winter Relief Organization – a perfectly innocuous joke, as it happens. Whereupon the old man was sentenced to a prison term of one year, the two Storks having sworn that he was not the slightest bit drunk at the time. Despite the fact that the chemist was declared unfit to go to prison by a doctor on the grounds that he was severely diabetic, he had to serve out the whole sentence. He was never quite right after that, and crept around the town silent and withdrawn, distrusting everyone, but most of all himself.

But Stork the schoolmaster and mayor had made an example of somebody – striking terror into the hearts of the lukewarm! – and felt pleased with himself. But of course the idiot had failed to foresee one consequence of his misdeed, which was that he was ostracized by every decent member of the local community – and there were still plenty of those. Nobody wanted to have anything more to do with this *provocateur* and informer, who in the first flush of victory had even boasted of his deeds. Everyone gave him a wide berth, nobody wanted to be seen talking to someone like that. In the monthly teacher meetings he was shunned, his own colleagues wanted nothing more to do with him. This had the unfortunate consequence that he retreated even more into his role in Mahlendorf. Here he had the whip hand, here people were dependent on him, here there was no shortage, unfortunately, of toadies and gossip-mongers; there were always people who for one reason or another wanted to suck up to the mayor. His liverish disposition was accentuated by this defeat, which had initially looked like a victory. He put the blame on others, anyone who didn't belong to the Party was a dubious character and should be eliminated. He stepped up his activities, the number of reports he wrote increased. He was too stupid to see that this didn't make him any more popular with his superiors either. He was just making more work for them with all his reports, and in most cases nothing ever came of it, because it was all based on gossip and rumour. All the same, a man like him was worth hanging on to – he had his uses. The Nazi Party and the government that emerged from it made a point of investigating every report from an informer, even the ones that were obviously motivated by spite or greed. Informers were useful people, perhaps not ideal candidates for preferment, but always serviceable. Stork couldn't grasp that. In himself he must have been weary of fighting these petty battles in a country backwater, and longed to bestride a bigger stage, which he hoped to obtain by denouncing more people.

By that time he had also tired of teaching. School was just a sideline for him, he wasn't interested in the children any more – he had ceased to be a good teacher a long time ago. His various official duties, the reports he was always writing, his trips to see the district council leader in the county town – these things took up most of his time. And then he had grown so used to hanging around on the village street, chatting and chinwagging, always on the lookout for some tit-bit, the worm he could use to bait his hook, that there was no room in his life for proper work any more.

His attitude to me and my family was very changeable. His position as mayor and the constant government regulations encroaching on people's private lives made it necessary to apply to him more and more frequently with questions, requests and petitions of one sort or another. Sometimes he was all smiles and affability, giving us everything we asked for, even things we thought likely to be refused. Another time he would brusquely turn down the most harmless request, only to agree to it three or four days later with an air of gracious beneficence. The truth is he was a coward. Like his eyes, which couldn't look directly at anyone, he was a cowardly, skulking, treacherous dog from the bottom of his soul. He never dared to attack openly, preferring to creep up and bite you from behind.

At the time I was having a minor dispute with a small farmer in the village, to whom our mayor lent his support. It was one of those long-standing country disputes that you just can't avoid in a small village, no matter how careful you are. One evening, just after we had moved to Mahlendorf, I came home from a walk to find a boy sitting in my plum trees and eating plums, while the boy's horses were busy eating my grass. I shouted at the lad and pointed out that twenty metres away, on the other side of the little stone wall that formed the boundary between our properties, were his father's plum trees, from which he could help himself just as easily, and rather more honestly. To tell the truth I was less bothered by the theft of the plums – boys will be boys, after all – than I was by having my grass flattened by his horses. This was the start of a long-lasting feud between my family and that of the small farmer, and it was not just me that they cut dead, but all the members of my family and the people who worked for me too. Village feuds are as uncompromising as they are silly.

Well, we could handle it, and we didn't take it too much to heart. One day the feud would pass: giving a boy a ticking-off was hardly grounds for undying enmity.

It must have been about a year later when my mason came to me and asked where he could get some large stones to make a border for a vegetable patch. I directed him to the low fieldstone wall on the edge of my field, and some time later I heard there was a story going around the village, claiming that 'Fallada has had a boundary stone removed!'

This is not a nice accusation, especially when it isn't true. And it must have been untrue, since to the best of my knowledge the boundary with my neighbour's property – that's the father of the plum-picking boy – was not marked with stones. That low wall marked the boundary, and according to the information given to me at the time of purchase, the whole of it stood on my land. But since the gossip wouldn't go away, and a boundary stone I had removed was rapidly becoming a boundary I had shifted in my favour, I went to the district council office and asked to have my boundary marked out with stones by the district surveyor. The big day arrived, the councillor turned up with his team of assistants and a stack of red-and-white poles and grey granite stones marked with an incised cross, while on the other side the small farmer – let's call him Mechthal – arrived under the protection of mayor Stork. There was a lot of whispering and cogitating between the two of them and the councillor, and it was all too apparent that the missing boundary stone, which had never existed in the first place, featured in the discussion again. The councillor didn't seem unduly bothered by any of this as he set to work measuring and sighting, looking at old maps, telling his men where to put the poles – 'More to the right!', 'A touch more to the left!' – peering through strange-looking telescopes and finally saying: 'The boundary stone goes here!'

We looked at each other, and I'm afraid I was mean enough to smile, because according to this survey not only the little wall belonged to me, but also . . . 'Oh I see', said I, as my smile grew steadily broader, 'so all the plum trees on your side of the wall also belong to me, Mr Mechthal – I had no idea.' But he wasn't smiling now, in fact he looked mightily peeved, and our good mayor had turned quite yellow, as yellow as a well-aged, overripe quince. I must confess that I didn't have the heart to enjoy my triumph to the full. In the event, although the plum trees on the far side of the wall did actually belong to me, I didn't make use of them – which didn't stop the opposing party helping themselves again every so often from the plum trees on my side of the wall. Now the other two fell to whispering among themselves, and then the mayor spoke up for the furious, but not very articulate Mechthal: 'Look here, Fallada has put up a high fence around his house and garden, and he's sited the fence so close to the road that the farmers get hitched up on it with a full harvest load. Surely that's not allowed, Mr Councillor?' The councillor looked at me, I looked at him, and then I said: 'Since we're doing the boundary stones, why don't we just carry on and mark out the whole property while we're at it? It'll cost a bit more, but we're not bothered about that, Mr Councillor.' So they set to work again, measuring and sighting and looking on the plans, and eventually the councillor said to my two adversaries: 'You're out of luck, gentlemen. Mr Fallada would be within his rights to site his fence another metre and a half further out into the road, and then nobody would be able to get past at all with a horse and cart! Count your blessings, I say – it could be a lot worse!' So I had won a double victory, but it cost me dear over time, earning me the undying enmity of the mayor and farmer Mechthal, who became the village's ranking SA officer during the war, and who now makes life uncomfortable for me and my family in every way he can. On the other hand, he and his family are at least speaking to us again; but I actually found their open hostility back then preferable to this bogus friendliness now, which seeks to do me harm wherever it can.

Here is another tale of our mayor's endless, unpredictable flip-flopping, all sunshine one day, thunder and lightning the next – though this is something that happened much later. We live in a heavily wooded area, and we had an abundance of timber almost up until the outbreak of war. Most people heated their homes with wood rather than coal, and we were no different. But as industry geared up for war, the forestry authorities became increasingly reluctant to let us have firewood, as every tree was needed for the production of rayon, which was made into fine silk stockings, soft, durable suiting fabrics, and even, I rather think, gunpowder. Eventually the responsibility for allocating firewood was handed over to the mayors of each locality, who were supposed to allocate supplies to each village resident based on the size of the house and the number of occupants. Our own mayor circulated a list, and from this I could see that he had allocated all of three cubic metres of wood to me. I have a fairly large house with a lot of people living in it, and with this allocation of three cubic metres, plus the coal allowance we also had, I would have been able to keep the kitchen range going all year round, plus just one heating stove for three months. So it really wasn't enough, it seemed to me, and I was enraged by this new dirty trick. But that was just his style, to sneak up and bite you from behind. At the same time I knew that losing my temper with this treacherous man would only make more trouble for me, and so I asked my wife to accompany me: 'You must come with me and make sure I don't fly off the handle. If it was up to me I'd slaughter the old bastard!'

'And much good it would do you!' replied my wife, and she was right, of course.

So we went to see mayor Stork together, and he received us in a very friendly manner. My own manner was equally friendly as I pointed out that there must have been some mistake with the three cubic metres of firewood I had been allocated. And I did the sums for him and showed him how long the briquettes and wood would last me, just enough for the kitchen range and one stove for half the winter. When I had finished, I felt very pleased with myself that I had made such a convincing case, and I looked expectantly at Stork.

He smiled and rubbed his hands together and replied in that smarmy way of his: that was all well and good, and I may well have got my sums right, but unfortunately there was nothing he could do about it – there was just no more wood to be had, and so he couldn't give me any more.

This did make my hackles rise somewhat, and I reminded Stork that I had two small children and a very old woman living in my house, amongst others, and that if I couldn't heat the place properly for them, I would effectively be leaving them to freeze to death. He smiled his smarmy smile again and said that was awful, of course it was; but 'you know the old saying: you can't get blood out of a stone', and there simply wasn't any more wood to be had.

My temper rising a little more, I pointed out that many people still had wood from the previous year or even further back stored in their yard, yet these people had all been allocated more wood than me, when I didn't have a single log left. Surely there was a double standard being applied here – ? At this point he became angry too, and said it was nothing to do with him how people chose to manage their stock of wood. If one person was sparing in his use while another burned the whole lot away in one year, that was up to them. At all events, I would not be getting any more wood than my allocation, no matter how much of a fuss I kicked up. I was welcome to lodge a complaint against him – we'd soon see who was in the right here!

I knew this already, and so I forced myself to calm down, especially as my wife now placed her hand over mine in a gesture of entreaty, and said that perhaps the mayor would get another allocation of wood later on, and might then allow us to have more. But he was not even prepared to send us away with that crumb of comfort. Instead he shook his head adamantly and repeated: there was nothing else apart from the three cubic metres, and there was an end to the matter. Done and dusted! But in the meantime I'd come up with a different idea, and I said: 'Mr Stork, there's a national census taking place soon, on 10 October, and wherever a person is resident on that date, that's where they pay their local taxes. Now, I'll tell you what I am going to do, Mr Stork: at the beginning of October I am going to move to Berlin with my entire family and stay in a hotel, which means I'll also be paying my taxes in Berlin – and the parish of Mahlendorf will have to see how it manages without its only real taxpayer!'

I'd become more and more worked up as I spoke, and the mayor was now equally worked up when he replied: 'So you think you can threaten me like that? I'll report you! I'm not going to stand here and be threatened by you!'

'You're threatening me with a lot worse!' I shouted. 'You're threatening me and my wife with illness and freezing to death!' 'That's enough now', said my wife. 'I think it would be better if neither of you said anything more! It's not going to do anybody any good!' And with that she hustled me quickly out of the room, because she could see that I was about to explode and say things that would have landed me in deep trouble.

But I wasn't ready to calm down yet, and I spent the whole night doing and redoing the sums to work out how much coal and wood we would need, and every time the numbers showed that we simply couldn't manage with that amount. Surely the mayor must see that for himself! I just couldn't get my head round the idea that the mayor simply didn't want to see it, that the whole point for him was to torment and harass me until I lost my temper and said things I would regret. I still thought that such cold, calculating villains only existed in the pages of books. And the mayor wasn't even that calculating. He was like his name, not '*stark*' – strong – but only 'Stork', only ever doing things by halves. And so it turned out again on this occasion: he phoned me two or three days later and asked me to drop by to discuss 'the wood business'. I did so, and he greeted me in the most genial manner and inquired with a smile: 'How much wood do you want, Mr Fallada?' I was caught off guard: was he just winding me up again? But

I stayed calm and said that I needed at least twenty-five to thirty cubic metres of wood for the winter. He beamed: 'You can have more if you want it! How much would you like?'

'Well, I wouldn't mind having fifty cubic metres.'

'You shall have them!' he said. 'I'll make sure they are allocated to you right away!'

I couldn't help asking the question: 'But how is it possible, Mr Stork? Three days ago there was not a single cubic metre to be had, and here you are today, knee-deep in wood!'

'That's my little secret', he said, and that's how we left it. I never did find out what his little secret was, of course. To this day I don't know if he really did have more wood all along, or if he managed to secure a fresh supply, or if my threat to withhold my taxes had any effect. All I know is that I was given more wood that winter than I'd ever had before, namely fifty cubic metres. But that was him all over, he never changed. He was always a bad lot, even if he did help me out once in a while. He never behaved well because it was the decent thing to do. In most cases I think it was fear that made him change his tune – fear of the consequences of his actions.

(5.X.44.) He had been living in our village for so many years now, and even a dimwit like him must have noticed that his situation was worse than when he arrived. He had had friends, was invited to people's houses, and now the friends had backed off and the invitations had ceased. In many cases relations had broken down as the result of a quarrel, but more often than not it was because of the very obvious way the Storks cultivated friends only so long as they could be useful to them. This was another delightful characteristic of our mayor that I have not mentioned before: he had perfected the art of getting people to do him favours, favours that were actually not favours at all but proper jobs of work, such as hauling firewood, ploughing fields and suchlike. He just took it for granted that all these things should be done for him free of charge. If someone asked for payment, that was

the end of good relations. The man would get his money eventually, if he was sufficiently persistent, but then the mayor was no longer his friend. So he actually lived a very isolated life in the village; he wielded absolute power, dispensed his favours or disfavours as he saw fit, but he had hardly any friends. And even tyrants have their hours of weakness, when they are in need of friends.

Another separate entry. I'm feeling fairly agitated; there is a possibility that I might be allowed to go home for a couple of hours to fetch some papers, escorted by a police officer, of course. But that would hardly stop me smuggling this MS out of this house of the dead, and hiding it at home. They may tell me their decision this evening. I can hardly believe they'll give me permission, but it would be such a relief! I'm living in a constant state of fear as I push ahead with my writing day after day, watched by so many prying eyes, and it is preventing me from enjoying my work – and disturbing my already fitful sleep. I'm not so much afraid for myself, I'm already living the life of a prisoner behind bars, so outwardly my life would not be very different up until the final hour, when I hope to acquit myself well. But all the others who would be caught up in this business – it's them I fear for! It was incredibly reckless of me to start writing this account here. And yet I could not do otherwise. And yet I carry on writing!

But if they would let me go to Mahlendorf for a few hours I would take this MS with me, and I would stop writing at the point I had got to by then, even though I have not yet written what may be the most important chapter, about the war. I wouldn't even be sorry to end it this way. I embarked on this project with great expectations, but now I'm rather disappointed. All the things I've been through come across as just a bunch of petty squabbles, it seems to me, which everyone else must find boring. At the time I felt anger, bitterness, and sometimes fear. But now, writing about these things much later, I haven't even felt that any more. So how am I to communicate anger, bitterness and fear to the reader? He'll be bored stiff reading it! And yet I say to

myself: what else could I have written? I wasn't living at the heart of
events, I wasn't the friend and confidant of ministers and generals, I
have no great revelations to make. I lived the same life as everyone else,
the life of ordinary people, the masses. And for those of us who were
not Party members, life in the Third Reich really was just one long
series of wrangles, small battles that we had to fight in order to make a
living and survive. Nothing big happened. Just as a publisher couldn't
publish books any more, but had to spend his time conducting a pointless correspondence with the authorities about every damn thing, so
the writer of books could not just get on with his work in peace; there
was constant friction, agitation and interference. When I think how
much I myself had to change in writing my books! I had to abandon
all thoughts of writing the books I really cared about. Any portrayal
of darker characters was strictly forbidden. I had to be optimistic and
life-affirming, in an era that was negating the very meaning of life
through persecution, torture and executions. Since *Wolf* I've not actually written anything that I really cared about. I've fallen back on 'light
fiction'. I've written books of memoirs, yes, and they've given people
a lot of pleasure; but they were just evasions too. I really don't feel so
old yet that I want to live off my memories – or my memoirs. It would
have been much nicer if I'd been able to write them ten or twenty years
later. But that's just it: they systematically took us away from our real
work, they wouldn't allow us to follow the call of our own heart. For
them there was only one call, and that was the sound of them calling
the shots. They are frightened of the individual and individuality, they
want the shapeless masses into which they can drum their slogans. And
they've done very well with that, especially now during the war. They
have introduced forced labour, they prohibit everyone from doing the
work they want to, the work they were born to, under threat of dire
punishment. They are destroying every human being – and the puppets
that are left give them no trouble at all.

What will Germany be like after this war? What kind of Germans
will one have to live with? A terrible thought! How few of them will
have retained vestiges of their true selves! And they won't even feel the

change that has happened to them! They'll just say: 'We were always like this!'

So I am not satisfied with what I have written. Although I don't know how I could have written it any differently. I'll just carry on, more doggedly than a mule. But if they do let me go back to Mahlendorf for a few hours, then I'll break off without any regrets or remorse. Perhaps my heart has been embittered by what I have written so far? I don't know. But I would be happy to hear a 'yes' this evening. I'd manage it somehow, smuggling the thing out – under the watchful eyes of the policeman! And then what a relief to think to myself: most of what you planned to write is safely tucked away in Mahlendorf! Then I could sleep more soundly again. Another task accomplished.

When the war came, mayor Stork told everyone who cared to listen that he had immediately volunteered for front-line service. Schoolmaster Stork promptly related this to his pupils, telling them how happy he would be if he could take up arms and show the Führer that he was one of his loyal warriors. Stork was in his early thirties at the time, robust and without visible ailments (except when his feelings of envy sometimes became too much and adversely affected his gall). But the months went by without Mr Stork marching off to war. Every now and then mention was made of the fact that he was indispensable as mayor, and that his local authority superiors would not release him for military service: but his own burning desire was still to be posted to the front. He often belittled the work he was doing here on the home front: 'But of course we must faithfully do our duty wherever the Führer has thought fit to place us!' The months turned into years, four years of the war had passed, and our mayor was still with us. (During these war years he was more insufferable than ever, but I will come to that later.) Then the news finally came through that our mayor was leaving us: he really was going to join the army as the war entered its fifth year. But again he was out of luck: denied the opportunity to take up arms and fight for his Führer, he was posted to the medical corps. He bore the disappointment heroically, but never failed to point out what a disappointment it was. Doubtless his wife did much to help him bear his fate with fortitude, going to visit him in the barracks nearly every week with suitcases filled to bursting. It was actually inconceivable that a man could eat so much in addition to the robust army fare. But doubtless Mr Stork put the principles of National Socialism into practice by giving much of it away. Though not so much to his comrades, so we heard, as to his superiors, in particular the all-powerful orderly room sergeant, who could make or break a man.

The training period passed quickly, and all of Stork's comrades were sent out to Stalingrad,[156] where a fierce battle was being fought. But destiny (and the all-powerful orderly room sergeant) once again had it in for Stork: of all his comrades he was the only one who had to stay at home and work in the orderly room. His frequently voiced disappointment knew no bounds: 'But I mustn't complain. I must do my duty wherever my Führer sends me.' While his comrades, engaged in heavy fighting on the Eastern and Western fronts, often went a year or more without getting leave, Mr Stork was allowed to go home on leave at least once a fortnight, and often weekly – and he was promoted more rapidly than the rest of them at the front. A true Nazi, and a March Martyr to boot, a dyed-in-the-wool loyalist – a man such as that wears his superiority like an unseen badge wherever he goes: he performs a more important service for his Führer back here in the homeland than any non-Party members fighting at the front. Many people in our village were too ignorant to understand this; they resented the fact that he was always home on leave, while they didn't get to see their own sons or husbands from one year to the next. But the Storks rose above such benighted sentiments, and continued to show themselves most Sundays, walking arm in arm on the village street. For sheer shamelessness and effrontery, they had always been in a class of their own. They had always followed the principle that Nazi rules and regulations imposing restrictions and privations on the population, especially now in wartime, only applied to others, never to themselves. And they followed that principle here: if you've got it, flaunt it! Meanwhile, by all accounts, petitions were being furiously penned by husband, wife and friendly, lower-ranking bureaucrats, arguing the urgent need to reinstate Mr Stork in his old post as mayor. The new mayor, it was claimed, was just not up to the job, and some recent political appointees in the village were already displaying alarming red tendencies. Unfortunately the Wehrmacht, which is of course not an arm of the Party, showed not the slightest inclination to release Private, or indeed Corporal, Stork from the medical corps on the strength of these petitions. On the contrary, rumour has it that the army pulled him out of the orderly room and sent him out to some large troop training ground in the East. Whether he is fighting for his Führer there with pen in hand again, or whether they are getting him ready to be shipped out to a fighting unit – perhaps one day schoolmaster Stork's fondest wish will be fulfilled after all, and now in this fifth year of the war he will get to hear a shot fired again, or even – God forbid! – loose one off himself!

But in relating all this I am anticipating events that occurred much later in the life of our mayor. Before he joined the military, he spent another four years of the war in Mahlendorf, and you may depend upon it that he made full use of the time to inflate his own sense of power and humiliate the local residents he didn't like. Even before this he could hardly have complained about a shortage of powers, and he had already become the absolute master in Mahlendorf – apart from the occasional need to refer back to his superiors on this or that matter. But all this was as nothing compared with the power that the war placed in the hands of this bitter, resentful little coward. How it must have tickled Stork, suddenly to have the power of life and death placed in his hands! He sat on the draft board that conscripted people into the armed forces, and if the mayor cast his vote to the effect that such and such a man could or could not be spared from his farm, that frequently decided the matter. He had never learned the meaning of shame, Mr Stork, and it wasn't long before we saw his enemies leaving the village to go and fight – and in some cases die – at the front, while his friends stayed at home on their farms year after year because they were indispensable to the war effort! His opportunities for tormenting and harassing his fellow men, already far too numerous, now grew exponentially. The system of ration cards[157] that regulated everyone's provisions, and which now made the most basic needs of life dependent on a decision by the mayor, made him all-powerful. The way he approved or denied requests for new shoes for poor girls, the way he used a worn-out bicycle tyre as a pretext to wreak revenge, and the way he was so open and transparent about it all, so that the mean motives behind his refusal were always plain to see under the thin cloak of his expressions of regret – it was just disgusting! How much worry he caused my wife when the children had their school holidays and Stork refused to issue the ration cards for them on one pretext after another, making it harder and harder to get bread for them! Stupid as the mayor was, he was ingenious enough when it came to devising such torments and thinking up endless new pretexts, if not for denying the fulfilment of legitimate requests, then at least for delaying it, and not for a moment was his conscience troubled by thoughts of a worried mother or hungry children. There is one story that casts a glaring light on the utter viciousness of this swine, who was protected by his official position and those who had appointed him. Here it is. Living in the village was a small woman, very young and not unattractive, married to a farm mechanic who had been sent off to the front on the first day of mobilization. Mrs Schote was a shy, kindly thing with a two-year-old daughter, and nobody in the village had a bad word to say about her. She had always been hard-working and frugal, and her child could not have had a better mother. She had the misfortune to live in the same house as the wife of a farm labourer, a thoroughly disreputable woman, debauched from an early age, one of those creatures who seem to regard immorality and shameless brazenness as their natural element from the day they are born. This woman, a certain Mrs Kock, had only married her husband, a three-parts idiot, in order to have a father for the child she was expecting – as she told him straight after the wedding, laughing in his face. She was as ugly as sin, as vulgar as a street whore, and as work-shy as an old drunk. While the two husbands had been living in the house as well, these two very different parties had been at daggers drawn; they never spoke to each other, never even gave each other the time of day. Mrs Kock had developed a special knack for pushing and pinching her neighbour's little girl when nobody was looking.

But with the outbreak of war the relationship between these two very different women started to change. They grew closer, they spoke to each other, they even formed a kind of friendship. Heaven knows how that came about! Mrs Schote would have been welcome company anywhere in the village – in the houses of ordinary folk, at least – but nobody wanted anything to do with Mrs Kock. It was probably Mrs Kock who initiated the rapprochement. With what she had in mind, she didn't want a spy in the house; and an accomplice would not spill the beans. And the shy little woman, lonely and abandoned, probably didn't dare to resist her coarse, vulgar neighbour; feeling defenceless and vulnerable, she knew her life would be hell if she didn't do what her neighbour wanted. That's how it must have started; later on, having once tasted of the forbidden fruit, she no doubt went along with it willingly enough. A rumour gradually spread through the village of indecent goings-on in the house of the two soldiers' wives. It was said that they received male visitors, and there was talk of night-time revelries too. In actual fact this was something that didn't concern anyone apart from those immediately involved, i.e. the two husbands, who were far away. But a village, and especially one that stands isolated on a peninsula, cut off from every breath of fresh life, has no such qualms, and is grateful for every bit of new gossip. When people started talking about these two women it wasn't long, of course, before the story reached the ears of our worthy mayor. It was no business of his either, whether in his capacity as mayor or as a private individual, and he promptly declared that he was not interested in Mrs Kock, allegedly because her immorality, renowned throughout the village, was ingrained and incurable, but in truth because he was afraid of her sharp, vulgar tongue. But he took a very different view of Mrs Schote's involvement. He lamented her youth and inexperience, set himself up to act on behalf of her husband in the field, and voiced dark fears that the nocturnal male visitors might be prisoners of war, with whom

Germans were forbidden to consort on pain of imprisonment. In short, he once again had no difficulty in finding reasons why he should poke his nose into somebody else's business, which, foul-smelling as it was, didn't concern him in the slightest. And having satisfied himself in this way that intervention was required, the coward picked a man from the village to assist him, an obnoxious old bachelor with a notoriously dissolute past of his own, and the two of them took up sentry duty outside the house of the two women at 9.30 in the evening. They had waited barely half an hour when two men did indeed slip into the house – not prisoners of war, not even men from Mahlendorf, but two soldiers whose job it was to guard POWs working on a nearby estate. The two spies now moved into position at the window of the one room where light was showing; because the blackout curtains did not close properly, and the old window frames no longer formed a tight seal, they were able to observe everything going on in the room and hear practically every word that was spoken. They were gratified to note how affectionately the two guardsmen were received by the two amorous women, how they took a bottle of wine and packs of cigarettes out of their pockets while the two women served up coffee and home-made cakes. They exchanged a running commentary in eager whispers, carefully noting every kiss, every cooing laugh, every fiery glance. But they soon discovered that they were not alone in enjoying the spectacle of these amorous dalliances. As is the way in village life, the news that the mayor was bent on putting a stop to the immorality of the POWs had spread from house to house in the immediate neighbourhood, and soon the two male observers were joined by half a dozen female ones, mostly old women, but there were also two young girls of sixteen and seventeen. As the hours passed, and the initial caresses and endearments turned into something altogether more serious and intense, and the amorous discourse of the lovelorn couples grew ever more explicit, the party assembled outside the window became steadily more boisterous and unrestrained. Each in turn excitedly pushed the other away from his (or her) listening post at the window, and spluttering with barely suppressed laughter they told each other in whispers what they had just seen; and mayor Stork, who had come here to keep watch in the name of morality and as the guardian of innocence, voiced no misgivings whatsoever about the fact that young girls were participating in this spectacle, shoving him aside and breathlessly following the cavortings with shining eyes. It was a classic Breughelesque scene from rural life, the natural product of wholesome living in a village, on the land, where, according to our Führer and his henchmen, all is purity, innocence and glowing health! No Darré[158] could have painted a more persuasive picture!

The lascivious snoopers held out at the window from 9.30 in the evening until 4.30 in the morning; even when the lights had gone out they stayed on – for there were still words to be heard, kisses to be counted and sighs to be recorded. The mayor justified this refusal to leave by claiming that he intended to confront the two adulterous soldiers who were abusing the wives of fighting men, and report them to their commanding officer. But when the two soldiers appeared at first light and hurried off through the village towards their estate, our hero, needless to say, didn't even have the courage to go up and speak to them. Instead he comforted himself and the others waiting with him with the thought that at least they knew who was involved, and that it was perhaps best not to get into an altercation right now, at this early hour of the morning. If the story so far gives ample insight into the dark depths of this exceptionally nasty character, then what he did next must condemn him even in the eyes of those whom he represented: the Party faithful. Or it should have: but they kept him on and allowed him to operate – to the greater glory of the Führer and the Party. The thing is, Stork did not summon the women to him and give them a warning, but left them to find out about the nocturnal spying activities from village gossip. Instead of speaking to them, he sat down and wrote a long letter to the husband serving at the front, in which he 'felt duty-bound' to inform him of his young wife's behaviour, taking care to assure him that he was not just passing on idle gossip, but that he, the mayor of the village, had personally witnessed these things. What the poor fellow, who was in love with his wife and fighting for his life on the Eastern front, went through when he read this letter we shall never know. But he was killed seven or eight weeks later. In the end, what dealt him the mortal blow was not a Russian bullet but the unbelievably cruel letter from the Nazi mayor; his wife heard nothing more from him after he received that letter. Vicious and cowardly people have always existed in the world, but it is the peculiar prerogative of the Nazi Party to have deliberately used such people as an instrument of their rule, promoting them to high office and inciting them to enslave their fellow citizens, giving them encouragement and rewards. Filth at the top and filth at the bottom, and everything plastered with empty slogans in which divine providence features prominently.

My family and I would have got off too lightly if Stork had been content to leave it at the minor torments I mentioned earlier. I hadn't spoken to him for ages, and if there was any business between us, my wife took care of it. I knew he hated me, and he had said often enough that he would get me one day. Fate dealt him one or two very good cards, and for weeks and months on end it looked as though I really was done for. During the war I had taken on an old gardener,[159] a man of nearly seventy, but still very glad of the work, well recommended by his former employers and personable enough in his demeanour. For a while things went very well with this man, we were well satisfied on both sides, and my wife and I were already saying how fortunate we were to have found such a good worker – when the problems began. The old gardener seemed to have taken against one of our young girls, and every time she brought him his meal there was always something wrong; sometimes he claimed he'd been given margarine instead of butter, and then the complaint was that she'd eaten the salami off his plate. (Which didn't make a lot of sense, since she had access to the whole salami, and therefore hardly needed to help herself to the slices on his piece of bread.) A few days later he had to wait five minutes for his supper, but instead of waiting he left and went home hungry. Next morning he showered me with angry reproaches. I let him carry on working and going without food. I tried to reassure him, and I succeeded once, twice; but the third time there were angry words from me too, he threatened me with a mattock, and I fired him on the spot. He went straight to the mayor and denounced me. He accused me of a whole series of offences and crimes contrary to wartime economic regulations: I was said to have claimed double my allocation of ration cards, bought and sold grain illegally, obtained coal entitlements by fraud – there were eight charges in all.

When this war began, my wife and I, who had both gone hungry in the previous war, had sworn that we would do everything possible in this war, including things that were strictly forbidden, in order to put food on the table for our children and ourselves, and that's exactly what I had done. It was not my war they were fighting, I did not wish Hitler's armies to be victorious, so I had not the slightest reason to respect the economic needs of this war. In short, the old snooper and spy had observed correctly: I had indeed committed all the offences and crimes that were now laid at my door, and a long prison or jail sentence now seemed certain. I need hardly add that these denunciations were grist to the mayor's mill. He sprang into action, interrogated half the village, and told everyone that Fallada was now going to jail. But I had not been idle myself, having got wind of this denunciation almost before it happened. I had spoken to my suppliers and agreed on our stories: we admitted everything that could not be denied, but contrived to cloak it all with a mantle of innocence. Meanwhile I had written to the old gardener's previous employers and asked for information about him – something I really should have done before hiring him. What lay behind those glowing references, it now turned out, were sundry attempts to offload a vexatious employee onto others by singing his praises. Every time he had been dismissed for making defamatory allegations; every time he had conceived a furious hatred for some female or other; every time he had harboured absurd suspicions against these girls or women; and every time he had ended up, as a long-standing Party member, by denouncing his employer to the authorities. The surmise of one particular employer, that the old man was suffering from advanced hardening of the cerebral arteries and was half-cracked, was particularly opportune: I made application for the 'sick' informer to be examined by the local medical officer.

I've told far too many stories already, so I won't go into great detail again. Suffice it to say that the battle went on for years, with interrogations, reports, house searches, claims and counterclaims. I fought the battle with utter determination, not for a single moment deterred by the thought that I was indeed guilty according to the strict letter of the law. I saw myself as innocent, and the laws passed by this criminal government could never have any authority whatsoever over me. By their definition, what I thought, and often enough said, ranked as high treason, and yet I knew that I was a decent man and a better German than the lot of them. But more than anything I did not want to hand them the right to haul me up before their courts as a delinquent caught in the act, to pass sentence on me in the name of a fraudulent legal system, and to condemn me. But ultimately – and this is perhaps what gave me the most strength – I was determined never to give my hated enemy, this mayor Stork, the satisfaction of seeing me laid low, brought down by his own hand! I went through many bitter times in this long battle, I lay awake brooding at night, I spent hours pacing up and down in my room working out my next moves. And throughout that time, with this sword hanging over my head, I blithely carried on supplying the needs of my smallholding by illegal means, under the spying eyes of half the village, I ran rings around these idiots, and refused to back off an inch. And what was the final outcome? On all eight counts the charges against me were dropped, either because I had done absolutely nothing illegal, or because nothing could be proved against me. All I got was a fine of fifty Reichsmarks for some technical violation. Stubborn as an ox, I even went and objected to this fine. And I won – the fine was revoked too. Oh how I laughed – and with what feelings of triumph I gazed into the jaundiced countenance of our mayor, too shamefaced to look me in the eye! I may not be the stuff of which soldiers in the field are made, but I can fight my wars and win my battles, in my own way.

(6.X.44.) We Germans felt the war in our bones long before it came. We kept on hoping that it could still be avoided, but somehow we never quite dared to believe it. It was already obvious before 1939 that Hitler had come to the end of his work-creation program. The Wehrmacht was now fully armed and equipped, and the countless factories with their vast numbers of workers would have to shut down, and unemployment would return, unless something new turned up. But what could that something new be? The something new that occurs to rulers in such situations is actually something very old, namely war, the father of all things, that insatiable destroyer that must be constantly fed – with work, with blood, with tears. What else was Hitler going to think of? Something really new? He never had a new idea in his life, his whole Party and its program was cribbed and cobbled together from the Fascism of Stalin and the Bolshevism of Russia. And the original mind of our brilliant Führer failed again when it came to solving the problem of unemployment: all he could come up with was war. One recalls the various stages along the way: the militarization of the Rhineland, the annexation of Austria, the Sudetenland adventure, Czechoslovakia. Each time he declared himself satisfied, only to come back with fresh demands. He wanted war – at any price. How he must have raged in his heart when people kept on giving in to him!

From the beginning I was very pessimistic. And so were many others. I recall one evening in Berlin when we'd been invited to the house of a doctor.[160] We talked about the future of Germany, and the spectre of the coming war weighed upon us like a dark shadow; even back then we were all certain that Germany would be defeated. (Evil cannot triumph.) What would become of the fatherland that we still loved so dearly? Memories of the occupation of the Ruhr and the excesses of the French[161] were still fresh in our minds, and the thought of the Russians with their primitive standard of living still made us feel very uneasy – little suspecting that in a few years' time Hitler's *Blitzkriege* would send our own standard of living plummeting to an all-time low. We talked it all over this way and that, mapping out the future we dreamt of. And we hoped for the future we wanted for Germany and for all true Germans. A journalist known for his caustic wit raised his index finger and whispered: 'One must always be prepared for the worst: we might lose the war and keep the Führer!' We laughed heartily. Then we agreed that the most desirable outcome, for us North Germans at least, would be to become a British mandated territory. The British would not interfere with the real substance of our cultural life. We would have to work hard and go without a lot of things, that much was clear. But it would be bearable. We would be more free under the rule of the British than under Hitler's brownshirts. It's strange when I think back to that evening, how we really were all of one mind. But when the war broke out in earnest, and the fast-moving campaigns in Poland, France and the Balkans were under way, and the radio carried 'special bulletins' almost daily about the latest brilliant successes of our armies, most people just rolled over. They listened as if besotted to these siren strains, forgetting completely that if these conquests ever ended in final victory, their lives would not be freer as a result, and the only beneficiaries would be the Hitler elite. Suddenly they believed every word of the official announcements, and argued passionately against me when I pointed out that the propaganda of Dr Goebbels was unlikely to be more truthful in time of war than it was in peacetime. It took several more years of war before these besotted dupes did another about-turn, and it was actually the increasingly heavy air raids on German cities that undermined their morale. But they now disowned the view that the best outcome for Germany would be to become a mandated territory under British rule. They were ashamed of such thoughts; somehow it was all right to think such things in peacetime, but not now, in time of war, when German boys were shedding their blood in every country across Europe. I have never shared this woolly, sentimental view. I wanted the Nazis to be defeated, and the sooner the better. Under no circumstances did I want Germany to become the dominant power in Europe: with the rise of National Socialism the country had just given another spectacular demonstration of its political immaturity. A nation that fell for every beguiling slogan without thinking for itself was not yet ready to become the leader of other nations.

But since Hitler's power could only be broken by losing the war – the Germans would never rid themselves of this tyrant by their own efforts – every additional drop of blood that was shed at the front brought the desired goal a fraction closer. The words of a Viennese film director,[162] spoken at the time of our terrible losses at Stalingrad, sounded shocking in their brutality, and yet he got it exactly right: 'A lot more blood needs to be spilt yet! Whole divisions must perish! Every man who dies out there is one less follower for the Führer! And if they are all killed, I for one shall rejoice.'

Around the time of the Sudetenland adventure[163] I was ordered to report for a medical examination at my local army recruiting office – the first time since 1914. I was determined not to play along with this soldiering lark. The army medical was very thorough as far as the externals were concerned: height and weight were measured, every missing or damaged tooth was carefully noted, and a painstaking check was made for haemorrhoids. The actual medical examination took much less time. The doctor, barely more than a boy, just placed his stethoscope on my chest and listened to my heartbeat. That was it. I took it upon myself to point out that I suffered with my nerves. He waved a dismissive hand: 'Not a problem!' I ploughed on regardless, and told him that in the First World War I had been discharged from the service after eleven days as permanently unfit for duty. He asked me: 'What are you – a writer? You'll be amazed how much good physical activity will do you. We don't recognize nervous conditions! Next!' I had to leave, and the note in my service record book said 'Fit for restricted duties'. I was determined not to accept this finding. I was working for some film company or other at the time, and I persuaded them to give me a certificate signed with the name 'Dr Goebbels', confirming that my work was important for the war effort and requesting that I be exempted for the time being from all military service. I submitted this certificate along with a request for a second examination by a medical specialist, citing my nervous disorder. And sure enough, I was called in for a second examination. The doctor appointed to carry it out was, if anything, even younger than his predecessor, and he was certainly no specialist. He confirmed as much himself, being somewhat more communicative than his predecessor. 'We don't carry out any examinations other than the purely physical one', he explained. 'But surely', I said, 'that means you'll be conscripting schizophrenics, epileptics, paraplegics and God knows who else!'

'So what?' he replied, without missing a beat. 'Some of them turn out to be excellent soldiers. And the rest, who are no good for anything, we just send home again. It makes no difference!' I took the view that it made quite a lot of difference, but I could see there was no future in arguing the point. I later discovered that people with hereditary diseases and those who had been sterilized by law were also conscripted into the military; although they were not worthy to beget children for the fatherland, they were welcome to die for the fatherland! I took my old service record book[164] out of my pocket and showed the doctor the entry confirming that I had been discharged after just eleven days of service, and had never had an army medical since. 'And I think you'll find that I haven't got any healthier in the intervening twenty-five years.' He just smiled, said vaguely: 'We'll see!' and set about examining me physically. He conducted a painstaking check for haemorrhoids, then placed his stethoscope against my chest and listened to my heart. His face took on an unexpected expression, he listened more closely, and then he murmured: 'You've got a serious heart defect!' He reeled off a few numbers to his clerk. And with that I was dismissed. I had to fetch my papers from the local army recruiting office. In the orderly room all the young sergeants and NCOs had a go at me. It seemed that my request for a follow-up examination by a specialist had touched a collective raw nerve. Here was one more thing, apparently, that was no longer allowed in Nazi Germany. 'You'll never be signed off unfit!' shouted a young sergeant. 'You're as fit as a fiddle, you are!' I really should have congratulated him on his X-ray vision, which had obviously discovered this through my clothing, but fortunately the door to the next room opened at this moment, and the major in charge of the recruiting office, disturbed by all the noise, stuck his head round the door and roared 'Quiet!!' Then he pointed to me: 'Who's this?'

'He's the one who requested the follow-up examination, sir!'

'I see!' For some time I was fixed with a rigid stare through the doorway; only the head of the major had joined us in the orderly room, his body stayed behind in the holy of holies. Then he waved to me: 'Come inside!' I was even permitted to take a seat in front of his desk. 'So you write novels and films?' he asked after scrutinizing me afresh. 'I've never heard of you.'

'No harm done, Major!' I reassured him.

He searched among the papers on his desk. As he searched he looked up again and asked: 'So is it worth it? Can you make a living from it?'

'Oh yes, Major!' I said. 'You can – or at least, I can.'

'Curious', he said. 'Very curious. I'd never have thought it.' Finally he found the piece of paper he was looking for, I recognized it straightaway: it was my certificate with the signature of Dr Goebbels. 'See here', said the major, tapping the sheet of paper with his hand. 'What your Dr Goebbels writes here is of no interest to us in the Wehrmacht. As far as we're concerned, he can write twenty letters, and we'll put you in the army all the same. We're not a bit interested in Dr Goebbels.' The major's voice was now sounding really annoyed; Dr Goebbels did not seem to be regarded with any great fondness in the Wehrmacht. Thank God, an orderly now brought in my service record book, with the note on the result of my follow-up examination. The major glanced at it. 'Fit for restricted duties', he read. 'Well, that settles it as far as we in the Wehrmacht are concerned. You won't get called for another medical unless there's a war.' I felt happy. The fact that the latest examination had shown that I had a serious heart defect didn't trouble me at all. Prior to this I had had the healthiest heart in the world, and as I soon established through a private follow-up examination, I still did. So the question is, did the young doctor make a genuine mistake, or did he make an *intentional* mistake in order to do me a favour? In any event, the Wehrmacht was no longer my concern. 'I expect you're pleased that you don't have to join the army?' the major suddenly asked me. He sounded quite kindly, more curious than anything. 'I'd have been nothing but trouble, Major', I replied. 'I'll never make a decent soldier as long as I live.' 'Curious! Very curious!' he said, and signed my service record book, deep in thought. 'Someone who'd rather write books than be a soldier – I'd never have thought it!'

He looked at me again, shaking his head. He gave me my service record book, and even shook my hand as we parted. To him I must have seemed a very rare and unusual specimen of mankind, a sort of museum curiosity.

A few years passed before I was called before another army selection board, and by now there really was a war on – in fact we were well into the war and it was 1944. I was told to report for a medical examination. This had already happened a few times, but so far I had managed to avoid it by reporting myself as 'sick'. But now I wanted to get this examination behind me once and for all. This constant threat hanging over me – of having to join up and fight – was irritating me more and more the longer it went on. I knew – everyone knew – that these army medicals were just a sham. The army needed more men, and it didn't care where they came from or what condition they were in. This new round of army medicals had already been dubbed 'the heroes' review board'. I was more determined than ever not to be reviewed as a hero. At the time I was in a bad way, mentally as well as physically. I looked terrible and I had lost a lot of weight. Nonetheless I decided to make a special effort for the army doctor this time and to prep myself for a diagnosis of 'heart defect'. I still had a few caffeine tablets, which I swallowed before reporting for the medical. At the door of the school where we had to assemble I met the army doctor who was conducting the examinations. We shook hands warmly. 'So you're one of my victims today!' he exclaimed with a laugh. I entered the classroom and began mechanically to undress. 'I'm screwed!!' I thought to myself. 'I'm screwed even before the examination begins!' The army doctor had been our family GP some years earlier, and we had not parted on good terms. As sometimes happens, doctor and patient had disagreed slightly over the treatment for an illness. 'He's never forgiven you', I said to myself. 'Now he's going to get his revenge. It's so easy for him: heroes' review board!' And already I saw myself as a raw recruit, doing things I hated, bawled at, hounded from pillar to post . . . We were all 'old' men gathered for this medical, all of us over fifty. Damn it, we weren't exactly a bunch of Greek gods! I simply couldn't imagine how these emaciated or overweight figures could be turned into soldiers. Yet I learned afterwards that of the hundred or more men who were examined during those days, only four were rejected as completely unfit for duty; all the rest were 'fit for restricted duties' or at least serviceable in some capacity. I entered the room where the draft board was sitting. At one end of the room was the board itself, consisting of officers, clerks, a few journalists, the mayors of the villages whose men were up before the board. At the other end of the room was the examining doctor. I had to wait, sitting half-naked on a bench. I noticed that our miller, a jaundiced, liverish man, was wearing a brightly coloured lady's bathing costume. Ah yes – the wearing of bathing costumes is permitted for 'awkward' people, and since our miller has never been swimming in his life, he has probably borrowed his wife's. For a moment I had to laugh: he just looked too comical, this man with thin, weedy arms and a yellow bird-like head, and below that the blue and red bathing costume, much too big for him of course! But then I grew serious again, and morose. 'I've had it', I thought to myself, and eyed the doctor with aversion. 'He'll check me out good and proper!' My heart, stimulated by the caffeine, was pounding like a trip hammer, it was really bothersome. 'What's up with you?' asked the doctor, looking at me askance in a most friendly way through his big, rimless glasses. 'Oh', I answered without thinking, allowing my bad mood to get the better of me. 'I'm done for, I'm sick of my life.' The doctor looked at me for a moment, then nodded. 'We're rejecting this man', he said, looking across to his clerk. 'Totally unfit for duty.'

By now my heart was beating so loudly that everyone in the room must have heard it. My precious caffeine – I could have saved it for when I had some difficult work to do, he didn't even listen to my heart! Discharged as unfit – so we'd managed to get out of that war too! Terrific! And when the next one comes along they won't even bother with me. A decent fellow after all, the doctor! He didn't take his revenge – some people are more decent than you think, but it's rare, very rare. Usually it's the other way round.

I stood before the colonel, the chairman of the heroes' review board. He was writing something in my service record book. 'So here we have Mr Fallada', he said, and gave me a friendly look. '*Little Man – What Now?*'? I nodded and was free to go. I no longer had a service record book, I had finally been written off by the German Wehrmacht. Half an hour later I was sitting in the hotel of our local small town, demolishing a plate of roast beef with raisin sauce accompanied by a youngish Bordeaux. And sitting at the large table across from me were the gentlemen from the draft board, also eating and drinking. I caught the doctor's eye, and raised my glass in greeting. He returned the greeting, smiling through his rimless glasses. It occurred to me that I had deceived the good doctor: I wasn't sick of my life after all, or at any rate, life felt good again now. Not bad at all, despite the fact that we were now in the fifth year of the war.

Back before in the last days of August 1939, when the dark storm clouds were gathering ever more menacingly over our heads, our eldest son, a boy of ten, was in Berlin. The easy-going teaching practices of his Nazi teachers had left him insufficiently prepared for the grammar school entrance exam, so we had had to send him to a school in Berlin for a year, where the teachers were rather more interested in their job and less interested in the gossip on the streets. But as what we all feared came to seem ever more inevitable, we decided to fetch the boy home to us for the time being – and never mind his schooling. Who could tell how things would turn out? My wife and I got the car out of the garage and made our last journey in peacetime. It was a lovely late summer day, the roads were almost empty, and we passed very few cars coming the other way. In the villages we saw people standing around by the public loudspeakers; as we passed they stared at us in silence, with an air of disapproval. No doubt the ever-diligent Joseph Goebbels had put the word out again: 'the entire German nation is gathered around the loudspeakers', and here we were again, conspicuously failing to gather. We were always stepping out of line. We were never in the vanguard of 'national comrades'.

But as we drove through the open countryside outside the villages, where the fields lay so quiet and deserted, and saw the stooks of corn standing there, waiting to be harvested, the sky stretching away so high and blue above us and the sun shining so warm and bright; as we saw the woods standing there in solemn silence, with only the warning cry of the jay occasionally shattering the stillness; and as we drove over bridges and saw the little rivers and streams below us, the clear waters purling swiftly over the gravel bed – it seemed to us impossible that this beautiful world might at any moment be plunged into a nightmare of blood and destruction! We looked at each other and said: 'Maybe it will pass us by again!' We couldn't believe it, but we wanted so much to hope again . . . This peaceful, beautiful world – why, oh why? The earth has room enough for us all – why, oh why? 'But what if it doesn't pass us by?' we said. 'Then we won't let this war speak for us two', we promised each other. 'If at all possible, we'll carry on living as if the war didn't exist.' We looked at each other again, and made each other a firm promise. It wasn't our fault that things worked out differently, that the war dragged us both in and changed us, that it destroyed our beautiful, peaceful world . . . Not our fault. Nobody can live through five years of war, and under a regime like that, without being changed. In the later years of the war especially, when the air raids got so bad, I sometimes played a kind of game, trying to imagine, as I was falling asleep, how we would have survived the war if I had foreseen what was to come . . . In my dream I construct a passageway from the cellar of our house in Mahlendorf, descending deep down into the earth, and I seal it off with nine secret doors, invisible even to the most practised eye, like something out of a classic Edgar Wallace novel.[165] But this is no hideous, dark tunnel of bare earth: an elegant flight of stone steps leads downwards, the walls are covered with stars, and electric lights are built into the vaulted ceiling. At the bottom you enter a fine antechamber, stepping straight from that into the vast living and working space, twenty metres below the ground. The walls are lined from top to bottom with books, of course, my beloved books, but there are also cupboards containing games for the children, there's a sewing corner for my wife, complete with sewing machine, and there's an open shelf with a huge stack of crossword puzzle magazines specially for my mother. But as a room with no windows would remind us constantly that we are living here deep in the bowels of the earth, which over time would be likely to affect our mood adversely, windows have naturally been provided. One of them looks out onto Potsdamer Platz in Berlin, another overlooks the square in front of Hamburg's Town Hall, and another has a view of the Outer Alster as seen from the Lombardsbrücke causeway. At the push of a button the people and cars and cyclists in these little panoramas come to life and start to move, the white steamers on the Alster ply busily from landing stage to landing stage, and the white sails of the yachts are unfurled. But perhaps the best thing is a set of three adjacent windows that house large aquariums. Wondrous fish, shimmering and brightly coloured, are slowly gliding between green water plants, a lobster is scurrying across the sand floor towards his hiding place in a pile of rocks, and sea anemones unfold their naked life. When we tire of all these sights, we make our own night; we draw the yellow silk curtains shut, and now the children are allowed to read for half an hour before they go to bed. Naturally arrangements have been made to ensure that the air in our subterranean home is not bad or stale: a ventilation system designed to introduce fresh air has one pipe reaching far out into the beech forest of the river island, where the intake is concealed among boulders in some inaccessible spot. The pipe brings fresh, clean forest air into our quarters. But we can also sniff the breeze that blows higher up: another pipe terminates on the highest hill in our area, hidden in an impenetrable thicket of blackthorn. The hill is only 126 metres high, but it often blows quite hard up there: we are bound to catch a little bit of that breeze down there in our home. And of course we have our cosy bedrooms down there, a fully electric kitchen, and then a whole series of storerooms, containing enough supplies for the next ten years: food, clothing, wine and tobacco, shoes, including things in larger sizes to allow for the children's growth. Naturally we have our own electricity generating plant and endless fuel bunkers for the diesel oil that drives the generators. The drainage system posed quite a few challenges, but this problem was also solved. We don't have just the one exit, you see, leading up to the cellar of our house – we have two other exits, for use in emergencies. One of them leads up to a sandpit, ending in a wall of sand just a metre and a half thick which only has to be shovelled away, and then we are outside. But the other emergency exit climbs gradually uphill and brings us to the lake, terminating in a small dock where a fast motorboat is moored ready for our escape; the gate that opens onto the water is possibly even more cunningly concealed than the door in our cellar, and underneath it runs our drainage pipe, which discharges into the water at the bottom of the lake. Our sewage is pumped through this pipe under pressure. It's all been carefully planned and worked out down to the last detail, and we would want for nothing even if the war were to last for ten years. There was no need to cut corners on the cost, so I was generous and set aside no less than 20 million of my own money for the fitting-out of our subterranean shelter.

And now imagine that on the first day of the war the Fallada family – father, mother and children – had shut up their house and announced that they were going on their travels. They had disappeared, lost in the upheaval of the great German war, nowhere to be found. Inside their house a layer of dust collects on the furniture, the garden is overgrown with weeds, and in the yard the grass is sprouting in the cracks between the flagstones. 'Where can the Falladas be?' people are asking. And the answer will be: 'They must have fled abroad!'

In reality, though, we are installed in our underground palace, and it should not be supposed that we are living a life of idleness down there! On the contrary, we have plenty to do. Each day is completely filled. While my wife has more than enough to do keeping the place clean, cooking the meals, washing and mending clothes, I'm in charge of the technical side of things. I look after the electricity generators, get the pump going, fire up the dynamo – and when all that is done I go into the passageway outside the windows and aerate the aquariums, feed the fish and dust off the Outer Alster with all its bits and pieces. Meanwhile the older children are sweeping the passageways, and when they have finished that they sit in the motorboat and tell each other stories about the world outside, where they once lived, and which is gradually becoming a fading memory for them as the months go by. They say words like 'sun' and 'moon', and tell each other everything they know about them. Then I come and turn them out and fetch them into the living room, where it's time for school lessons, and as the years pass I find it harder to explain to them all the things that are out there in the world: trees, and countries, and oceans. I look at our youngest, so absorbed in playing with his toys down here, who can no longer remember the world up above, and I wonder how I shall teach him, my very own Kaspar Hauser . . . Such is our life, and the months slip by, and we try to forget that a jinxed war is raging outside. Once a year, though, we put a mild sleeping draught in the children's soup at supper-time, and when they are sleeping soundly we two parents creep quietly up the stairs to the cellar door; there we wait, listening for any sound, and then we gently open the door and enter the cellar of our old house. The rats and mice scurry away, the floor is littered with dry leaves, blown in through a broken window by the wind, which rustle softly as we walk across the room. Cobwebs hang down before our eyes and get caught up in our hair. We climb the steps, but we do not enter the rooms where we once lived and were happy – we prefer not to see them in their present sorry state. We step straight out into the yard, breathing in deep lungfuls of fresh air, which I have to say is sweeter than our filtered forest air down below, and for a long time we gaze up at the stars, twinkling and shining, and we feel our hearts beating and we whisper: 'How lovely! How magnificent!' Then we head on deeper into the dark, blacked-out village, and we find that nothing has changed, everything looks exactly the same as it did a year ago. We don't see the war, don't feel it, don't taste it – only the blacked-out windows everywhere tell us that the war is still going on. We whisper quietly to each other, and ask ourselves if we are doing the right thing by robbing our children and ourselves of the chance to breathe freely and live a real life, keeping them in an artificial world with all these toys and gadgets. And then I remind my wife what kind of man our village schoolteacher is, and how he didn't scruple to show photos of butchered Germans, murdered by the Poles, to eight- and ten-year-old children, photos full of shocking, hideous details, designed to teach the children to hate the Poles from an early age. 'We're protecting them from all that, and from much worse!' say I. 'But afterwards, will they be able to live in the other world again afterwards, when they've not stood up to the wind for so long, and not been hardened by any kind of resistance?' says my wife. And we walk on, until we reach the other lake, and hear the waves lapping over the sand, while the wild ducks quack softly in the reeds. 'It's time to go back', says Suse, and we wander back home through the sleeping village. We also go into the orchard – it's autumn by now, and the village youngsters have actually left us some apples on our trees. We pick what we can, filling every pocket as well as Suse's skirts. We make our way through the sleeping, echoing house, through the secret door, and down the steps again to our hidden home, our refuge from the war. At first the descent seems harder and harder with every step I take, it feels as if we are entering a prison. But then, as we stand beside our children's beds while they are fast asleep, and as we place a few apples on the chair beside them, we just say: 'This is the right thing to do! We're saving them from so much!' And then the next day, this glorious day, almost better than Christmas, when the children find the red-cheeked apples next to their beds, and the youngest one doesn't even know that you're supposed to eat it, and wants to play ball with it instead – he hasn't seen fresh fruit before. We get all our food out of tins and jars and from various types of grains, and our vitamin requirements are supplied in the form of tablets, taken in accordance with a plan carefully drawn up by doctors. And then we have to explain to them that the apples are for eating, and we tell them about the gardens that grow in the light, about the wells, the rain, the sun, the bees that pollinate the flowers, about the clouds that sail across the land, and they listen intently to us as we listened to fairy stories when we were children. Now that is a very special day indeed. But sometimes when I am falling asleep I imagine other things entirely, as if to prove to myself that it is necessary to live like this in the bowels of the earth. I imagine that we cannot open the cellar door, something has wedged itself against it, and so we have to use the emergency exit to the lake. We then discover that not only our house but the whole village is burnt out and in ruins, abandoned by every living soul. And now begins a very different life for us and the children: we carry on living in our refuge, but we also live up above, among the abandoned ruins. We find a few animals that have been gassed: a goat, a few rabbits, some hens. But we have to keep a sharp lookout for enemy aircraft, and also for marauding gangs of people. Once we nearly get caught, at the last moment we manage to snatch our youngest away, almost under the noses of our pursuers, and escape down to our refuge. For weeks on end we dare not venture out again, because the search is on for the people who vanished so mysteriously.

There are many dreams that can be triggered by the idea of 'refuge', such as the one where one of our children gets out through a door that has been carelessly left open, and where we only manage to get him back again after much fighting and searching and braving many dangers. And then there's the dream where we are besieged in our refuge by Hitler's men, and we are left with no choice but to blow up all the emergency exits,

(7.X.44.) the passageways collapse, and now we really are cut off from the world outside, living forgotten and abandoned in the bowels of the earth. But when a long period of time has passed, many months later, we set to work to clear one of the passageways with shovels. We face immense difficulties and hardships; the earth caves in, large boulders, too heavy for us to lift, block our path, and the main problem is always: where are we going to put the spoil? We have to sacrifice one room after another, we are living on top of each other in an increasingly confined space, and it's still a long way to the exit. Then disaster strikes and I am buried by falling earth, Suse and the children work frantically to dig me out. But for a long time after that I lie ill, and just can't seem to recover properly. How long have we been living down here? Years and years!

What is the world like outside now? Peaceful? Has the thousand-year Reich finally collapsed? We look into each other's faces, which have become so pale and translucent, and only when I compare how we look with the coloured pictures of people in books do I realize how much we have changed. And then the day finally comes when we reach the exit. We are standing in our cellar, but the broken window has been replaced, there are no more rustling leaves underfoot, the spiders have been banished, and the shelves have been filled again with neatly organized supplies. We look into each other's faces, and take each other by the hand: 'How my heart is pounding!'

'Mine too!'

'Does this mean peace?!'

'New life in our old house!'

'Quiet! Listen!'

And we can clearly hear a child crying upstairs. We stand there, tears welling up in our eyes. A child is crying, children are being born again, not in order to be torn to pieces in hideous wars, but for the sake of a better future! But we dare not go upstairs, we retreat back down to our refuge. We look at each other. We've become so scared over the years! We're afraid of the people who have endured all the things that we fled from. We're afraid of the bright daylight, the loud laughter, a harsh word. We're afraid of the gaze of other people: even to each other we look like ghosts now. If it was just ourselves, we would remain in this self-imposed isolation. But we have to think of the children – children whose nerves, like ours, have become stretched thin as gossamer, whose ears would flinch at every loud noise, whose eyes would be dazzled by the daylight.

But then one day there we are, outside in the garden of our house, with our children. It is a very dull morning, at the start of summer, before sunrise. The strangers living in the house, our house, are still asleep. The children are really enjoying being outside in the open air, every flower, every blade of grass excites them and prompts a hundred questions. The birds are stirring, and in our shed a cow moos. More excitement, more questions! And then all of a sudden, close to where

I am standing, the door from the house onto the veranda is pushed open, and a tall, slim woman is standing in the doorway. She looks at us, hesitantly, questioningly. Suse and I get up and walk towards her. We look at each other. We see a look of horrified astonishment spread across her face, we must look very different, and move very differently, from the normal human population. I try to speak, I want to ask what I already know, I just want to say: 'It's peacetime again, isn't it?' But all that comes out of my throat are strange, distorted sounds, suddenly I break into sobs, tears well from my eyes, I am weeping, all I can do is weep. The woman is leaning back, her body pressed against the doorframe, her hand is laid on her heart and her eyes are wide open and staring. 'I know', she whispers. 'I know who you are. You are the buried ones that people talk about round here. You are the ones who were buried alive, and now you have risen from the dead!' She stares at us again. 'It's you', she says again. 'I can tell by looking at you. Buried alive. How could you do it? How could you do that to your children?' Suddenly she turns round and picks up a large bowl from the table on the veranda, which is piled high with red cherries. She calls out in a loud voice: 'Come here, children! I've got some cherries here. Cherries for you to eat!' And our children, ignoring us completely, run straight past us to this unknown woman.

Among the many dreams that I dream at night during this time of war, which would fill more than one stout volume if I were to relate them in detail, is one that I should at least mention briefly, because it is so different from the ones I have recounted so far. Our underground refuge features in this dream too, but in addition to the rooms I've already described there is another passageway, a long passageway lined with cells, proper prison cells. When we move into our refuge they are all empty, but gradually they fill up. By a combination of guile and brute force I manage to capture all my worst enemies and lock them up in these cells, starting of course with mayor Stork and his wife, but also including quite a few others who became my enemies, such as the small farmer Mechthal. I lock them all up, and to all my other occupations I now add that of jailer. I keep them there year after year, nobody ever speaks to them, all they ever hear is the sound of their own voice. I feed them, dressed in a long, dark robe and with a black mask over my face. And I see how the engrained brutality of mayor Stork starts to break down, how this pitiful scrap of a human being now stands naked before me in all his wretchedness. I hear him screaming and crying, praying and cursing. I have made a gramophone recording, and the record catalogues every villainous deed of his known to me: listening at the window of Mrs Schote, his cowardly victory, dodging war service, withholding ration cards, denying people new shoes – there is so much to list that one record actually isn't large enough. On many days I put this record on, and the litany of all his crimes is relayed through the microphone in his cell day and night, night and day, until he begins to scream in agony, rant and rave, beat the walls of his cell and bang his head against the steel door. But when he wakes from his dazed state, the gramophone is still playing the same record, he has no more tears, all that's left to him is despair. He sits there, silent and stupefied, occasionally raising his forefinger and nodding, and sometimes laughing quietly to himself. That's how I deal with him, that's my way of pre-empting divine retribution, which is far too lenient. His wife, on the other hand, I feed up with all manner of fattening foods, I stuff her and force-feed her the way one stuffs and force-feeds a goose, and I get her to the point where this once-mercurial woman just sits in her bed like a lump of fat, virtually immobilized, and unable to think of anything except food. And then I put the couple together in the same cell and watch the burning hatred erupt between them, between the greedy, overfed woman, who begrudges her jaundiced little husband every mouthful, and the half-broken liar, constantly pestered by his scheming, self-satisfied wife. This too is one of my dreams. But I'm ashamed of it really, which is why I have related it here – precisely because I am ashamed of it.

But what does it all signify? Is it just the pathetic attempt of a weakling who can't handle everyday life to escape into a world of dreams? I fight my corner stoutly enough by day, I don't avoid confrontations. They often cost me a lot of nervous energy, and I hate them – but I stand my ground. No, this is no cowardly flight on my part. But it is like an island, to which I return in the evening in my boat after a hard day's work, and where I can be alone with myself and those who are dear to me. I never felt so strongly as I did under Hitler's rule that when a man's very survival is constantly under threat, he needs somewhere to escape to with his hopes and dreams. An inner certainty that one day the evil enemy will have lost the game is not enough to get us through the worst of times. Because we need strength each day to endure the constant little stings and torments of everyday life, we have to have something that gives us this new strength one day at a time. A distant certainty is good – but also distant. My dream of a refuge deep in the bowels of the earth takes me away from my enemies each day, and strengthens me for the day to come. I was alone, and down here, twenty metres below ground, I'm out of reach. Here the banned books line the shelves, the walls are hung with degenerate art, and traitorous thoughts run through my brain – free from interference! Here is the source of my strength, which no Nazi can violate!

Unfortunately it is not the case that this source flows freely every day. Some days it seems to be blocked, and it's no use summoning up my old plans; they have faded, they no longer work. I rack my brains for new ideas, but to no purpose – nothing comes to me. I lie in bed at night, inconsolable, it's hard to get to sleep, the following day is almost unbearable. Then all of a sudden, maybe weeks later, my refuge is open and waiting for me again.

Separate entry: It took two days longer than I expected to hear whether my visit to Mahlendorf would come to anything or not. The chief prosecutor could not be reached. During that time I carried on working as before. My heart is more at peace again. I knew that if this way of smuggling the MS out of the building myself were to fail, there were two other ways. Admittedly not ways I would freely choose, because then the MS would pass through the hands of other people, and would remain in the hands of other people for some time. But at least it would be away from this closely guarded building, where it poses a constant threat to our lives. But none of that is necessary now: the chief prosecutor has granted permission. Tomorrow I shall be going home with the senior nurse. Someone has already called ahead, they are expecting me. At long last I'll be able to eat my fill again of food that I enjoy. I'll be able to walk in the bright autumn sun, which is shining today too. People will stare at me. I shall smile, I shall be carrying the MS on my person, and I shall hide it away in a safe place. Until the end of the war. It's a strange thing: sometimes, as I write these lines, it feels as if the war really is over already, as if I am writing this in retrospect, in a time of peace. Yet the last two nights, and yesterday lunchtime, the air-raid siren sounded again. Through the bars of my window I watched large formations of aircraft heading for Berlin in the sunny skies: there bombs were falling, houses were collapsing or going up in flames, people were running for their lives and suffering terrible torments – while I carry on writing, as if in peacetime. And tomorrow I shall get the MS to a place of safety.

Of course, I regret that I was not able to complete it. Another ten days, or maybe just a week, and I would have finished the chapter about the war and the one about my trip to France. But I can't let this favourable opportunity slip. It won't come again. And once I get back here safely, I won't be writing any more. There'll be time for that later. I've written the worst of it out of my system: the old hatred of the Nazis is still there, but it doesn't hurt so much. And if this whole work is a sorry failure, without merit or interest, what harm is done? I've unburdened my soul! In twenty-four hours we'll have the rail journey behind us, the senior nurse and I (a good job they didn't pick a police officer as my escort) will be walking along the shore of the lake towards Mahlendorf. My naturally suspicious nature keeps telling me there may still be some danger lurking somewhere: an unannounced inspection, someone telling me to hand over the MS before my trip. But my rational mind tells me this is just my paranoia speaking. I have just packed up my dirty laundry in my suitcase to take with me. The senior nurse – the strictest in the building – stood by and watched me. I held up an envelope, in which I had placed the letters I had received in prison and already attended to, and said: 'These are old letters, Mr Holst. Do you want to look through them? It's not as if I'm trying to smuggle anything out!'

'And I wouldn't expect you to!' replied the senior nurse, leaving me to put the letters into my suitcase without examining them.

On our last excursion in peacetime, through the villages clustered around their loudspeakers, through the peaceful fields, meadows and forests, we didn't drive into the centre of Berlin. We were going to fetch our son, who was in a sanatorium on the northern outskirts of the city, to which he had been evacuated by a doctor of our acquaintance.[166] We drove up to the front of the sanatorium, nobody came out to welcome us, and we climbed the steps: no son rushed to meet us. We entered the large office. There were a lot of people sitting or standing around. Our son glanced across at us, nodded and then carried on listening. The doctor shook hands with us briefly and offered my wife a chair. We were all listening now. We heard the Führer's voice issuing from the microphone: German troops have entered Poland . . . etc., etc. (check with Ibeth[167] and see what Horkenbach has to say[168]). And then the same old spiel about the shameful Treaty of Versailles, the just demands, the madness of the Corridor, and how Danzig is a German city.[169] How nauseating it was even back then, this empty claptrap that never spelled out the real reason! And how meaningless it has since become! Who cares about the Corridor and Danzig today? Today the very survival of the German nation is at stake! We have sacrificed ten times more people than the entire population of Danzig, we have had hundreds of times more houses reduced to rubble than make up the whole of Danzig. How this war, just by virtue of the fact that it has lasted five years now, has unmasked the lies of that idiot! How the real reasons have emerged more and more clearly: Hitler's insatiable hunger for power, his unbridled need to dominate others, his craving for everything that is good and lovely in this world, which, despite his best efforts, he cannot destroy! We stood by the radio in silence.

What the others were thinking, I have no idea. A few women and an older girl were in tears. One young thing appeared bored by it all. A woman in the corner was scribbling furiously in her shorthand book; I fear she was not transcribing the Führer's speech, but writing a letter to her beloved. We kept on hearing the word 'war' coming out of the loudspeaker – 'war', 'war', 'military involvement', and more war . . . I looked at my boy, he was nine years old. I gave this war at least four years (and I was mocked constantly for this prediction during the first two years of the war). My son would be fourteen, fifteen years old by the time this war ended. In all probability he would hardly be aware that it was happening. (Back then nobody had any notion of the terrible air raids to come.) And how is it looking now? The war has just entered its sixth year, and the boy has already been digging trenches out East. Next year he has to leave grammar school and serve as an anti-aircraft gunner somewhere (carrying on with school lessons in his spare time – officially!). No indeed, the war will not spare him. The little town where his school is situated has been targeted by American bombers. Miraculously his grammar school, the largest building in the place, has escaped unscathed. But for how long? How we have learned to endure the constant fear for the safety of our nearest and dearest, getting up with it in the morning and going to bed with it at night! How we have changed! And how the boy has changed! War has come to seem like a normal way of life for him (even if he doesn't like it) – but for his father it is still something to be rebelled against at every turn.

The Führer has spoken. Solemn silence – then the German national anthem followed by the Nazi Party anthem, the Horst Wessel Song. 'Raise high the flag, close tight the ranks, SA marches on . . .' Silence. The doctor has quickly turned down the volume knob on the loudspeaker to mute the sound. He glances at the people around him, and I do the same: quite a few of them are sporting Party badges in their buttonholes. 'Another incorrigible chancer', I think to myself. 'They'll take it out on you for not letting the Horst Wessel Song play out to the end when war was declared.' And I smile at him. It's the same doctor who shares my view that Germany would be better off as a British mandated territory. Incorrigibly rash, and incorrigibly true-hearted. He whispers to me: 'All the same, I hope we win. The German soldier . . .' Incorrigibly true-hearted? Incorrigibly German. This *furor teutonicus* that seizes even the best of men when the call to arms comes! Poor, incorrigible Germans!

A despatch from the house of the dead.
Afterword

It feels, he says, as if he is writing 'in retrospect', as if he is writing 'in a time of peace'. While the bombs are falling in Berlin and houses are going up in flames, Hans Fallada is sitting in his cell in the Nazi custodial institution in Strelitz and writing a memoir that could cost him his life. With unflinching candour, caught up in his own contradictions, he relates his experiences in Nazi Germany. At the end these notes seem to him too slight, a failure even; the tone of them is too tame for what he has been through. But still: he has 'written the worst of it out of my system'. So what are we to make of this despatch from the 'house of the dead'?

The Prison Diary from the autumn of 1944 is more than just an exercise in self-examination, more than just introspective monologue. It speaks to an imaginary reader, and makes use of all the literary devices that Hans Fallada the story-teller had at his disposal. For an important part of his attempt to process the past, not to say its underlying motivation, is the need to defend his own actions, his 'inward emigration'.

It is no coincidence that the opening scene reminds us straightaway of one of Fallada's lighter novels. With practised skill the writer paints a picture of the high-spirited atmosphere in 'Schlichters Wine Bar'. Into this cosy scene bursts the waiter who brings the fateful news that the Reichstag is on fire. It is 27 February 1933. The fascist character of the new regime is now laid bare. On the very next day the 'Edict of the Reich President for the Protection of the Nation and the State' suspended key articles of the constitution, and the constitutional state was irrevocably transformed into a police state, which took brutal action against its opponents. It was not long before National Socialist cultural policy was also put into effect. The 'thorough moral cleansing of the body politic' announced by Hitler meant in practice the suppression of an independent, free press. Once the press had been brought into line with Nazi doctrine, other measures against writers' organizations soon followed. The '*Schutzverband deutscher Schriftsteller*' (SDS – Association for the Protection of German Writers) was 'purged', and its members were henceforth required to proclaim allegiance to the National Socialist state. In July 1933 the SDS was subsumed into the newly founded '*Reichsverband deutscher Schriftsteller*' (RDS – Reich Association of German Writers). The Reich Chamber Law of 22 September 1933 established the statutory basis for the regimentation of cultural life in general. Under Goebbels' supervision the Reich Chamber of Culture, established under the aegis of the Propaganda Ministry in November 1933, would now decide who could work as an artist and who could not. Jews and political dissidents were no longer allowed to write for a living. The campaign of terror against writers unpopular with the regime had already taken on a new dimension with the burning of books on 10 May 1933. Among those whose books were burned were Anna Seghers, Lion Feuchtwanger, Thomas and Heinrich Mann, Kurt Tucholsky, Sigmund Freud and many others. Hans Fallada was not on the list. Those who, like him, wished to remain in the country and continue to publish had to reach an accommodation with the powers that be – whether they liked it or not.

The gaiety and bustle of 'Schlichters Wine Bar', the haunt of Berlin's *boheme*, belonged to the past. As this opening scene already makes clear, Fallada treats his memories as material for literature, telling stories about ordinary people and the famous, creating characters, dialogue and scenes. The interspersed 'separate entries' are a repeated reminder of the conditions of his confinement and the emotional stress he is living under.

In the autumn of 1944 Hans Fallada had reached the nadir of his existence. The most important wellsprings of his life were drying up: literary success, and his relationship with his wife Anna Ditzen. His drug addiction was getting the better of him again in a life that was gradually turning into a nightmare.

In 1935, two years after they moved out into the country, the Nazis declared him an 'undesirable writer', following the publication of *Once a Jailbird* and *Once We Had a Child*. In 1938 Fallada was back on the blacklist again. The literary failures of the next few years did not leave him unscathed. 'The dream of becoming a great artist is over' was the bitter conclusion of a writer who had settled for churning out light-weight novels. In 1943 he lost his publisher, after nearly 25 years as one of his established authors. The many compromises, and the battles with the Nazi authorities, had left their mark.

By the autumn of 1944 Carwitz, once an enchanted island in a 'storm-tossed world', had long since ceased to be an idyllic haven where he could work in peace. The war had come to this village too. The house afforded a refuge for Fallada's mother, Elisabeth Ditzen, and a number of Anna's relatives. The previous year Fallada had encouraged them to move in, but now he was developing an aversion to the many 'strange faces'. He found an outlet for his anger by engaging in target practice in the garden. In the village, meanwhile, people were gossiping about an affair of the writer's. In these notes Hans Fallada relates with brutal honesty and unconcealed hatred how the petty-mindedness and tale-telling of the villagers had poisoned his life over the years. He makes sure that the 'informers and malicious gossips' will not readily be forgotten. In contrast to the descriptions in *Our Home Today*, the book of 'evasions', the Prison Diary of 1944 has little to say about the joys of writing in leafy seclusion. The clashes with the Nazi bigwigs of the village and the constant run-ins with the hostile local farmers, all the disputes and legal proceedings going on year after year – these things made his everyday life a hell. And on top of all this Fallada now felt himself consigned to a 'Strindbergian hell' in his own home. His resentment against his wife of many years grew stronger. In the end he moved out of the house and into the gardener's flat in the barn.

And he agreed to a divorce. On 2 May 1944 the lawyer Dr Rehwoldt in Neustrelitz was instructed to act for him, and was simultaneously informed that the couple had reached a 'gentlemen's agreement'. They carried on living together on the farm in Carwitz, which remained home to their three children. On 5 July 1944 the marriage was dissolved in a hearing before the district court in Neustrelitz. But that did not put an end to their wrangling. Fallada fell head over heels in love with the young refugee widow Ursula Losch, and they began to make plans for the future. But the relationship did not bring him greater peace of mind. On 28 August a quarrel broke out between him and Anna Ditzen that was to have serious consequences. A shot was fired from Fallada's pistol. He wasn't aiming at her, they both testified later. The doctor who was called to the scene summoned the police, and Fallada was led away under guard. On 31 August 1944 the district court in Neustrelitz ordered him to be temporarily committed to the Neustrelitz-Strelitz psychiatric prison.

While the lawyer sought to persuade the court that the whole thing had been an unfortunate accident, pointing out that the accused was a renowned German author, Fallada himself sought refuge in literary work. The prison authorities had supplied him with some paper – not enough for someone who now wrote at manic speed, but Fallada's handwriting was small and condensed, and there was space between the lines that could also be used. The first work to emerge from a veritable fever of creativity was the novel *The Drinker*, in which Fallada comes to terms with the painful end of his own marriage. He then turned to his 'experiences during twelve years of Nazi terror', as he called these notes when he was preparing them for publication in 1945. In *The Drinker* he recounts the decline of the respectable citizen Erwin Sommer, who feels inferior to his 'remorselessly capable' wife, eventually taking refuge in alcoholism. He becomes violent towards her and ends up in an institution. Fallada's hero is finally overtaken by the fate that he most feared for himself – preventive detention under Section 51. For him too this was a very real possibility.

He had to wait three months for the court's verdict. On 28

November 1944 the district court in Neustrelitz ordered him to serve three months and two weeks in prison, with full allowance for the time already spent in custody. He was released from custody on 13 December 1944.

This crisis in Fallada's life coincided with the collapse of the Hitler regime. He and the rest of the country were physically ravaged and mentally exhausted. While Germany was on the point of losing a catastrophic war, the writer Fallada was sitting at his desk in prison uniform; closely guarded, surrounded by thieves and murderers, he reconnected with his life through the act of writing. The Prison Diary and *The Drinker* mark the start of the final series of 'genuine Falladas' (the author's own description of his novel *Wolf among Wolves*, which he wrote in 1937 after a series of more lightweight works), which addressed the conditions of life in Germany in an impressive and convincing way – among them *Alone in Berlin*, his 1946 book about grass-roots resistance to the Nazis.

Fallada reclaimed his reputation as a significant writer. It was, as the Prison Diary shows, a painful process. His hatred of the Nazis finally found an outlet: 'They are frightened of the individual and individuality, they want the shapeless masses into which they can drum their slogans.' The brutal candour of the notes put the author's life at risk, and in all its contradictions, sudden mood swings, crass judgements and errors it is both taxing and revealing for the modern reader. Fallada sought to exorcize the oppressive past by casting it in literary form. With supreme mastery he plays with that past, making contemporaries and colleagues such as Ernst Rowohlt, Emil Jannings, e.o. plauen and Peter Suhrkamp into the 'heroes' of his story, inventing dialogue and inner monologues for them, embroidering and embellishing scenes. Memory and imagination merge, fiction and truth are conflated. And raw emotions are constantly erupting into the text, wildly erratic and ambivalent in the extreme: hatred and sadness, hope and fear, self-pity and self-recrimination, discerning insight and blindness. The Prison Diary stands before us not as the documentary record of a controlled and sustained process of thought and reflection, but as the testimony of a highly conflicted personality, damaged by Nazi terror and trapped in the internal contradictions of his own actions.

This 'unpolitical writer' is here making his first profession of political faith. It is revealing and instructive – but it fails to convince. Fallada is one of that group of artists who did not leave Germany during the Nazi years. So his memoir sets out to justify his actions. With his 'catalogue of sins' as a writer he finds himself the target of accusations and reproaches. His account reveals the bitterness and contradictions of those artists who felt they had no choice but to 'stick it out' in Germany and do what they could to defend the great German 'civilized nation' against the primitive violence of ethnic nationalism and racism. Like Ernst Jünger, Fallada believed that he had shared in the 'tragedy of his people'. Those who emigrated, fleeing into 'comfortable' exile, were 'slinking away to a life of ease' in the country's 'hour of affliction and ignominy'. He claimed to have thought about emigrating on several occasions, and had packed his suitcases more than once: but in 1938, when the family had made all the necessary preparations to travel to England via Hamburg and was ready to go, he simply could not bring himself to leave Germany. And so he stayed – for 'the trees and the bees'. As a writer, he said, he could not imagine living anywhere except Germany, and 'probably couldn't do it anywhere else'. Fallada paid a high price for staying, as these notes from 1944 testify.

The phrase 'inward emigration' was coined by Frank Thiess as early as 1933 – he too rejected the idea of German exile from the outset. After 1945 the rift between the émigrés and 'those who had stayed behind at home' grew deeper. The claim made by Thiess – that by 'sticking it out' in Germany he had acquired a 'rich store of insights and experiences' – culminated in the imputation that it had been harder 'to preserve one's identity here than to send messages to the German people from over there'. This egregious defamation of German authors in exile elicited an unusually sharp riposte from Thomas Mann. He argued that the literature of 'inward emigration' had forfeited any claim to the status of resistance literature. 'It may be superstition, but in my eyes any books that could be printed at all in Germany between 1933 and 1945 are less than worthless, and not the kind of thing you want to pick up. The smell of blood and infamy clings to them. They should all be pulped.'

However, writers like Ricarda Huch and Ernst Barlach can claim with some justification to be practitioners of 'inward emigration', since they took a public stand against National Socialism. But what of Hans Fallada? Did he seek to offer any kind of 'intellectual opposition' to the prevailing 'spirit of evil'? Certainly, in a novel such as *Wolf among Wolves*, he gave readers a work of fiction that did not conform in any way to the tasteless triumphalism of approved Party literature. Nor is there any doubt about his aversion to fulfilling the regime's expectations. And yet he is compromised by the revised ending to *Iron Gustav*, rewritten along the lines suggested by Goebbels. Indeed, Fallada found himself having a lot more to do with Goebbels' Propaganda Ministry than he was comfortable with – as the Prison Diary also attests. So we see the author who was celebrating in 'Schlichters Wine Bar' in February 1933 turning up five years later in the Hotel Kaiserhof, where the Nazi state held court, and where Fallada now took part in discussions about a proposed project with the 'National Actor' Emil Jannings. The claim of the authors who had 'stayed behind at home' that they had opposed the regime, even if their opposition had to be read between the lines of their texts, was dismissed early on by Thomas Mann as a strategy doomed to failure.

Fallada too misread the political situation and his own role in it. And he vilified the émigré writers. He claimed he would rather perish with this 'unfortunate but blessed nation' than 'enjoy a false happiness in some other country'. He defended himself against his critics in exile by lashing out at them, deploying the standard arguments used to justify 'inward emigration'. The idea that artists had a special role and a special responsibility for the sorely afflicted country also surfaces in the diary of Wilhelm Furtwängler. In 1945 he writes: 'Here I was able to do more for the true Germany, and thus for peace and the arts worldwide, than anywhere else.' In Fallada we read: '[. . .] not everything has lost its savour [. . .] we were the salt of the earth.' A proud boast, and a foolish one. Like Furtwängler, Fallada invokes Germany's cultural heritage and celebrates the nation that produced Goethe and Beethoven: 'I love this nation, which has given [. . .] imperishable sounds to the world.' The exhortations of the émigrés to engage in active resistance are decisively rejected by Fallada: he refuses to 'commit suicide cheered on by a bunch of émigrés'. Here too he is following the standard line of argument used by 'those who stayed behind at home'. Thus in 1945 Frank Thiess asserted that it had been a great deal harder to live through the 'German tragedy' in Germany than to pass comment on it from the 'boxes and orchestra seats of other countries'.

Above all else, the Prison Diary documents the failure and the growing despair of an unpolitical writer. The fact that his own notes fail to satisfy him in the end, that he finds them 'without merit or interest' even (he has 'no great revelations' to make), undoubtedly has something to do with his inability to analyse National Socialism critically. Political reflection was not Fallada's forte – and there is no reason why it should be. He tells us that he has never thought in terms of Jews and Aryans, that Jews had always been part of 'an entirely random mix' of friends and acquaintances. When he was arrested by the Nazis in 1933, a female Jewish friend was staying in the house. The way he describes the situation shows how he failed to grasp the very real danger. He says he has not wasted mental energy on such things as 'learning to tell the difference between all these silly uniforms'. Was it a 'Standartenführer' who arrested him on that occasion? 'A "Rottenführer"? A "Scharführer"? I've no idea.' All that mattered to him was that 'a good old country policeman' was there too, 'wearing the familiar green uniform', who could at least be expected to see that things were done in a 'legal' manner. After his release from protective custody at the end of April 1933 Fallada notes that they are still 'entirely unpolitical people', and many things are just a 'closed book' to them: he has no idea 'what the lawyer and the district council leader talked about in private, regarding conspiracies against the person of the Führer, good and bad political jokes, and Mr von Salomon.'

His political innocence and 'naivety' are also evident in another area. Shortly after the Nazis seized power in 1933, Fallada moved into a 'Jewish' guesthouse, and, as he puts it, 'gaily started sending out' his letters from there. His friends warned him that his imprudent behaviour – 'given the growing number of spies and informers' – was tantamount to suicide, but he blithely dismisses their concerns: 'But I like it there! If they ban Aryans from living in Jewish guesthouses, then I'll move out. But until then, I'm staying put!'

While anti-Semitism now became *de facto* government policy, and the Jews were discriminated against, humiliated and persecuted, Fallada, who describes himself as a 'philosemite', makes a few observations that 'give me pause'. The Jews, he writes, really do have 'a different attitude to money'. Fallada comes out with anti-Semitic remarks despite himself, describing the typical 'Jewish' face in terms redolent of a caricature in *Der Stürmer*, and characterizing someone as 'a little, degenerate Jew'. He writes about the 'deep instinct for quality that so many Jews have', their capacity for self-irony, in which they 'so excel', and he is fiercely critical of the anti-Semitic propaganda of the National Socialist regime, which he says 'had always sickened' him – and which nevertheless dictates the terms of reference for his own arguments. The 'unpolitical' writer was becoming politicized without even noticing it. When he reluctantly accepts a commission from the Propaganda Ministry in 1941, he does so under the dubious premise that if he does it at all, then he will write a 'non-anti-Semitic, anti-Semitic novel'.

He makes no secret of the fact that he despises the Nazis. He attacks their viciousness and inhumanity with utter disgust and growing hatred, calling them 'brutal', 'primitive', 'thugs', 'an entrenched gangster culture'. In his description of an 'archetypal SA visage' (with 'that thick neck with its six or seven rolls of fat') he voices an emotive rejection that 'had absolutely nothing to do with politics'. And Fallada writes very movingly of the victims of the Nazi dictatorship, one of whom was the music teacher Sas, who was arrested for illegally keeping a portable printing press in his house, and then had to endure endless torments until he was finally hanged in Plötzensee prison. An 'everyday story of German life', as Fallada puts it.

In May 1945 Fallada was back at work on his notes, which he had written only a few months previously at the risk of his life. He now wanted to adapt his memories and experiences to the changing times. The Red Army had entered Feldberg, and the town was under the control of the Soviet town major. Fallada was revising and editing his account, because now, finally, he saw a real prospect of getting it published. His proposed title was 'The undesirable author – My experiences during twelve years of Nazi terror' – even though the work has little to say about the struggles of the 'undesirable author'. But in May 1945 it seemed desirable, indeed necessary, to give the text sharper political definition. The foreword he wrote for it reads like a mission statement for the task of revision and emendation he is about to undertake: 'These reminiscences clearly bear the traces of the circumstances in which they were written. Constantly interrupted and laid aside, concealed from the gaze of the prison warders, they were never going to be a work of calm contemplation. They are not serenely detached, but sad, angry and full of hatred; I have suffered too much. They are driven solely by the single-minded resolve that kept me going for twelve years: the resolve to root out every trace of Nazism from this unfortunate German nation, which has brought calamity upon nearly all of Europe through its deluded faith in the crazed "Führer". Never again must anything like Nazism be visited upon mankind; these reminiscences, which show that everything Hitler did, big or small, was rotten to the core, may hopefully help to prevent that happening.'

With these words Fallada began to transcribe his notes on 9 May 1945, the day after the war ended. 136 pages of the typescript he prepared have survived, amounting to approximately half of the original hand-written pages. The text breaks off in mid-sentence partway through the entry for 30 September 1944. It is impossible to say now whether Fallada stopped work at this point and never resumed, or whether he finished the text and the remaining pages have simply gone missing. At all events, the surviving typescript shows significant changes in content and style. There is a very obvious attempt to emphasize just how much Fallada hated the Nazis. So the 'ruthless men' of the manuscript now become 'ruthless thugs'. Similarly Fallada makes more of his own sufferings at the hands of the Nazi dictatorship. In the first version Fallada had to wait 'five or six days' for a response from his lawyer when he was arrested in 1933; in the typescript this has been stretched out to two weeks. And there is also a marked shift in his attitude towards the German people: in September 1944 he speaks of this 'unfortunate but blessed nation', but in May 1945 he takes a much more distanced and pessimistic view, referring only to 'this unfortunate nation'. Fallada also radically revised the memorable portrait of his publisher and friend Ernst Rowohlt. As well as adding further details, he paints an even more favourable picture, in order to do his old colleague a good turn – in 1945, as a former member of the NSDAP, Rowohlt was facing a denazification tribunal. So Fallada emphasizes Rowohlt's international standing and praises his ambitious publishing list, which included many foreign authors and a number of Jewish ones.

There were other changes besides. The anti-Semitic remarks are toned down in the typescript intended for publication. The assertion that the Jews have a 'different' attitude to money is now contextualized as a 'first impression', which on mature reflection he rejects as mistaken. The power of National Socialist propaganda, he belatedly realizes, has influenced even the staunchest opponents of Nazism. What was intended as a criticism in the autumn of 1944 – that it was the Jews themselves who had 'erected this barrier between themselves and other nations' – now gives way to a recognition that the Jews were right to stick together in their hour of danger. After all, 95 per cent of Germans had elected the Führer and supported his policies, so 'why should the Jews, whose lives were constantly in danger, believe that we happened to belong to the other five per cent who had rejected him?' The later toning-down and revision of anti-Semitic remarks undoubtedly stemmed in part also from the new revelations about the horrific scale of the Holocaust. The reports from the concentration camps and extermination camps that were gradually emerging showed for the first time the full extent of the persecution and the enormity of the crimes that had been committed.

In May 1945 Fallada found himself in a changed situation, both personally and politically. The new revelations and discoveries were incorporated into the typescript. Sometimes whole passages were excised in the course of revision. Fallada was becoming increasingly aware of his own political naivety. In the autumn of 1944 he still took the dubious view that it was not the Germans 'who did the most to pave the way for National Socialism', but rather the French and the British. In May 1945 he acknowledged self-critically that he was 'a perfect example of the political folly of the Germans', who hoped in their millions that 'it wouldn't be so bad', and in the end learned to their cost that things had turned out a great deal worse 'than anyone in their wildest fantasy could possibly have imagined'. So in May 1945 he chooses to emphasize the political 'naivety' of the Germans rather than dwell on their 'attitude' to National Socialism, seeking thereby to defend his fellow countrymen – and himself.

A portion of the typescript, the first section of the notes from the Reichstag fire to Fallada's arrest at the beginning of April 1933, was revised and edited in 1945 under the Soviet military administration and published in the *Tägliche Rundschau* under the title 'Celebrating Easter 1933 with the SA'. Fallada edited the text down for print, cutting the portrait of the conservative Ernst von Salomon to a minimum and condensing the story of the Sponars, whose name was changed to 'Donner'. Published in serial form in November and December 1945, the text served above all to present Fallada as a victim of the Nazis.

But let us now return to the original, hand-written version. The Prison Diary of 1944 begins as an apologia. Fallada feels compelled to explain why he chose to 'stick it out' in Germany. He wheels out a series of friends and contemporaries such as Rowohlt and e.o. plauen in order to show by their example – vicariously, on occasion – the trials, perils and struggles endured by those who stayed behind at home. As the example of Peter Suhrkamp shows (see note 67), the account he gives can sometimes be clouded by errors and personal animosities. Subjective assessment and stylization occasionally win out over the true facts. But Fallada's reckoning with the past documents a growing disillusionment and resignation. At the beginning Fallada draws a clear distinction between the good Germans and the Nazi mobsters, between victims on the one hand and perpetrators on the other. But from the experiences he recalls and the stories he tells, a picture gradually emerges of a nation of fellow travellers, cowards and informers. Decent men and women are sold down the river.

'We had had enough of fighting these losing battles, which, as people without rights, we could never win', writes Fallada of the events of autumn 1933, when he had to flee to Berlin at a moment's notice after his arrest in Berkenbrück. For the first time in his life he had suffered 'a patent injustice', having lost the roof over his head after being denounced: 'Child that I was, I still didn't get it: since January 1933 Germany had ceased to be a country under the rule of law, and was now a police state pure and simple.' But even in Carwitz, his place of refuge, the suspicions and accusations continued. Quickly identified as a man who hated the Nazis, the author was kept under close watch by the villagers. For the first time Fallada writes openly about everyday life in National Socialist Germany, where someone like the village mayor is described as 'this pitiful scrap of a human being [. . .] in all his wretchedness'.

The nation that he began by defending has become alien to him; the country, his homeland, no longer seems like home. And his hopes for a possible new beginning, for a peaceful and civilized Germany, have vanished. The feeling of resignation culminates in a final, escapist dream vision: the sheltering cave beneath his own house. 'In my dream I construct a passageway from the cellar of our house [. . .] descending deep down into the earth, and I seal it off with nine secret doors, invisible even to the most practised eye [. . .]. But this is no hideous, dark tunnel of bare earth: an elegant flight of stone steps leads downwards, the walls are covered with stars and electric lights are built into the vaulted ceiling. At the bottom you enter a fine antechamber, stepping straight from that into the vast living and working space, twenty metres below the ground.' Fallada imagines his 'underground palace' in increasingly elaborate detail – his metaphor for 'hibernating' through the winter of National Socialism. A final bastion against the trials and impositions of the age: a desperate idyll. But it all ends in a bitter guilty verdict: 'Buried alive. How could you do it? How could you do that to your children?'

The Prison Diary of 1944 is a record of growing resignation and despair, written in the hope of bearing witness.

The genesis of the Prison Diary manuscript

The original text of the Prison Diary from the autumn of 1944 forms part of the so-called 'Drinker manuscript', which is kept at the Academy of Arts in Berlin. The manuscript consists of 92 sheets of lined, A4 paper – i.e. 184 pages – with page numbers inserted by the author. On pages 1–6 Fallada wrote the short story *Little Jü-Jü and Big Jü-Jü* and the first five pages of the novel *The Drinker*: this portion of the manuscript was lost in the chaos of the post-war era. The surviving text begins on page 7: the rest of the novel *The Drinker* (pp. 7–131) is followed by the short stories *Looking for Father* and *The Story of Little and Big Mücke* (pp. 131–41, line 7).

Fallada had begun writing these literary works on 6 September 1944. As he was able to write relatively undisturbed in his confinement, he soon embarked on a highly dangerous undertaking: here of all places – 'inside these four walls' – he sets about writing down his memories of the Nazi period. On 23 September 1944 he writes the date at the top of the last page (page 184) – '23.IX.44.' – and adds the title of a short story *Der Kindernarr* as a cover for the compromising content of his memoir. He then goes back to p. 141, line 7, inserts the same date again – '23.IX.44.' – and begins to write the account that we now know as the Prison Diary: 'One day in January 1933 . . .'

In the weeks that followed he produced a highly intricate and virtually indecipherable manuscript. Fallada wrote 24 lines per page in the German form of cursive handwriting known as Sütterlin, until he reached the last line of page 183. At the end of the page he began a new sentence with the word 'And'. On page 184, where the date – '23.IX.44' – and the title *Der Kindernarr* were already noted at the top, he now wrote the short story of that name. When he got to the bottom of page 184 – having now used up all the 92 sheets of paper allocated to him – he turned the page upside down, wrote the page number 185 on the bottom edge, and continued writing in normal Latin script between the existing lines of Sütterlin script. He proceeded in the same way with the remaining pages: they were turned upside down, numbered in sequence, and Fallada carried on writing between the existing lines of text. On page 189, line 1, he ends the short story *Der Kindernarr*. On page 183 Fallada picks up the sentence he began earlier with the word 'And' and continues to record his memories, in Latin script, until he reaches page 202, where he interpolates the short story *Swenda – A Dream Fragment, or My Troubles*. As the 'Swenda story' is an integral part of the Prison Diary, it has been included here. It follows on from one of the three 'separate entries' in which Fallada provides a commentary and an update on his present situation in the psychiatric prison.

The Prison Diary account is continued on pages 204 to 228 in Latin script. Fallada now inserts up to three additional lines at the top of the pages and up to two more lines at the bottom. Page 228 brings him back to the first page of his memoir – page 141. He continues to write between the lines of this page in Latin script, then inserts the page number 229 between the first and second lines at the top of the page; from this point he carries on writing between the lines again, this time in Sütterlin script, until he reaches page 241.

The last 14 pages – 228 to 241 – each contain three sets of hand-written lines, amounting to at least 72 lines on each page. The highly compromising notes became a kind of secret code or cryptograph, the minuscule handwriting zigzagging back and forth for up to eighty lines a page. The text ends with a final entry dated 7 October 1944.

The editors would like to thank the staff of the Archive Collection at the Academy of Arts in Berlin for their kind assistance in making the manuscript available, as well as the Hans Fallada Archive in Carwitz for the opportunity to examine the later typescript version. The School of Applied Language and Intercultural Studies at Dublin City University, Ireland, facilitated the completion of the edition by granting Jenny Williams a period of sabbatical leave.

Chronology

1893   21 July: Rudolf Ditzen, alias Hans Fallada, is born in Greifswald.

1899   The family moves to Berlin.

1911   Attempts suicide in a pact with his friend Hanns Dietrich von Necker.

1912   Committed to Tannenfeld sanatorium (until 15 September 1913).

1919   Meets the publisher Ernst Rowohlt. First course of treatment for morphine addiction in Tannenfeld.

1920   Debut novel *Der junge Goedeschal* [*Young Goedeschal*].

1922   Employed as a bookkeeper on the Neuschönfeld estate near Bunzlau (present-day Bolesławiec in Poland).

1923   Sentenced to six months in prison for embezzlement; the novel *Anton und Gerda* is published.

1924   Imprisonment in Greifswald.

1925   Arrested again for embezzlement; sentenced to a prison term of two and a half years.

1928   Released in the spring from the Central Prison in Neumünster.

1929   5 April: marriage to Anna (Suse) Issel.

1930   Joins the staff of the Rowohlt publishing house – Rowohlt Verlag – in Berlin. Birth of first son Ulrich (Uli).

1931   Publication of *Bauern, Bonzen und Bomben* [*A Small Circus*].

1932   *Kleiner Mann – was nun?* [*Little Man – What Now?*] is published and becomes an international best-seller. The family moves to Berkenbrück.

1933 7–22 April: held in protective custody in Fürstenwalde.

18 July: birth of twins, of whom only one, the daughter Lore (Mücke), survives.

Purchase of the smallholding in Carwitz.

1934 Publication of *Wer einmal aus dem Blechnapf frisst* [*Once a Jailbird*] and *Wir hatten mal ein Kind* [*Once We Had a Child*].

1935 May: suffers nervous breakdown as a result of attacks in the Nazi press and money worries.

September: following the publication of *Altes Herz geht auf die Reise* [*Old Heart Goes on a Journey*], Fallada is declared an 'undesirable author'.

October: finishes writing *Das Märchen vom Stadtschreiber, der aufs Land flog* [*Sparrow Farm*].

November: another nervous breakdown.

Early December: his status as an 'undesirable author' is revoked.

1936 Publication of *Hoppelpoppel, wo bist du?* [*Hoppelpoppel, Where Are You?*].

1937 *Wolf unter Wölfen* [*Wolf among Wolves*] is published, and is an unexpected success. Signs a contract with the Tobis Klang Film Company to write 'the story of a German family from 1914 to 1933 or thereabouts'. The project secures the backing of Joseph Goebbels, Emil Jannings is lined up to play the leading role.

1938 Goebbels insists that the story of the family in the film be continued into the Nazi period. Fallada agrees, but the project is shelved anyway. The material is published as a novel, *Der eiserne Gustav* [*Iron Gustav*], with a revised ending approved by the powers that be. Renewed attacks in the Nazi press. Publication of *Die Geschichten aus der Murkelei* [*Stories from a Childhood*].

1939 The Rowohlt publishing house is incorporated into the Nazi-controlled Deutsche Verlags-Anstalt. Writes *Kleiner Mann, grosser Mann – alles vertauscht* [*Little Man – Big Man, Roles Reversed*].

1940 3 April: birth of son Achim.

October–December: hospitalized again.

1941   Publication of *Damals bei uns daheim* [*Our Home in Days Gone by*].

1943   January: suffers severe depression, admitted to the Kuranstalt Westend, a clinic in Berlin. Publication of *Heute bei uns zu Haus* [*Our Home Today*]. Undertakes three tours abroad on behalf of the Reich Labour Service (RAD).

        November: Rowohlt Verlag is closed down for good. Fallada is readmitted to the Kuranstalt Westend.

1944   Meets Ulla Losch. 5 July: divorced from Anna Ditzen.

        28 August: during an argument with Anna Ditzen, Fallada fires a shot from his pistol. He is committed to the Neustrelitz-Strelitz psychiatric prison, where the novel *Der Trinker* [*The Drinker*], a number of short stories and the memoir of the Nazi period are written.

        13 December: he is released.

1945   1 February: marriage to Ulla Losch. Following the entry of the Red Army into Feldberg, he is appointed mayor of the town.

        August: suffers another nervous breakdown and is admitted to a hospital in Neustrelitz for treatment of his morphine addiction. Later moves to Berlin and meets Johannes R. Becher. Contributes to the *Tägliche Rundschau*.

1946   Further stays in various clinics and hospitals. The last novels *Der Alpdruck* [*The Nightmare*] and *Jeder stirbt für sich allein* [*Alone in Berlin*] are written.

1947   5 February: Hans Fallada dies in Berlin.

Notes

1 Incorrectly dated: the Reichstag burned down on 27 February 1933. Fallada had to rely entirely on memory when writing these reminiscences, so there are occasional errors and misdatings.

2 The publisher Ernst Rowohlt (1887–1960). Fallada met him through Egmont Seyerlen (1889–1972). Seyerlen's wife, Anne Marie (Annia) Seyerlen (1885–1971), had encouraged Fallada to write. His first novel *The Young Goedeschal* was published by Rowohlt Verlag in 1920, and all Fallada's subsequent works up until 1943 appeared under this imprint. Over the years Fallada and Rowohlt, who always addressed each other with the more formal second person form 'Sie', became not just business associates but close friends. The scene in 'Schlichters Wine Bar' described here paints a fairly accurate picture of their relationship in February 1933. In November 1944, when Rowohlt was making plans to set up a new publishing house after the war, he went to see Fallada in the Neustrelitz-Strelitz facility with a view to securing his collaboration and support. On the relationship between Fallada and Rowohlt, see Hans Fallada, *Ewig auf der Rutschbahn. Briefwechsel mit dem Rowohlt Verlag*, edited by Michael Töteberg and Sabine Buck, Reinbek bei Hamburg 2008.

3 'Schlichters Wine Bar' in Lutherstrasse, which had been established in the 1920s by Max Schlichter, a brother of the painter and printmaker Rudolf Schlichter; popular with Berlin's bohemian set and a regular haunt of Bertolt Brecht, Theo Lingen, Heinrich George and others.

4 Anna Ditzen (1901–1990), Fallada's wife since 1929, and Elli Engelhardt (no biographical data available), Ernst Rowohlt's third wife, to whom he was married from 1933 to 1941.

5 The novel *Little Man – What Now?* (1932) marked Fallada's national and international breakthrough. By the end of June 1932 more than 2,000 copies had been sold; four months later sales had reached 21,000. A film contract was soon signed; translation and reproduction rights were sold. Fallada was bombarded with inquiries from newspapers and devoted readers. He wrote to his parents on 16 July 1932: 'We are really happy, now we can easily move to a larger apartment, furnish it nicely, pay off our debts, and above all have a longer summer holiday.' (Letter to Wilhelm and Elisabeth Ditzen, Hans Fallada Archive, Neubrandenburg)

6 The novel *The Good Earth* by the American writer Pearl S. Buck (1892–1973) was published in German for the first time in 1933.

7 The famous epic of the deep South by the American writer Margaret Mitchell (1900–1949) appeared in June 1936, and immediately became one of the biggest best-sellers in the history of American literature. The film of the same name had its US cinema release in 1939, and became one of the most successful films of all time.

8 A chronological slip. Fallada was working on the novel *Once a Jailbird* in January 1933, but did not begin writing *Once We Had a Child* until November of that year.

9 Hermann Göring (1893–1946) was the Prussian Minister of the Interior at the time of the Reichstag fire (and as such in charge of the entire Prussian police force); in April 1933 he became Prime Minister of Prussia and Commander-in-Chief of the Luftwaffe. Göring played a key role in the establishment of the Nazi dictatorship; it was at his instigation that the first concentration camps were set up, initially as prison-like facilities where opponents of the regime were incarcerated by the police and the SA. He was also responsible for the establishment of the secret state police, the Gestapo.

10 From 15 November 1932 to 23 April 1933 Fallada occupied the upper floor of the villa at Rother Krug 9 in Berkenbrück/Spree, to the east of Berlin.

11 The Jewish paper wholesaler Leopold Ullstein (1826–1899) had founded a newspaper publishing company in Berlin in 1878, which revolutionized the newspaper market of the day with the *Berliner Illustrirte Zeitung*, the first German mass-market weekly. When he died the company was

taken over by his five sons – Hans (1859–1935), Louis (1863–1933), Franz (1868–1945), Rudolf (1874–1969) and Hermann (1875–1943) – who built it up into an influential publishing enterprise producing newspapers, magazines and books. It is not clear which of the sons is referred to here.

12 Emil Ludwig (1881–1948), son of the Jewish ophthalmologist H. Cohn, was the author of successful biographies of Goethe, Napoleon, Rembrandt, Bismarck, Wilhelm II, Michelangelo and Lincoln. His books were burned on 10 May 1933. Six days later the board of directors of the Association of German Booksellers pronounced his work to be 'detrimental to Germany's international standing', and recommended that it should not be disseminated. That same month Ludwig resigned from the German branch of the PEN Club. From 1940 onwards he lived in exile in America, moving back to Switzerland after the end of the war.

13 In *Die Weltbühne*, which had been founded in 1905 by Siegfried Jacobsohn as a theatre journal (*Die Schaubühne*) and later turned into a political weekly, Kurt Tucholsky denounced militarism and the lack of democratic principles in many of the institutions of the Weimar Republic. In the article 'Militärbilanz' ['The state of the military'] (22 April 1920) he called for 'the dissolution of the Reichswehr, the creation of a standing army of 100,000 men, as permitted under Article 160 of the Peace Treaty, a civilian police force, under the command of democrats. Summary dismissal of all officers who display even the faintest hint of monarchist sympathies.' Tucholsky was particularly exercised by the issue of the Reichswehr, as he explains in a later article: 'The barrack rooms are awash with imperial insignia, pictures of the Kaiser, nationalist pamphlets and newspapers. The officers, whether elderly staff officers or young pups, all have exactly the same outlook on life and on the state, and it is the backwardness of their outlook that led us into that catastrophe. Their political reliability does not bear close inspection.' ('Die Reichswehr', in: *Die Weltbühne*, 23 February 1922)

14 *Das Tage-Buch*, the weekly intellectual journal first published by Rowohlt Verlag in 1920, carried articles on literature, theatre, cinema and the press. In the first issue, which appeared on 10 January 1920, the founder Stefan Grossmann set out the aims of his new journal: '*Das*

Tage-Buch can and will serve no political party, but I am hoping for a conspiracy of creative minds alongside, above and in despite of political parties.'

15 The American journalist and Pulitzer Prize winner H.R. Knickerbocker (1898–1949) had been living and working as a foreign correspondent in Berlin since 1928. In the early 1930s he published a series of books on current political issues, which were published by Rowohlt Verlag – including *The Red Trade Menace* (1931).

16 The much-discussed book by Weigand von Miltenberg (pen name of Herbert Blank, 1900–1959) had appeared under the Rowohlt imprint in 1931; it contained a savage critique of Hitler's *Mein Kampf.*

17 The book by Walter Oehme and Kurt Caro, which was published by Rowohlt Verlag in 1931, was a critical assessment of the NSDAP and its leading functionaries. The authors dismissed Hitler's 'propagandistic doctrines' in *Mein Kampf* as 'a demagogue's Bible'.

18 In 1932 the journalist and author Konrad Heiden (1901–1966) published his *Geschichte des Nationalsozialismus. Die Karriere einer Idee* under the Rowohlt imprint; 5,000 copies were printed. Heiden, who was one of the earliest critical observers of National Socialism, published the first serious biography of Adolf Hitler in 1936, when he was living in exile in Switzerland.

19 In March 1933, as part of an 'initiative to combat the un-German spirit', the German Student Union organized a campaign against Jewish, Marxist and pacifist writers. This culminated on 10 May 1933 in public book burnings on the Opernplatz in Berlin and in twenty-one other German cities, when tens of thousands of works by proscribed authors were consigned to the flames by students, university professors and National Socialist agencies.

20 Fallada takes the view that the terms imposed by the Allies under the Treaty of Versailles (1919) – and in particular the vast sums demanded in war reparations – had weakened parliamentary democracy in Germany from the very outset and encouraged the rise of National Socialism. In the later version of the text that Fallada revised for publication (1945 typescript), the paragraph 'And I'll say it here and not mince my words . . . in which we are now living!' has been cut out. In its place Fallada has inserted a new paragraph: 'I myself, the author of these lines,

am a perfect example of the political folly of the Germans: despite all the bad omens, despite my own bitter experiences, I kept on believing that the Nazis would settle down, that they really weren't that bad after all, until they finally dropped the mask altogether in the war and the atrocities of their SS and SA, of their Gestapo and concentration camps, taught me that they were a lot worse than anyone in their wildest fantasy could possibly have imagined. The fact that I never became a Nazi, that I felt nothing but utter hatred for them right from the start, has to do with reasons that are much more "bourgeois": because I despised their crudeness, their constant resort to violence, their stupidity and their philistinism. But the last few years have seen to it that there was nothing bourgeois about that hatred any more; it wasn't just political, it was something elemental.' (Hans Fallada, *Der unerwünschte Autor. Meine Erlebnisse während zwölf Jahre Naziterror.* Typescript 1945, Hans Fallada Archive, Neubrandenburg, pp.10f.)

21 Winter Relief Organization [WHW in the German – *Winterhilfswerk des Deutschen Volkes*]; it was established in September 1933 under the control of the Propaganda Ministry as an emergency aid initiative. Through door-to-door collections and street collections, plus the sale of badges, the WRO raised 358.1 million Reichsmarks in its first winter, which were used to help the unemployed and homeless.

22 During a hospital stay (21 January–22 February 1944) Fallada witnessed the heavy bombing raids on the German capital. In a letter to his sister Elisabeth Hörig of 2 March 1944 he mentions 'the series of terror attacks, which were probably the worst thing I have ever experienced'.

23 As well as the Prison Diary the 'Drinker manuscript' contains the novel *The Drinker* and five short stories, two of which are stories for children: *Der kleine Jü-Jü und der grosse Jü-Jü* [*Little Jü-Jü and Big Jü-Jü*] and *Die Geschichte von der grossen und der kleinen Mücke* [*The Story of Little and Big Mücke*] (published in: Hans Fallada, *Drei Jahre kein Mensch*, Berlin 1997, pp.79–95).

24 Anna Elisabeth Rowohlt (1930–?).

25 Ulrich (Uli) Ditzen, the eldest son of Hans Fallada, was born on 14 March 1930 in Berlin.

26 In his account of the events of Easter 1933 Fallada gets some of the dates wrong. The correct sequence of events is as follows: Friday 7 April

1933: visit from Ernst von Salomon; Sunday 9 April (Palm Sunday): arrival of Lore Soldin, a family friend, who appears in Fallada's account as 'a Jewish lady'; Wednesday 12 April: Fallada is arrested by the SA; Monday 17 April (Easter Monday): Lore Soldin leaves; Tuesday 18 April: Anna Ditzen visits her husband in Fürstenwalde; Wednesday 19 April: a second prison visit does not work out; Saturday 22 April: Fallada is released.

27 The writer and Freikorps combatant Ernst von Salomon (1902–1972); in 1922 he was sentenced to five years in prison as an accessory to the murder of Germany's Foreign Minister, Walther Rathenau. In 1930 Rowohlt Verlag published his autobiographical novel *Die Geächteten* [*The Outcasts*]. In 1933 Rowohlt hired him as a publishing editor. Ernst von Salomon took over the position of Franz Hessel, who – just like Paul Mayer – had to be dismissed because of the Nuremberg Laws. From 1936 Salomon became increasingly interested in cinema, and in 1939 he moved to Upper Bavaria to devote himself exclusively to film projects.

28 Probably Horst von Salomon; no detailed information available.

29 Bruno von Salomon (1900–1954).

30 Between 1918 and 1920 the Baltic Armed Forces or *Landeswehr* fought against Bolshevist troops and subsequently the Red Army; the Iron Division under Major Josef Bischoff took Riga on 22 May 1919. Ernst von Salomon joined the Freikorps in the Baltic in the same year.

31 Underground nationalist terror organization during the Weimar Republic; founded by Hermann Ehrhardt after the failed Kapp Putsch, the organization sought to undermine the political system of the young Republic by carrying out political assassinations (including that of Walther Rathenau). Ernst von Salomon was one of its most prominent members.

32 Walther Rathenau (1867–1922), Reich Foreign Minister, was murdered in Berlin on 24 June 1922 by members of the Consul Organization. Ernst von Salomon had been involved in the preparations for the assassination, and received a five-year prison sentence.

33 In the novel *Die Geächteten* (1930) Ernst von Salomon reappraises his part in the assassination of Rathenau from a critical perspective. Fallada's account of the book here is therefore quite misleading.

34 In the novel *Die Stadt* (1932) Ernst von Salomon describes his part

in the *Landvolkbewegung* [agrarian protest movement] in Schleswig-Holstein in 1928/29. Fallada's novel *A Small Circus* (1931) is set against the background of the same events.

35 The autobiography of the Communist Max Hölz (1889–1933) was published by Malik Verlag in 1929; Kurt Tucholsky called it 'an outstanding document of our times' (*Auf dem Nachttisch*, 1929). Max Hölz, who in 1921 had organized an armed uprising of workers in the industrial heartland of central Germany, was charged with the murder of an estate owner in Saxony and sentenced to lifelong imprisonment. A public appeal by leading scientists and artists, including Thomas Mann, Albert Einstein and Ernst Rowohlt, led to his amnesty and release in 1928.

36 The literary journal which appeared between 1930 and (May) 1933, edited by the anarchist publisher and writer Kurt Zube (1905–1991).

37 The decree issued by Göring on 3 March 1933 removed all existing restrictions on the use of force by the police.

38 Julius Streicher (1885–1946) started the anti-Semitic paper *Der Stürmer* in 1923; from 1925 until 1940 he was Gauleiter of Middle Franconia, later Franconia. From March 1933 he headed the 'Central Committee for Defence against Jewish Atrocity and Boycott Propaganda'. In the SA he held the rank of Obergruppenführer.

39 Protective custody was introduced on 28 February 1933 under the provisions of the Reichstag Fire Decree; it was used for the political repression of regime opponents and any others who were *persona non grata*. The first wave of arrests following the Reichstag fire was directed principally against Communists; in March and April 1933 at least 16,000 people were arrested by state agencies in Prussia alone. Persons held in protective custody could be detained indefinitely; they were not entitled to legal aid. They were initially housed, like Fallada, in police jails and prisons, later in concentration camps.

40 Anna Ditzen was born in 1901 in Geestemünde and grew up in Hamburg.

41 Hugo von Hofmannsthal's poem *Terzinen I. Über Vergänglichkeit* [*On Transience*] (first published in: *Blätter für die Kunst*, March 1896).

42 Börries Freiherr von Münchhausen's ballad *Graf Egisheim* (1919).

43 Established shortly after the end of the war in 1918 by the reservist army

officer Franz Seldte, the 'Stahlhelm, League of Front-line Soldiers' was a paramilitary defence organization that was seen as the armed wing of the German National People's Party (DNVP). When the Nazis seized power, the organization underwent 'voluntary assimilation' in 1934. To avoid forcible dissolution, the majority of members voluntarily joined the NSDAP as a self-contained paramilitary unit; renamed the 'National Socialist German League of Front-line Combatants', the 'Stahlhelm' was incorporated into the SA as 'Reserve I'. In 1935 it ceased to exist as an association with a historical identity of its own.

44 Theodor Düsterberg (1875–1950) joined the 'Stahlhelm' in 1923, and in 1924 became joint chairman with Franz Seldte. In 1932 he campaigned on behalf of the 'Stahlhelm' and the DNVP against Adolf Hitler for the position of Reich President; in 1933, following the Nazi seizure of power, he declined the offer of a place in Hitler's cabinet. In 1934 he was briefly incarcerated in Dachau concentration camp during the wave of arrests that followed the Röhm Putsch.

45 Franz Seldte (1882–1947), the founder of the 'Stahlhelm', became Reich Minister for Labour in Hitler's first cabinet; he remained in post until 1945. In April 1933 he joined the NSDAP, in August he was made an Obergruppenführer in the SA, and was later appointed Reich Commissioner for the Volunteer Labour Service.

46 Alfred Rosenberg (1893–1946), a leading NS ideologue, stoked up anti-Semitism by distributing numerous pamphlets on racial ideology. In 1922 he became editor-in-chief of the *Völkischer Beobachter*. In 1929 he founded the 'Militant League for German Culture', with the aim of combating 'the culturally corrosive aspirations of liberalism', and in 1930 the *Nationalsozialistische Monatshefte* [*National Socialist Monthly*]. 1930 also saw the publication of his book *Der Mythos des 20. Jahrhunderts* [*The Myth of the Twentieth Century*]. In January 1934 he was appointed 'Commissioner of the Führer for supervising all aspects of the intellectual and philosophical training and education of the NSDAP'. Part of the remit of the 'Rosenberg Office' was the 'cultivation of literature'. Rosenberg was sentenced to death at the Nuremberg Trials and executed on 16 October 1946.

47 Ernst Rowohlt had married the actress Emmy Reye in 1912. This marriage soon ended in divorce. In 1921 he married Hilda Pangust, a native

Latvian. From 1933 to 1941 Rowohlt was married to the German-Brazilian Elli Engelhardt.

48 The lawyer Dr Alfons Sack (1900–1944); he had successfully defended the Communist Ernst Torgler in the Reichstag fire trial.

49 The Stössinger guesthouse was situated in Berlin-Charlottenburg, at Lietzenburger Strasse 48, close to the Kurfürstendamm. Fallada lived here with his family from 23 April to 8 May 1933. Following a nervous breakdown he went to Waldsieversdorf in the Märkische Schweiz area east of Berlin, first to a hotel and then to a sanatorium. On 20 June Fallada and his family moved back to Berlin and the Stössinger guesthouse; on 8 July Anna Ditzen gave birth to twins, one of whom died soon after birth. On 15 August Fallada and his son Uli and the family nanny moved to Feldberg, where he supervised work on the house in Carwitz. On 14 September he collected his wife and daughter from the clinic. On 7 October 1933 the family moved into their new home in Carwitz.

50 Identity unknown.

51 The Reich Chamber of Literature was one of the seven sections of the Reich Chamber of Culture established by Joseph Goebbels in November 1933. It claimed to be a 'professional association' for writers. From 1934 every writer who wanted to publish had to be a member of the RCL. Fallada's claim that he was never a member of the RCL is incorrect: membership card No. 841 in the name of Rudolf Ditzen/Hans Fallada was issued on 11 July 1934 by the Reich Chamber of Literature in Berlin. See *Hans Fallada. Sein Leben in Bildern und Briefen*, Berlin 1997, p. 125.

52 Paul von Hindenburg's memoirs *Aus meinem Leben* were published in 1920 by Hirzel Verlag in Leipzig; the Swedish translation *Ur mitt liv* came out in 1920, published by Bonniers (not 'Bonnier') in Stockholm.

53 Identity unknown.

54 Identity unknown.

55 Identity unknown.

56 Identity unknown.

57 In his comments on the 'Jewish' physiognomy (later Paul Mayer is described as 'a little, degenerate Jew weighing barely 35 kilos, and grotesquely ugly'), on the 'different' attitude of the Jews to money and

on the 'difference in blood', Fallada draws on the same anti-Semitic stereotypes that were being peddled by the Nazis in their inflammatory pamphlets and caricatures. In this respect the Prison Diary is a document of its times – alarmingly so. Fallada gives a forthright account of the change he underwent after the Nazis took power. He sees the behaviour of the victims as a confirmation of anti-Semitic prejudices. Fallada claims not to be a 'victim' or adherent of Nazi propaganda, yet the Prison Diary shows the extent to which he had internalized anti-Semitic arguments. In the 1945 typescript Fallada revised and 'corrected' these passages; see note 59.

58 Lore Soldin; cf. note 26.

59 The anti-Semitic stereotype of the Jews' greed for money was revised by Fallada in the version of the text he edited for publication (the 1945 typescript). He adds the following explanation: 'That was my first impression at the time, perhaps influenced after all by the constant Nazi propaganda pointing out that the Jews were a quite different (and of course inferior) race of people. Later I reflected further on these matters, and it eventually dawned on me that for one thing there were many among my many Jewish friends who thought and felt exactly as I did. And on the other hand it occurred to me that there were also thousands, tens of thousands of *my own race*, the so-called Aryans, who were prepared to put up with anything for the sake of money, who not only endured humiliations but were also willing to commit any crime if there was money to be made – witness the good old Sponars, Aryans through and through.

There really is something very insidious about the odious form of propaganda practised by Mr Goebbels. Repeating the same old thing in every speech, month after month, year after year, over and over again! In the end the poison seeps into even the healthiest of bodies, and if you don't recognize that, and don't fight against it, you are lost.' (Hans Fallada, *Der unerwünschte Autor. Meine Erlebnisse während zwölf Jahre Naziterror.* Typescript 1945, Hans Fallada Archive, Neubrandenburg, p. 82)

60 Paul Mayer (1889–1970) was a publishing editor at Rowohlt Verlag from 1919 to 1936, and oversaw the publication of Fallada's early novels, including his global best-seller *Little Man – What Now?* Mayer emigrated to Mexico in 1938, returning to Germany in 1948.

61 Cf. notes 27 and 33.

62 Cf. note 11. At the beginning of the 1930s Rowohlt Verlag was two-thirds owned by Leopold Ullstein. Ullstein Verlag was expropriated on 30 June 1934 as a 'non-Aryan concern' and taken over by the pro-Nazi Cautio Treuhand GmbH, which sold it on to Eher Verlag, the central publishing house of the NSDAP.

63 In the 1945 typescript this passage has been rewritten. Fallada revised the notion that it was the Jews themselves who had 'erected this barrier between themselves and other nations'. The later version reads: 'During that time I came to understand that in the hour of danger a Jew feels closer to another Jew, however much they disagree and differ, than to his friend of non-Jewish blood from happier days. I must admit that at first I was shocked by this discovery, and I observed our dear Paul Mayer with sadness and disappointment. The fact that he shared secrets with an empty-headed man-about-town like Leopold Ullstein, secrets which he kept from me, his loyal friend – I found this very hurtful. It took a while for me to realize that what had now happened was exactly what the teachers in the jail in Fürstenwalde had predicted: in their hour of danger the Jews of every country stuck together, and a huge wave of national feeling swept through world Jewry. They were right to view us as outsiders: we *were* outsiders. The danger that constantly threatened the Jews did not affect us. Their cares were not our cares. We could be outraged, horrified by the vile behaviour of the Nazis, we could have the most profound sympathy for our Jewish friends, but as for helping them, there was absolutely nothing we could do. And they didn't need our pity. After all, we belonged to a nation that had elected the Führer with 95 per cent of the vote, and vociferously applauded all his measures – why should the Jews, whose lives were constantly in danger, believe that we happened to belong to the other 5 per cent who had rejected him? Especially as there was no shortage of people who immediately set about exploiting the plight of the Jews. Jewish property was expropriated at ludicrous valuations and then flogged off at even more ludicrous prices to the upstanding Party followers and all the parasites who fell greedily upon these spoils.' (Hans Fallada, *Der unerwünschte Autor. Meine Erlebnisse während zwölf Jahre Naziterror.* Typescript 1945, Hans Fallada Archive, Neubrandenburg, p. 85) At this point in the typescript

Fallada interpolated a story about the Jewish features editor Monty Jacobs (pp. 85f.). Through such additions, corrections and explanations he sought to underline his pro-Jewish attitude in 1945.

64 See note 48.

65 The political caricature *De Podenas – Mr Pot de Naz* by Honoré Daumier (published in *La Caricature* in 1833).

66 Robert Ley (1890–1945) was made head of the Deutsche Arbeitsfront (DAF – German Labour Front) in 1933, when Germany's trade unions were broken up and replaced by the DAF, which now represented all 'German workers of brain and brawn'. Walther Funk (1890–1960), who had been editor of the *Berliner Börsen-Zeitung* until 1931, became Minister for Economic Affairs in 1938 and President of the Reichsbank in 1939. For Julius Streicher, see note 38.

67 Peter Suhrkamp (1891–1959) studied German language and literature after the First World War and worked part-time as a teacher. In 1929 he gave up teaching and moved to Berlin, where he worked as a freelance contributor to the *Berliner Tageblatt* and the monthly magazine *Uhu* published by Ullstein. In 1932 he joined the staff of S. Fischer Verlag, initially as the editor of the journal *Die Neue Rundschau*. In 1936, two years after the death of Samuel Fischer, he bought up the share in the Fischer publishing business that Gottfried Bermann Fischer was not able to transfer when he went into exile in Vienna. Suhrkamp ran the publishing house until April 1944, when he was arrested by the Gestapo for high treason and sent to Sachsenhausen concentration camp. After the war Suhrkamp was granted the first publishing licence in Berlin by the British military government. He collaborated initially with Bermann Fischer, but they parted company in 1950 and Suhrkamp set up his own eponymous publishing house. Carl Zuckmayer gives the following assessment of Suhrkamp's conduct during the Nazi period: 'There is absolutely no question that Suhrkamp ever approved, supported or endorsed anti-Semitic measures or tendencies, nor did he exploit the plight of others, but rather took on a highly complicated and difficult task.' (Carl Zuckmayer, *Geheimreport*, Göttingen 2002, p. 22) The factually untenable accusations that Fallada levels against Peter Suhrkamp here owe a great deal to personal antipathy. This dates back to the summer of 1933, when Suhrkamp successfully negotiated an end

to the difficult situation in Berkenbrück on Fallada's behalf. Fallada felt that Suhrkamp had treated him like a schoolboy: 'It was a case of once a teacher, always a teacher with him, and he could be really acerbic and downright scathing when playing that part.' Then Suhrkamp wrote a review of *Once We Had a Child* in which he criticized the ending, which Fallada particularly liked. Rowohlt often sought Suhrkamp's opinion, and in a letter to Fallada of 4 March 1935 he passed on Suhrkamp's view that the title of the new novel *Und wenn der letzte Schnee verbrennt* [*Even If the Last Drop of Snow is Burned*] was too frivolous. It had also been suggested that Fallada could have saved himself a lot of trouble if he had made a few judicious cuts to the two previous novels (*Once We Had a Child* and *Once a Jailbird*). This kind of intervention led Fallada to suspect that Suhrkamp was trying to drive a wedge between him and Rowohlt. On 6 March he informed his publisher that he wished to have nothing more to do with Suhrkamp, and would not tolerate any further interference in his work. This personal animosity was evidently still there in 1944, when it found expression in the malicious gossip about Suhrkamp the 'legacy-hunter'.

68 The novels of the French writer Gustave Flaubert (1821–1880): *Madame Bovary* (1857), *Salambo* (1862), *La Tentation de Saint Antoine* (1874). Flaubert was a celebrated perfectionist, who took five years to write *Madame Bovary*, four years for *Salambo* and twenty-five years for *La Tentation de Saint Antoine*.

69 The monthly magazine *Uhu* put out by Ullstein Verlag from 1924 to 1934 published *Ein Mensch auf der Flucht* [*A Man On the Run*] in 1931 (Vol. 7, No. 12, pp. 43–51); *Gegen jeden Sinn und Verstand* [*Against All Reason*] in 1932 (Vol. 8, No. 8, pp. 39f.); *Mit Metermass und Giesskanne* [*With Ruler and Watering Can*], also in 1932 (Vol. 8, No. 10, pp. 25–34); and *Fünfzig Mark und ein fröhliches Weihnachtsfest* [*Fifty Marks and a Happy Christmas*] in 1933 (Vol. 9, No. 3, pp. 23–38 and 104–6).

70 Eva Schubring (1903–1994), who was working as foreign correspondent of the *Vossische Zeitung* in 1932. In 1934 she married the writer Ottfried Graf Finck von Finckenstein (1901–1987).

71 Emil Jannings (real name Theodor Friedrich Emil Janenz, 1884–1950) returned to Germany in 1929 after a successful period in Hollywood, where he had won the first Oscar awarded to an actor. In 1930 he took

on the role of Professor Unrat in the film of the novel *The Blue Angel*. He stayed in Germany throughout the Nazi years; after 1933 he collaborated on a number of propaganda films and was honoured by the regime, becoming 'Staatsschauspieler' [National Actor] in 1936 and Reich Senator in 1938.

72 Friedrich Kroner (1865–1932).

73 Samuel Fischer (1859–1934).

74 Cf. note 67. Since 1932 S. Fischer Verlag had been run by Brigitte and Gottfried Bermann Fischer. In 1936 Bermann Fischer emigrated to Vienna, taking part of the publishing business with him. In 1938 he moved to Stockholm. The remaining part of the business in Berlin was managed by Peter Suhrkamp on behalf of the family. The challenging task of keeping the prestigious publishing house intact during the Nazi period led to quite a few misunderstandings and misinterpretations. The 'legacy hunter' accusation was the subject of widespread rumour. In Fallada's account the hand of the literary artist is unmistakable. He uses the relationship between Suhrkamp and Samuel Fischer to tell a story, inventing scenes, bringing them vividly to life, and treating the persons involved as characters in a work of literature. Each episode serves to create tension and drive the action forward.

75 The poem *Üb immer Treu und Redlichkeit* . . . (1775) by Ludwig Hölty was set to music by Wolfgang Amadeus Mozart in 1791.

76 Mark 8, verse 36 [quoted here in the Authorized Version].

77 Brecht left Berlin with his family on 28 February 1933 and fled in the first instance to Vienna via Prague, then on to Switzerland and Denmark. This account of how Peter Suhrkamp helped him to escape is not supported by any evidence.

78 The book of memoirs *Our Home Today*, published in 1943.

79 The property at Büdnerei 17, described by Fallada in a letter to his parents (25 October 1933) as 'a plain, simple country house', was on the edge of the remote fishing village of Carwitz in Mecklenburg, where Fallada lived from October 1933 to December 1944.

80 A fictional name for Carwitz, possibly suggested by the famous windmill [German: *Mühle*] at the entrance to the village.

81 Between 1928 and 1935 Franz Fein translated eighteen books from English for Rowohlt Verlag. With the exception of Halliday

Sutherland these were all books by American authors: Sinclair Lewis (8), Knickerbocker (5), Floyd Gibbons (1), Joseph Hergesheimer (1), Edward Albert Filene (1), William Faulkner (1).

82 The American writer Sinclair Lewis (1885–1951) won the Nobel Prize for Literature in 1930. His novels from 1928 to 1934 were published in German translation under the Rowohlt imprint. Franz Fein translated *Elmer Gantry* (1928), *Mantrap* (1928), *The Man Who Knew Coolidge* (1929), *Dodsworth* (1930), *Our Mr Wrenn* (1931), *The Trail of the Hawk* (1933), *Ann Vickers* (1933), *Work of Art* (1934).

83 The book *Die schlimme Botschaft* by Carl Einstein (1885–1940) was published by Rowohlt Verlag in 1921.

84 Rowohlt published the three collections of poems *Allerdings* (1928), *Flugzeuggedanken* (1929) and *103 Gedichte* (1933).

85 Anton Kippenberg (1874–1950) ran the Leipzig-based Insel Verlag from 1905 until his death. He formulated his publishing program in a letter to Hugo von Hofmannsthal of 1 December 1906: 'To serve the cause of world literature in the Goethean sense, to match the form of a book to its content, to raise awareness of the art of the book and even of the book as luxury object, and to publish little in the way of contemporary literature, limited as far as possible to works that promise to endure.' (As quoted in: S. Binder, review of *Anton Kippenberg. Der Briefwechsel mit Julius Petersen 1907–1941*, in: *Goethe-Jahrbuch*, Vol. 119, edited by Jochen Golz and Edith Zelm, 2002, p. 294.)

86 In the 1945 typescript this passage has been revised and extended. The changes show Rowohlt in an even more positive light. In the typescript, for example, he is no longer presented as a 'gambler', and his 'waywardness' is toned down; the fact that he publishes American writers is emphasized instead. It is quite possible that Fallada was trying to do Rowohlt a good turn here, since his old publisher was facing a denazification tribunal in May 1945. The revised passage reads as follows: 'In Germany it was never seen as one of the top-ranking publishing houses. The publishing director, Rowohlt himself, was much too wayward for that. He never followed a clear, straight line with his publishing program, as Dr Kippenberg famously did with his Insel Verlag; instead Rowohlt, who always liked to be around people and needed the company of other people, was always much more attuned to

current social trends. He had a unique instinct for finding the book that people were waiting for, often without realizing it themselves. So for all the apparent waywardness his publishing house did have a guiding sense of purpose, bringing out more and more books over the years that reflected the contemporary zeitgeist. The fact that Rowohlt always sought to promote foreign novelists as well as German ones is entirely consistent with that aim. Ideally he wanted foreign authors who did not tread the conventional path, but who were themselves contemporary in a higher sense. So for example he published – often at great sacrifice – the work of American authors who seemed to him (and not only to him) to sound an entirely new note, such as Hemingway, Thomas Wolfe and Faulkner. He knew that these men would never be widely read by the German reading public, but he published them anyway, despite this, or perhaps because of it. He was never the kind of man who wanted to turn a publishing house into a purely money-making enterprise: instead he was always prepared to reinvest the profits from a current best-seller in an author who was only ever likely to make a loss for him.' (Hans Fallada, *Der unerwünschte Autor. Meine Erlebnisse während zwölf Jahre Naziterror.* Typescript 1945, Hans Fallada Archive, Neubrandenburg, pp. 121f.)

87 The novel was written between July 1936 and May 1937, and represents a return to the realism of *A Small Circus* and *Once a Jailbird.* The story takes place in 1923/24 in Berlin and on a country estate east of the river Elbe. The novel deals with the effects of inflation, the 'desperate plight of a desperate people'. *Wolf among Wolves* became an unexpected success on its publication in September 1937: the first edition (10,000 copies) had sold out by mid-November. The Nazi authorities saw the novel as a critique of the hated Weimar Republic, which ensured it would be well received. The reading public was pleased to have another 'genuine Fallada', which promised to be an entertaining but challenging read.

88 Illegal paramilitary organizations that were encouraged, and in some cases actually operated, by the official German Reichswehr, in defiance of the Versailles Peace Treaty of 1919. They were opposed to the Weimar Republic. The Black Reichswehr plays only a background role in *Wolf among Wolves*; its representative, Lieutenant Fritz, is depicted as a 'cold adventurer'.

89 The novel portrays a range of different social milieus. The featured characters include prostitutes, criminals, drug addicts and gamblers.

90 After the departure of Paul Mayer, Friedo Lampe (1899–1945) was hired in 1937 to replace him. He worked as a publishing editor at Rowohlt Verlag until 1939; his novels *Am Rande der Nacht* (1933) and *Septembergewitter* (1937) were also published by Rowohlt.

91 The biography *Adalbert Stifter* by Urban Roedl (real name Bruno Adler, 1889–1968) was published by Rowohlt Verlag in 1936. The book led to a ban on Ernst Rowohlt practising his profession as a publisher, on the grounds that he had allowed Jewish authors to carry on working under cover.

92 Clara Ploschitzki (no biographical data available) had been Ernst Rowohlt's secretary since the publishing business was first established in Leipzig. At his denazification tribunal Rowohlt claimed his Jewish secretary had worked for him for twenty-five years before he was forced to let her go in 1936 (?). (Ernst Rowohlt, *Memorandum*, in: Hans Fallada, *Ewig auf der Rutschbahn. Briefwechsel mit dem Rowohlt Verlag*, edited by Michael Töteberg and Sabine Buck, Reinbek bei Hamburg 2008, p. 417)

93 The 'Reich Pogrom Night', more commonly known as 'Reichskristallnacht', on the night of 9/10 November 1938.

94 The headquarters of the Berlin police from 1890 to 1945, the office building on Alexanderplatz was increasingly used by the Gestapo after 1933. It also served as the central collection point for prisoners from all over the Reich, who were then taken from here to the Gestapo headquarters at Prinz Albrecht Strasse 8 for interrogation or transported straight to a concentration camp.

95 Gustav Kilpper (1897–1963), managing director of the Nazi-controlled Deutsche Verlags-Anstalt (DVA). Following its takeover by DVA on 1 January 1939, Rowohlt Verlag remained in existence initially as a subsidiary; until it was closed down on 1 November 1943 it was run by Heinrich Maria Ledig-Rowohlt, the eldest son of Ernst Rowohlt. The last book to be published under the Rowohlt imprint was Fallada's *Our Home Today* (1943). Nothing of Fallada's was ever published by DVA.

96 Fallada's debut novel *The Young Goedeschal* (1920), which he had given to Rowohlt in 1919 (not 1918, as stated here), was not 'lost'; Fallada thought the book a failure, and consequently disowned it.

97 Rowohlt Verlag used green envelopes for its correspondence.

98 Here Fallada is mistaken: Ernst Rowohlt did not return from Brazil until December 1940.

99 Ernst Udet (1896–1941), German First World War fighter pilot, on whom Carl Zuckmayer's play *Des Teufels General* was based; in the 1920s and early 1930s he played parts in a number of films with an aviation theme, including (alongside Leni Riefenstahl) *Die weisse Hölle von Piz Palü [The White Hell of Pitz Palu]* (1929) and *S.O.S. Eisberg [S.O.S. Iceberg]* (1933). In 1935 Göring made him a colonel in the newly established Luftwaffe. Udet was appointed Inspector of Fighters and Dive-Bombers, and in 1939 he became the Director of Air Force Ordnance; in 1940 he rose to the rank of Colonel General. After the failures of the Luftwaffe air offensive against Britain, and the resulting accusations levelled by Hitler and Göring, Udet took his own life. Nazi propaganda presented his death as a flying accident. Rowohlt, who had also trained to be a pilot, had got to know Ernst Udet during the First World War.

100 The correct dating is 1927.

101 Cf. note 35.

102 Carl Froelich (1875–1953), film director and pioneer of German film, founded Froelich-Film GmbH in 1920. He was one of the most highly regarded film directors in the Third Reich. He was appointed a professor in 1937 and president of the Reich Chamber of Film in 1939.

103 Erhard Milch (1892–1972), German army and air force officer (appointed Field Marshal General in 1940), served from 1933 to 1945 as secretary of state at the Reich Air Ministry and Inspector General of the Luftwaffe; following the death of Ernst Udet in November 1941, be became Director of Air Force Ordnance until July 1944. His Jewish ancestry is debated to this day. The rumours current at the time are also recorded in Victor Klemperer's published diaries; in the entry for 18 October 1936 we read: 'And Marta talked about Milch, the air force general, who had a Jewish father and an Aryan mother: he claims he was the offspring of his mother's adultery with an Aryan.' (As quoted in: Victor Klemperer, *The Klemperer Diaries 1933–1945*, abridged and translated by Martin Chalmers, London 2000, p. 189.) Göring is said to have remarked, à propos Milch: '*I* decide who is a Jew!'

104 Ernst Alfred Schmidt (1895–1943); the nickname is an acronym, derived from his birthplace Schlegel in eastern Germany, close to the Czech-Polish border: Ṣchmidt ạus Ṣchlegel [Schmidt from Schlegel]. After the First World War, from which he returned a convinced pacifist, Sas trained as a music teacher, and in 1929 he found a full-time job teaching in Leipzig. At the beginning of the 1930s he joined the KPD, and was arrested by the Gestapo for the first time in 1933. In 1934 he moved to Berlin, where he set up a private music school close to the Kurfürstendamm. Here he made contact with the resistance group around Hanno Günther, and in the autumn of 1941 he was arrested along with other members of the group. Released in March 1942, he was arrested again in July. On 9 October 1942 he was sentenced to death for plotting high treason, and executed on 5 April 1943 in Plötzensee. Fallada met Sas in 1937 through the actress Marga Dietrich (1897–1978), with whom he had been on friendly terms since the stage adaptation of *A Small Circus* by her first husband, Heinz-Dietrich Kenter (1896–1984), in 1931. Marga Dietrich had been Sas' live-in partner since 1934. (See Manfred Kuhnke, . . . *dass ihr Tod nicht umsonst war!*, Neubrandenburg 1991, pp. 51–5.)

105 Marga Dietrich; see previous note.

106 The letter that Fallada apparently planned to incorporate into his manuscript later reads as follows: 'My dearest, the letter that will reach you via the prison authorities is written. I've also written one to Schlegel, which is just as much for you as the one to you is for the folks in Schlegel. I just want to tell you about my great love for you, how it makes me so happy at this particular time, and that I now bequeath that happiness to you, to be with you at all times on your journey through life, and eventually, some day, far in the future, in your final hour. May my love be so great and powerful that, after a short time of tears, it enfolds you all the days of your life, protecting you, bearing you up, warming you: for ever and ever and ever. I saved some bread from breakfast and the bigger half I have just eaten, slowly. The other half I shall send to you. Our wedding breakfast. (People get married by proxy, after all, so why not this?) Eat as I have eaten, so that I am as much in you as you were in me when I ate: then get on with your life and grab it with both hands! For the real purpose of my life (so it seems to me at least, although at this moment

it no longer matters to me) remains unaccomplished. I'm only going to be leaving this body now (not this world!!!), at the very most we would have had maybe 30 years together. It has been my privilege that the shortness of my days has been more than made up for by the richness of my life (and never forget, it was your love that made this possible). You now remain behind. Whatever befalls you, whatever makes you happy, joyful, strong, good and reverential in the face of life, people and the unknowable: in all this I will be coming to you and I will be present with you: in music, paintings, books, in our kindly Mother Nature, in the strivings, errings and attainments of the human heart's desire. Do not grieve for longer, or more deeply, than is natural. There is no reason why you should. Think of it this way: I am no longer flesh and blood, and therefore not usurping anyone else's place. The time has come. Be good to Sas by being good to those around you. I kiss you, my one and only wife, in fondest love! sasil.' (Reproduced in: Volker Hoffmann, *Der Dienstälteste von Plötzensee. Das zerrissene Leben des Musikerziehers Alfred Schmidt-Sas (1895–1943)*, Berlin 2000, pp. 230f.) It was through his close friendship with Marga Dietrich that Fallada learned about the letters and poems that Sas had written in his death cell.

107 This defamation of German émigré authors, which serves first and foremost to justify Fallada's own decision to remain in Germany, contains the central argument of 'inward emigration', which was wheeled out after 1945 in the increasingly bitter argument between 'those who had stayed behind' and the 'émigrés'. So for example Frank Thiess (1890–1977), who famously clashed with Thomas Mann on the issue, claimed that it had been a great deal harder to live through the 'German tragedy' in Germany than to pass comment on it from the 'boxes and orchestra seats of other countries'.

108 Pseudonym of the illustrator and cartoonist Erich Ohser (1903–1944); the 'Father and Son' comic strip stories, which appeared in the *Berliner Illustrirte* between 1934 and 1937, made him famous.

109 Ohser drew some 800 cartoons for the National Socialist weekly *Das Reich* between its launch in May 1940 and his arrest in 1944. He did not align himself with the policies of the Nazi regime.

110 The cartoon was first published in 1972 as the illustration for February in the literary calendar put out by the East German publisher Aufbau

Verlag. In 1993 it featured on a commemorative stamp issued by the German Post Office to mark the centenary of Fallada's birth, and has remained one of the best-known portraits of the writer ever since. (See Manfred Kuhnke, *Der traurige Clown und der Elefant auf dem Seil. Hans Fallada und e.o. plauen*, Neubrandenburg 2003.)

111 Eugenie Marlitt (1825–1887), a popular novelist who wrote entertaining stories for the illustrated family magazine *Die Gartenlaube*. Her most successful novel was *Das Geheimnis der alten Mamsell* (1867).

112 Erich Ohser and his friend Erich Knauf were reported to the Gestapo by Captain Bruno Schultz and his wife Margarete. On the morning of 28 March 1944 Ohser and Knauf were arrested. Erich Ohser took his life in unexplained circumstances during the night of 5 April in the Alt-Moabit detention centre. Erich Knauf was condemned to death on 6 April 1944 by Roland Freisler, president of the People's Court, and beheaded on 2 May 1944 in Brandenburg prison.

113 Fallada inserted three of these 'separate entries' into the Prison Diary, on 30 September, 5 October and 7 October. In these pages he writes about his situation in the prison, about his cellmates and the notes he is now writing.

114 The correspondence with Friedrich Hermann Küthe began in March 1933: the unemployed librarian wrote to the author he so admired and asked for a portrait photograph. Although the correspondents never met in person, and always addressed each other formally as 'Mr Fallada' and 'Mr Küthe', their correspondence from the years 1933 to 1946 suggests a relationship of closeness and trust. They discussed books, and Fallada had words of encouragement for his unemployed pen-friend. In 1940 Küthe, now serving with the army in France, sent silk stockings and sweets to Carwitz. In 1943 he was seriously wounded on the Eastern front and spent some five months in a field hospital in Chemnitz. The letter that reached Fallada in the prison at Neustrelitz-Strelitz does not appear to have had any negative consequences for Küthe. The bundle of letters is kept with Fallada's literary estate in the Academy of Arts in Berlin.

115 The story was first published in: Hans Fallada, *Drei Jahre kein Mensch*, Berlin 1997, pp. 109–13.

116 The nurse Friedrich Holst (born 1900). He accompanied Hans Fallada to Carwitz on 8 October 1944.

117 As part of the drive to align the film industry with National Socialist ideology, Tobis AG was taken into state ownership in 1935. Tobis star Emil Jannings became a member of the supervisory board in 1937, and he used this position to further his own career. Fallada signed the contract with Tobis on 12 November 1937 and delivered the manuscript on time on 28 February 1938.

118 This is incorrect: Fallada is confusing Rudolf Virchow with Robert Koch. Koch's life was made into a film in 1939 by Hans Steinhoff under the title *Robert Koch, der Bekämpfer des Todes*; Emil Jannings took the title role, Werner Krauss played Rudolf Virchow.

119 See note 102.

120 Jannings played the village judge Adam in the film version of Kleist's *Der zerbrochene Krug*. The film's premiere took place in Berlin on 22 October 1937.

121 The Hotel Kaiserhof, which opened in 1875 as Berlin's first luxury hotel, was located at Wilhelmplatz 3/5, across from the Reich Chancellery in what was then Berlin's government district. In the 1920s the hotel's owners sympathized with right-wing nationalist organizations and made their premises available to anti-republican groups. In 1931 Hitler had a meeting in his suite with leading German industrialists, and in 1932 he moved into the hotel permanently. During the election campaign the upper floor of the Kaiserhof became the provisional party headquarters of the NSDAP. Other Nazi functionaries were also living in the hotel. In April 1935 Hermann Göring held a lavish wedding reception at the Kaiserhof when he married his second wife Emmy. Joseph Goebbels' memoirs dealing with the 'time of struggle' leading up to the takeover of power were entitled: *Vom Kaiserhof zur Reichskanzlei* [*From Kaiserhof to Reich Chancellery*]. In November 1943 the Kaiserhof was completely destroyed in a British bombing raid.

122 Joseph Goebbels; as a child he fell ill with osteomyelitis, which caused his right lower leg to atrophy and left him with a club foot. At around 165 cm he was also relatively short. Abroad, and on the street in Germany, people openly lampooned his physical handicap; Goebbels was mocked as 'the Teutonic dwarf' and 'Humpelstiltskin'.

123 The fictional character Gustav Hackendahl is based on the Berlin horse-drawn cab driver Gustav Hartmann (1859–1938), who was nick-

named 'Iron Gustav' for his opposition to motorized taxis. He became a celebrity in 1928, when he took his horse-drawn cab from Berlin to Paris and back. Jannings was much taken with Fallada's manuscript, since it offered him a meaty role as the eponymous cab driver. However, Goebbels insisted on changes to the text: he wanted Fallada to continue the story up until the time the Nazis came to power. Fallada agreed and wrote a new ending that satisfied the Propaganda Minister. The film project was approved by Goebbels, but fell foul of Alfred Rosenberg's objection to any involvement of Hans Fallada in a German film project. When the novel appeared in 1938, it was savaged by the National Socialist press.

124 The American film *Cavalcade* (1933) directed by Frank Lloyd, based on the play of the same name by Noel Coward, won three Academy Awards in 1932/33, including Best Film and Best Director. The film was also a big hit in Germany in the 1930s.

125 The Carl Froelich Film Studio was incorporated into the Ufa concern in October 1937. A power struggle ensued between Carl Froelich and the head of production at Ufa, Ernst Hugo Corell. In 1939 Corell was fired.

126 The actress and chanteuse Gussy Holl (Auguste Marie Holl, 1888–1966) had been married to Emil Jannings since 1922. In the 1920s Kurt Tucholsky and Walter Mehring wrote chansons for her, which she performed in the Berlin cabaret 'Schall und Rauch'. Gussy Holl was the third wife of Emil Jannings.

127 On 12 September 1935 Fallada was officially declared an 'undesirable author'. From now on his works could only be published in Germany, and foreign translation rights could no longer be granted. On 4 December 1935 his 'undesirable' status was revoked.

128 The screenwriter and author Thea von Harbou (1888–1954), who wrote screenplays for Carl Froelich in 1935 (*Ich war Jack Mortimer*) and for Emil Jannings in 1937 (*Der zerbrochene Krug*). On 23 July 1938 Goebbels noted in his diary: 'Long discussion with Jannings. I pointed out all the weak points in his film script. He cut up rough, but then calmed down. The ending will be completely revised and given a more positive twist.' That same afternoon a meeting took place in Jannings' lakeside house at St. Wolfgang, at which Thea von Harbou and Goebbels were present: 'Further protracted debate about the film.

With Jannings, Krause, K. . ., Mrs Harbou. The discussion became quite heated. But in the end everyone came round to my point of view.' The film project under discussion can only have been *Iron Gustav*, because Fallada was told on 28 July that Goebbels had approved the project in principle and was only insisting on one change: a new ending. (Joseph Goebbels, *Tagebücher*. Vol. 3: 1935–1939, Munich/Zurich 1992, p. 1240)

129 The novel, which is a plea for reform of the justice system and more humane treatment of criminals, prompted the first furious attacks on Fallada in 1934 by the Nazi-controlled press.

130 Fallada was caught in the middle of the power struggle between Goebbels and Rosenberg to control literary policy. As early as January 1938 a savage review of *Wolf among Wolves* appeared in *Bücherkunde*, the official organ of the 'Rosenberg Office' for the 'cultivation of literature'. In October 1938 Rosenberg succeeded in blocking the film project with Fallada, which had the support of Goebbels (cf. note 123). In a letter to his mother of 17 October Fallada says that a spokesman for the 'Rosenberg Office' had recently stated in Berlin that 'the position of the Reich Chamber of Literature is essentially that all Fallada's writings, past and future, are entirely unsuitable' (letter to Elisabeth Ditzen, 17 October 1938, Hans Fallada Archive, Neubrandenburg). When *Iron Gustav* appeared on 28 November 1938, the 'Rosenberg Office' conducted a smear campaign against Fallada.

131 During the filming of *Die Patrioten* (directed by Karl Ritter, with Lída Baarová and Mathias Wieman in the starring roles) a showdown apparently took place between Goebbels, his mistress Lída Baarová and her partner Gustav Fröhlich, which ended with a slap in the face for the Propaganda Minister. Fröhlich had indeed found Goebbels and Lída Baarová in a compromising situation, probably in January 1937, and had slammed his car door in the Minister's face. The affair between Goebbels and Baarová became public knowledge, and Goebbels was even prepared to get a divorce because of Baarová. But Hitler intervened at the instigation of Magda Goebbels and ordered Goebbels to end the relationship.

132 Mathias Wieman (1902–1969) gave a reading from *Wolf among Wolves* on the radio on 5 November 1937. He and his wife visited Fallada in

Carwitz at the beginning of December. Fallada and Wieman kept in contact over the next few years. Wieman visited Fallada for the last time in Berlin in November 1945.

Fallada's account of the relationship between Wieman and Goebbels takes a few liberties with the facts. Wieman, who staged *Das Frankenburger Würfelspiel* [a historical open-air pageant cum morality play] during the Olympic Games, had been in close contact with Goebbels since 1936. In January 1937 he was awarded the honorific title 'Staatsschauspieler' [National Actor] and invited to join the supervisory board of Ufa in April of that year. The falling-out with Goebbels occurred when in August 1937 the Minister strongly criticized Wieman's portrayal of a general staff officer in the film *Unternehmen Michael* [*Operation Michael*]: Wieman, he claimed, was not right for the part of an army officer. With reference to discussions about a film project telling the story of 'Dr Peters and the colonies', Goebbels notes: 'But not Wieman for the lead role' (diary entry for 20 October 1937). Wieman's appearance in the film *Die Kadetten* [*The Cadets*] was also judged by Goebbels to be 'a failure' (diary entry for 30 July 1939). Wieman moved to Hamburg, where in 1940 he performed in *Faust* under the direction of Gustav Gründgens. In 1941 he was back in Berlin, where he had a part in the film *Ich klage an* [*I accuse*] (1941). During the war Wieman continued to work in films and on the radio, where he recited German poetry in the regular Sunday series 'Das Schatzkästlein'.

133 Alfred Rosenberg gave an address at the University of Halle on 4 November 1938 under the title 'Ideology and doctrine'.

134 In his principal work, published in 1930, Rosenberg elevates the myth of 'blood purity' to the status of National Socialist state religion; cf. note 46.

135 Working title of the film *Der höhere Befehl*, made for Ufa in 1935 by Gerhard Lamprecht. Fallada is confusing this film, in which Wieman did not appear, with *Operation Michael*; cf. note 132.

136 Identity unknown.

137 Deutsche Verlags-Anstalt; cf. note 95. The list of authors published by DVA included Ina Seidel, Josef Ponten, Jochen Klepper, Börries von Münchhausen and Detlev von Liliencron.

138 The journalist and author Jochen Klepper (1903–1942); his book *Der*

Vater. Roman des Soldatenkönigs [*The Father. The Story of the Soldier King*] was published by DVA in 1937 in two volumes. Klepper's wife Hannelore and his two adoptive daughters were of Jewish origin; faced with the imminent deportation of one of the daughters, the family committed suicide on 11 December 1942.

139 Gustav Kilpper was replaced in 1943 (?) by Joachim Schmidt; see Hans Fallada, *Ewig auf der Rutschbahn. Briefwechsel mit dem Rowohlt Verlag*, edited by M. Töteberg and S. Buck, Reinbek bei Hamburg 2008, p. 362.

140 Probably Gertrud von Le Fort (1876–1971), whose novel *Der Papst aus dem Ghetto. Die Legende des Geschlechts Pier Leone*, published by Transmare Verlag in 1930, tells the story of the Jew Baruch Leone, who was baptized, and whose son Petrus became Pope Anaklet II in 1130.

141 *Das Märchen vom Stadtschreiber, der aufs Land flog* [*Sparrow Farm*] was published by Rowohlt in 1935.

142 Here Fallada is mistaken: the farmer Tamm character does not appear in *Sparrow Farm*, but in *Altes Herz geht auf die Reise* [*Old Heart Goes on a Journey*] (1936). It was because of this novel that Fallada was declared an 'undesirable author' – which is presumably why the manuscript had 'ended up on somebody's desk' at the Propaganda Ministry.

143 Cf. note 95.

144 For his fiftieth birthday Fallada received 'a drawing of the zodiac done for me by Kubin, with delicate pastel tinting, dominated by Leo the lion, my own birth sign' (letter to Ernst Rowohlt, 26 July 1943; as quoted in: Hans Fallada, *Ewig auf der Rutschbahn. Briefwechsel mit dem Rowohlt Verlag*, edited by M. Töteberg and S. Buck, Reinbek bei Hamburg 2008, p. 361).

145 Cf. note 139.

146 The books in question were *Die Stunde, eh' du schlafen gehst* [*Before You Go to Sleep*] (Goldmann Verlag, Munich 1954), *Der Sohn des Staubes* (published under the title *Ein Mann will hinauf* [*A Man Wants to Get On*] by Südverlag, Munich 1953) and *Der Jungherr von Strammin* [*The Master of Strammin*] (published under the title *Junger Herr – ganz gross* by Ullstein Verlag, Berlin 1965).

147 Following the closure of Rowohlt Verlag, DVA refused to negotiate with Fallada, and so for the first time since 1919 he found himself without

a publisher. In January 1944 he entered into discussions with the Dresden-based publishing house Wilhelm Heyne, and signed a contract with its publishing director Franz Schneekluth in the second week of March.

148 Cf. note 146.

149 In the summer of 1941 Fallada was gathering material in the Reich Ministry of Justice about the Jewish banking house Barmat und Kutisker, and a celebrated fraud case of the 1920s. When the Propaganda Ministry got wind of Fallada's project, they gave him their official backing in June 1943. He talks about this in a letter to Heinrich Maria Ledig-Rowohlt of 11 August 1943: '[. . .] I fear that the novel's point of view will not be what they are expecting.' On 30 November 1944 he announces in a letter to his wife from the psychiatric prison at Neustrelitz-Strelitz that he finished the novel two days ago (Hans Fallada, Anna Ditzen, *Wenn du fort bist, ist alles nur halb. Briefe einer Ehe*, Berlin 2007, p. 424). According to Günter Caspar, Franz Schneekluth, the senior editor at Wilhelm Heyne Verlag, received the manuscript before the end of the war; see the 'Nachwort' by Günter Caspar in: Hans Fallada, *Der Trinker/Der Alpdruck*, Berlin and Weimar 1987, pp. 563–76. The premises of the publishing house were destroyed during the bombing of Dresden on 13 February 1945. The Kutisker novel is thought to be lost.

150 In the subsequent account of events in Mahlendorf (Carwitz), Fallada uses fictitious names for most of the places and persons mentioned.

151 Dora Hertha Preisach (no biographical data available) typed up the manuscripts of *Once a Jailbird* in the autumn of 1933, *Once We Had a Child* in February 1934, and *Old Heart Goes on a Journey* in June 1935 in Carwitz. In the summer of 1935 she emigrated to Haifa with her father.

152 Fallada's portrayal of the bailiff character was based on Hans-Joachim Geyer (1901–1972), whom he had got to know in Radach in 1923; thereafter they exchanged letters and met up occasionally. Geyer visited Fallada for the last time in the Charité hospital in Berlin in December 1946.

153 Nickname for Gustav Schwanecke, who was Fallada's and Geyer's employer in Radach.

154 *Nationalsozialistische Volkswohlfahrt*: founded in 1932 as a local self-help

association in Berlin, it grew to become the second-largest National Socialist mass organization. By 1943 it had some 17 million members.

155 The 'Blood Order' was the highest decoration conferred by the NSDAP and was first awarded in 1923 to those who took part in the Beer Hall Putsch in Munich.

156 The battle of Stalingrad began in August 1942 with the assault launched by the 6th Army, and ended early in 1943 with the encirclement and capitulation of the German forces.

157 The first food rationing cards were distributed on 27 August 1939, just before the outbreak of war. They were used for the rationing of certain foodstuffs and other commodities.

158 Richard Walther Darré (1895–1953) was the 'Reich Farmworkers' Leader' and Reich Minister of Food and Agriculture from 1933 to 1942, head of the SS Central Office for Race and Resettlement from 1931 to 1938, and the author of numerous manifestos on National Socialist 'blood and soil' policy, including *Neuadel aus Blut und Boden* (1930). In 1932 he founded the monthly journal *Deutsche Agrarpolitik* (renamed *Odal* in 1939), in which he propagated his vision of a new 'farming aristocracy'.

159 Presumably the 72-year-old Mr Lamprecht, whom Fallada took on as a gardener in July 1942. He made a good impression at first, but was dismissed on 4 December 1942.

160 Willi Burlage (1893?–1943), a friend from Fallada's schooldays in Leipzig, had been director of the 'Heidehaus' sanatorium in Zepernick, just to the north of Berlin, since 1935. He treated Fallada in his clinic on a number of occasions between 1935 and 1940.

161 When the Allied Reparations Commission discovered in December 1922 that Germany was in arrears with its reparations payments, the entire Ruhr region was occupied on 11 January 1923 by one Belgian and five French divisions. The occupying troops punished any breach of their regulations. The Reich government called for a campaign of passive resistance, but the economic and political repercussions were so devastating that this had to be suspended on 26 September 1923.

162 Identity not established. From October 1941 to February 1942 Fallada was writing the screenplay *Eroberung von Berlin* for Wien-Film GmbH, a large Austrian film production company that came under Nazi control

in 1937. Fallada met the head of production, Karl Hartl, at the end of November 1941 in Berlin; the production manager, Fritz Podehl, visited Fallada in Carwitz twice in October 1942. Although the screenplay was reworked several times, the film was never made: the book version appeared in 1953 under the title *A Man Wants to Get On*, published by Südverlag in Munich.

163 The Munich Agreement (29 September 1938) provided for the cession of the Sudetenland to the German Reich, as demanded by Hitler. In return Britain and France guaranteed the continued existence of the rump Czechoslovak state. The Agreement lapsed with the entry of the Wehrmacht into Czechoslovakia (15 March 1939) and the establishment of the 'Protectorate of Bohemia and Moravia'.

164 Fallada was given his service record book when he was discharged from the 19th Saxon Supply Corps on 22 September 1914 as permanently unfit for military service.

165 Edgar Wallace (1875–1932) is one of the most successful writers of crime fiction in English. His crime novels had been appearing in German translation since 1927.

166 Cf. note 160.

167 Elisabeth (Ibeth) Hörig (1888–1979), Fallada's older sister, who was politically informed and – like her brother – hostile to the Nazis.

168 The standard work by Cuno Horkenbach, *Das deutsche Reich von 1918 bis heute*, was published in 1930.

169 Under the terms of the Treaty of Versailles (1919) Danzig with its surrounding territories was separated from the German Reich and on 15 November 1920 it was declared the Free City of Danzig. On 28 April 1939 Hitler announced in the Reichstag: 'Danzig is a German city, and wants to be reunited with Germany.'

Index